I0812439

IMAGES
of America

OMAHA'S EASTER TORNADO OF 1913

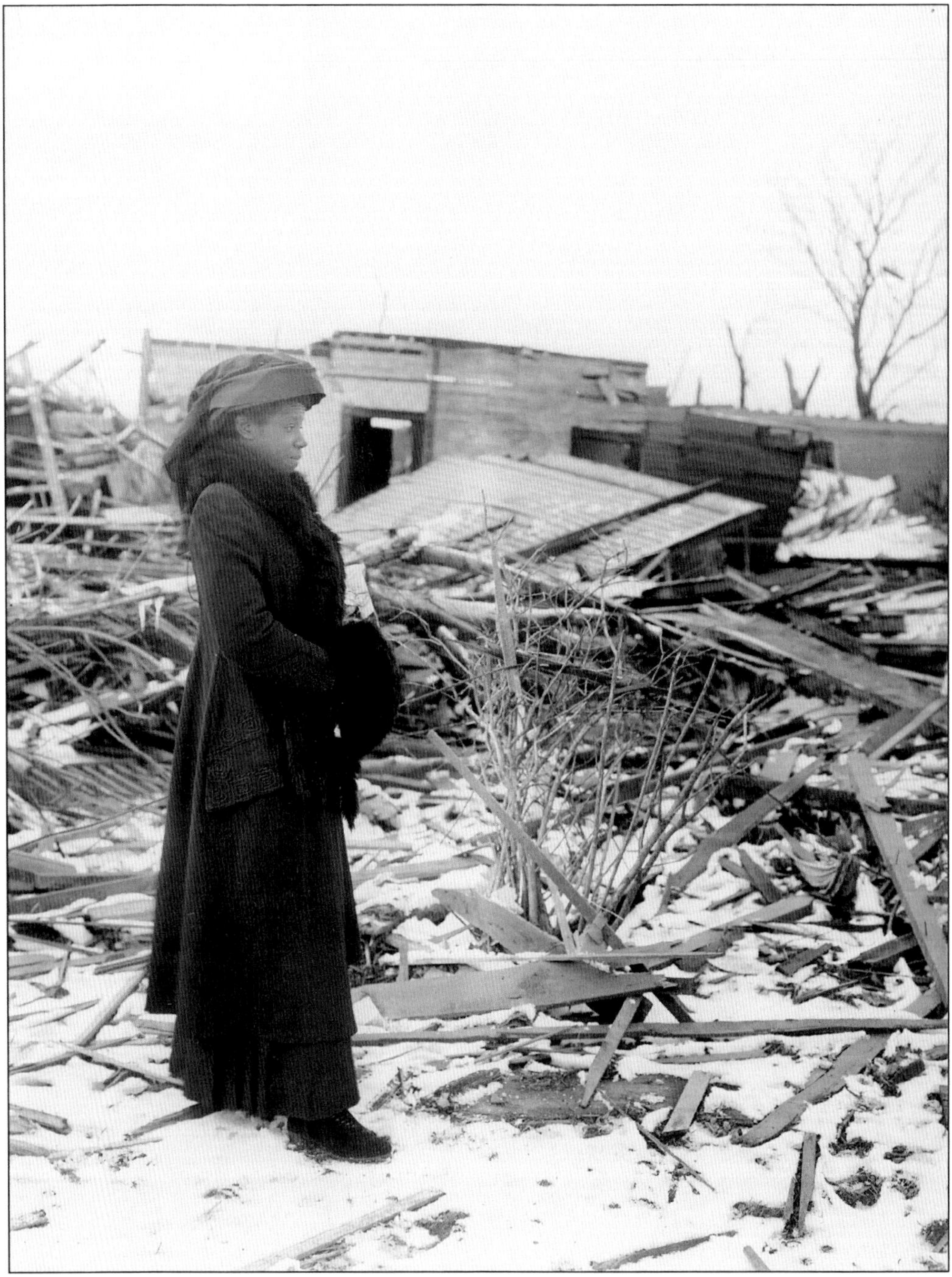

Lady in Black. This finely-dressed, unidentified woman sadly surveys the ruins of north Omaha near 26th Street and Patrick Avenue. (Bostwick-Frohardt Collection, Durham Western Heritage Museum.)

IMAGES
of America

OMAHA'S EASTER TORNADO OF 1913

Travis Sing

ARCADIA
PUBLISHING

ISBN 978-0-7385-3184

Published by Arcadia Publishing
Charleston, South Carolina

Printed in the United States of America

Library of Congress Catalog Card Number: 2003108861

For all general information contact Arcadia Publishing at:
Telephone 843-853-2070
Fax 843-853-0044
E-Mail sales@arcadiapublishing.com
For customer service and orders:
Toll-Free 1-888-313-2665

Visit us on the Internet at www.arcadiapublishing.com

This book is dedicated to my wonderful wife, Linda,

and tornado victims everywhere.

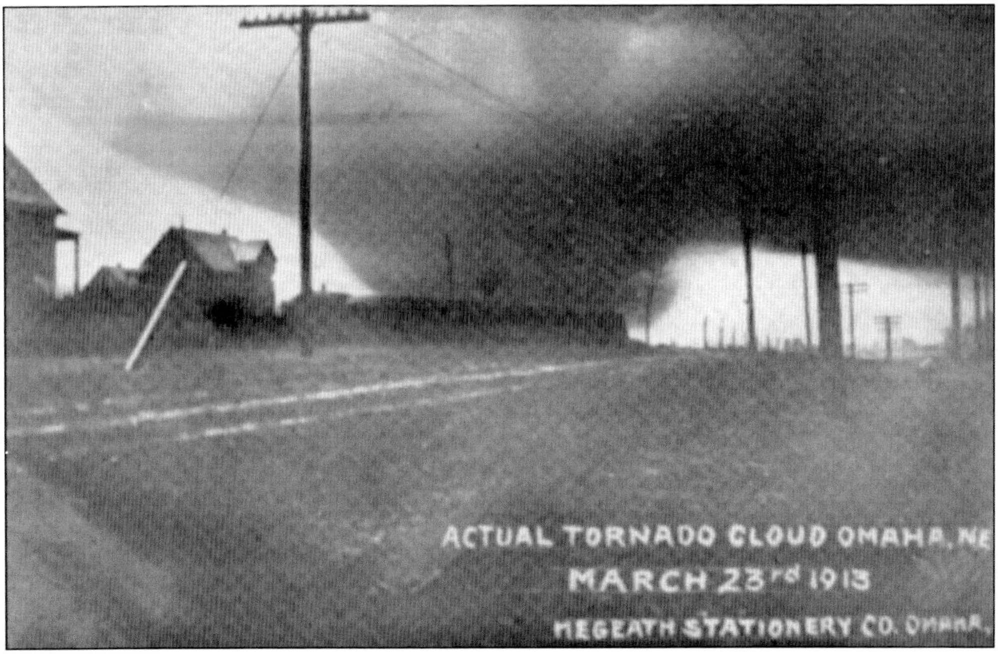

ACTUAL TORNADO CLOUD. At approximately 5:45 p.m. on March 23, 1913 (Easter Sunday), this tornado ripped through Omaha, leaving a swath of destruction over a quarter of a mile wide and nearly five miles long.

Contents

ACKNOWLEDGMENTS

Burnice Fiedler has my profound gratitude for graciously allowing me to utilize her vast and superb Omaha postcard collection; Dr. Oliver B. Pollak, who encouraged me to pursue an *Images of America* project, and put me in touch with Burnice; Elizabeth Remmen for help with scanning; the Boswell family for the 1913 souvenir booklet; Janelle Lindburg and the Durham Western Heritage Museum Photographic Archives; Don Snoddy, Jo Ann Meyer, and Rita Jerins at the Douglas County Historical Society Library/Archives Center; Jan Gorman at the Frank & Velma Johnson Ralston Archives Museum/Baright Library; Laura McKee Hickman at Duchesne Academy of the Sacred Heart; Patty Tipler and the Child Saving Institute; Jo Grebenick at Joslyn Castle, Christine Dahlin at Joslyn Castle Institute For Sustainable Communities; Tom Heenan and Joanne Ferguson Cavanaugh at the Dale W. Clark Omaha Public Library; Mary Nash at Creighton University Reinart/Alumni Memorial Library; the photographic department at the Nebraska State Historical Society, Carrie Marsh at the Honnold/Mudd Library of Claremont College, and a big thank you to Maura Brown at Arcadia Publishing for her guidance, diligence, and faith in this project.

All images from the Bostwick-Frohardt Collection are owned by KMTV and on permanent loan to the Durham Western Heritage Museum, Omaha, Nebraska.

INTRODUCTION

Those who have inhabited Nebraska, from American Indians to the pioneers to members of the modern age, have always been at nature's mercy. Blinding blizzards, scorching heat, flash floods, and terrible tornados are just a few things that make Nebraskans hardy people. This is, after all, the heart of the nation and the middle of Tornado Alley. It is rare for tornados to strike major metropolitan areas, but when they do, the damage is immense.

In 1913 weather forecasting was relatively primitive, and the first scientific tornado prediction was not made until 1948. Some placed credence in an "Indian legend" that held Omaha was protected from tornados by the surrounding hills. At the time, the only means of quantifying tornadic strength was through the loss of life and property damage.

The modern Fujita-Pearson scale (often called the Fujita scale, F scale, or FPP scale) was developed in 1971 by Drs. Theodore Fujita and Allen Pearson. While not a perfect system, it is practical. The scale rates the intensity of tornados, and measures the path's length and width. Through careful analysis, the Easter tornado is considered an F4, or devastating tornado. F4 tornados produce winds in excess of 200 miles per hour, are able to level well-constructed homes, and generate dangerously large debris.

On an unseasonably warm evening, the citizens of Omaha were given reason to believe the wrath of God was bearing down upon them. At approximately 6:00 p.m., a large tornado ripped through the city. This tornado was only one that occurred during an outbreak of severe weather. On that day, no less than seven tornados formed over eastern Nebraska, and some passed into western Iowa.

Downtown was spared, but the fashionable neighborhoods of the city's western fringe and the ethnic neighborhoods of north Omaha were ruined. Approximately 135 lives were lost, and the storm incurred millions of dollars in property damage. It was such a cataclysm that it made national and international headlines. This event still ranks as the worst tornado disaster in Nebraska history, and one of the worst in United States history. By comparison, the Omaha tornado of May 6, 1975, caused great property damage, but due to weather radar and tornado sirens, loss of life was minimal.

The Easter tornado first touched down and ripped through the tiny manufacturing community of Ralston. It soon entered southwest Omaha, cutting a swath of destruction from West Farnam to Bemis Park, and north to the intersection of 24th and Lake Streets. Homes, schools, churches, and businesses were all affected.

Darkness soon fell and citizens sifted through the rubble by lantern light, while others haphazardly wandered, searching for missing family members. Numerous fires were started by ruptured gas lines, communications were cut off, and looting was taking place. Soldiers from Fort Omaha mobilized to bring order to the blighted areas, and were supplemented by the

Omaha Police Department. Omaha firefighters were joined by the department from Council Bluffs, Iowa. Rain came in the evening, which greatly reduced the severity and number of blazes. The beneficial rain was soon followed by sleet, and then a quick return to seasonable weather treated the city to several inches of early-spring snow. Coupled with freezing temperatures, it hampered the recovery process.

Mayor James C. Dahlman initially refused aid from President Woodrow Wilson. Dahlman replied to Wilson, "We all deeply appreciate your offer of aid, but I believe we can handle the situation." Once the city fathers realized the storm damage was greater than they originally believed, aid was reluctantly accepted. The Red Cross established relief stations at key areas. An appeal was issued for contributions of money, clothing, and food. Soon after the tornado, a medical contingent arrived from Des Moines, Iowa, and students from Creighton University Medical College did what they could to help the injured.

Scant research has been performed and very little written on this topic in the last 90 years. Valuable information was found in Omaha's three daily newspapers from the era: *Bee*, *Daily News*, and *World-Herald*. Several 1913 books about weather featured a chapter or chapters about Omaha's Easter tornado. Numerous souvenir booklets were published by newspapers and printing houses. First-hand accounts by survivors were discovered in local archival collections.

In the wake of the tornado, hundreds of photographs were taken by several professional photography houses, and even some amateur photographers. Because of the extensive photographic record, it is considered the best-documented single event in Omaha history, and probably Nebraska history by that fact. There are approximately 1,000 extant images from the days and weeks following the storm. Private and archival collections in Omaha still hold these treasures. While most images merely document the material and human toll, some are composed so well that they rival the best documentary photography of the era, especially the fine work of Louis Bostwick.

The sheer number of images was both a blessing and a curse. It was a difficult task to choose the very best for this project, but it was a beneficial dilemma. Some images were not of printable quality, and many original prints have been lost or destroyed in the intervening years. Most postcards were replete with a caption or title that revealed information about the scene depicted. Other images did not have any ready information, and none could be found, rendering them unsuitable. Some images provided only the barest information, and occasionally were dedicated hours of research to uncover the full story. Another challenge was provided by the images that were mislabeled and required correction.

The larger goal of this project is not only to demonstrate the magnificent power of tornados, but to reveal the incredible power of spirit, both the individual human spirit and the community spirit. The human element is so strong that figures are in nearly every photograph in this book; they include government officials, soldiers, relief workers, cleanup crews, and families thankful they survived the storm. These memorable images convey the compelling story of the 1913 Easter tornado.

One

THE STORM

To the eye it had the distinctive funnel-shaped twisting character of the typical tornado, sweeping along at a furious rate of speed. To the ear it conveyed the sound of crashing din and a mighty rush of water. It was accompanied by a lurid brass-yellow luminous atmosphere followed immediately by dense darkness and a heavy downpour of rain lasting nearly an hour.

—The Track Of The Tornado *souvenir booklet, 1913*

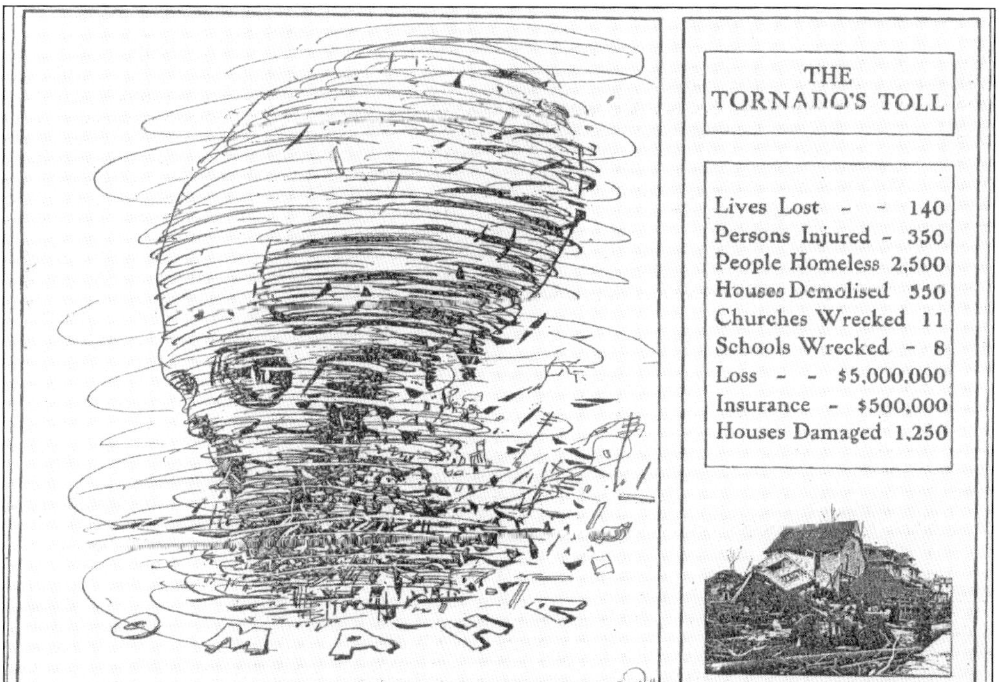

SKULL VORTEX. This illustration appeared on the front page of the *Omaha Bee* following the horrific storm. Illustrator Doane Powell captured both the death and destruction inflicted by the tornado by portraying it as a skull-shaped vortex.

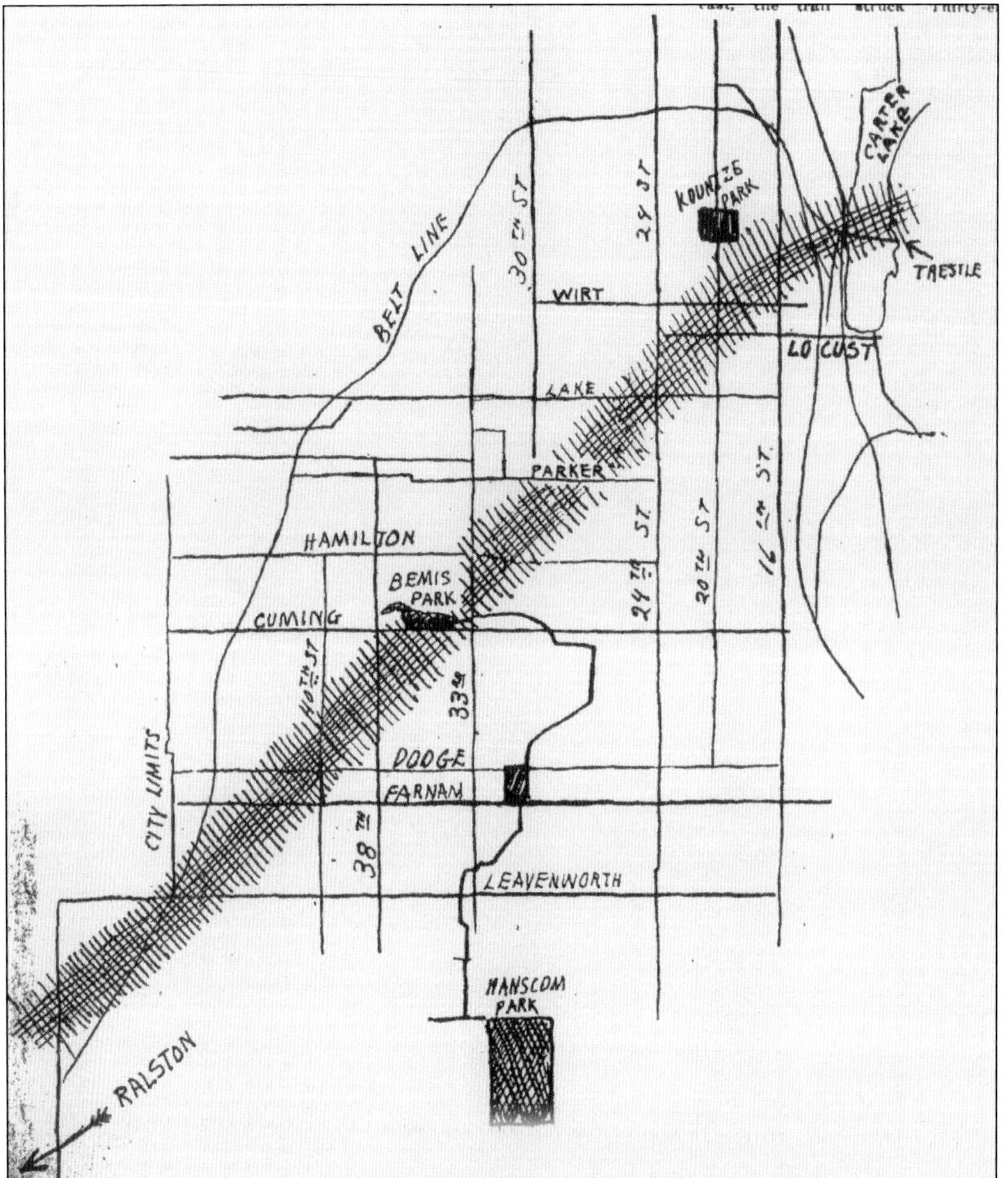

TORNADO PATH. This map shows the path the tornado took through Omaha, moving northeasterly through the city.

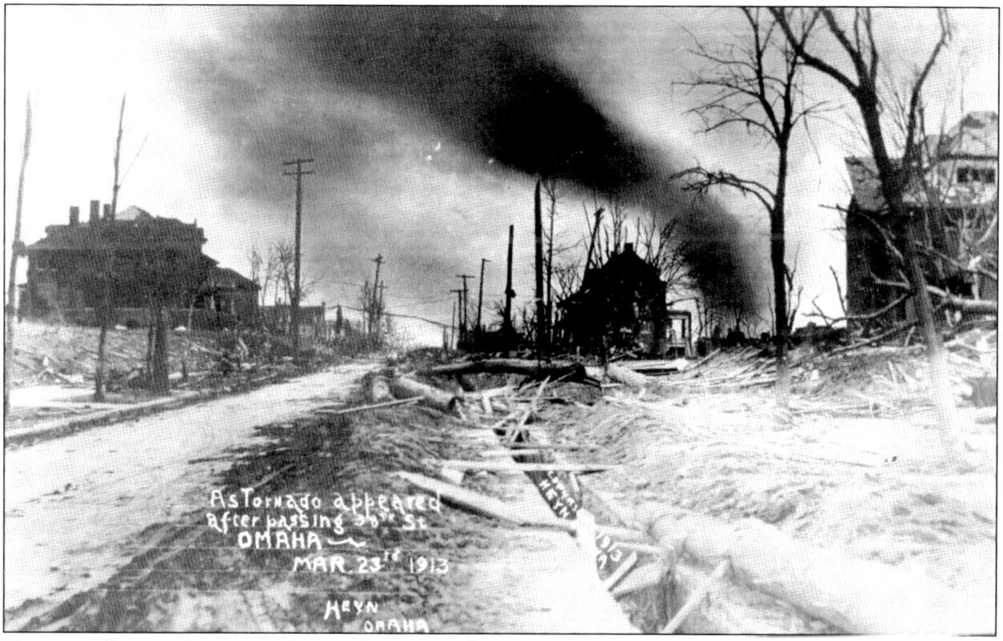

Funnel Cloud Passing 38th Street. This view of the funnel, looking northeast towards the Cathedral neighborhood, was taken at 38th and Arbor Streets. It was poetically called the "death-dealing cloud," the "grey reaper," and the "king of furies."

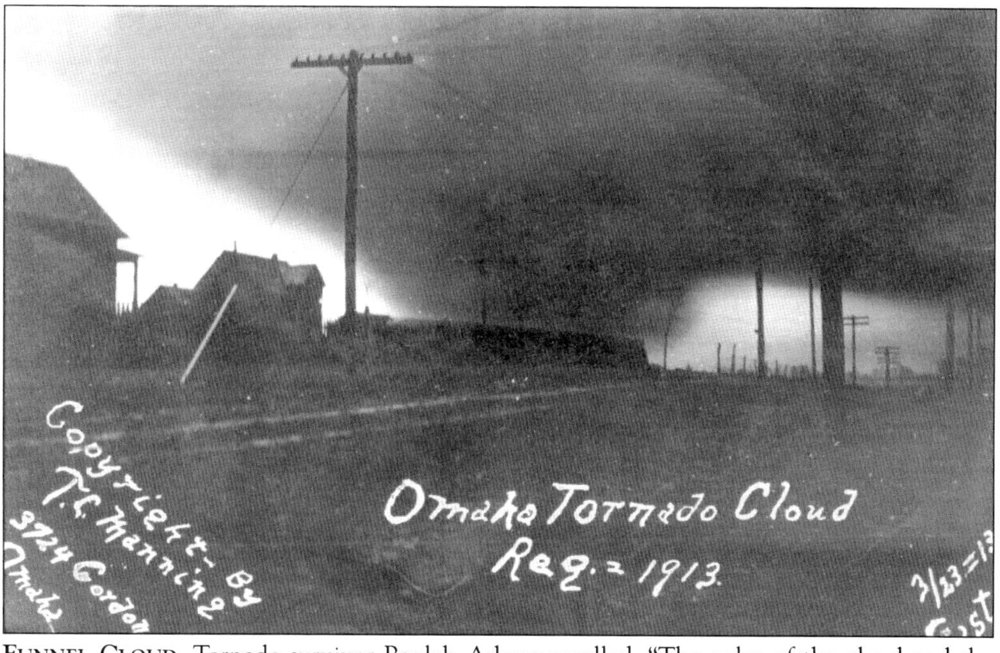

Funnel Cloud. Tornado survivor Beulah Adams recalled, "The color of the cloud and the sticks and black cloth whirling around appeared something like a big black cloud of smoke with leaves and scorched paper flying around . . . ."

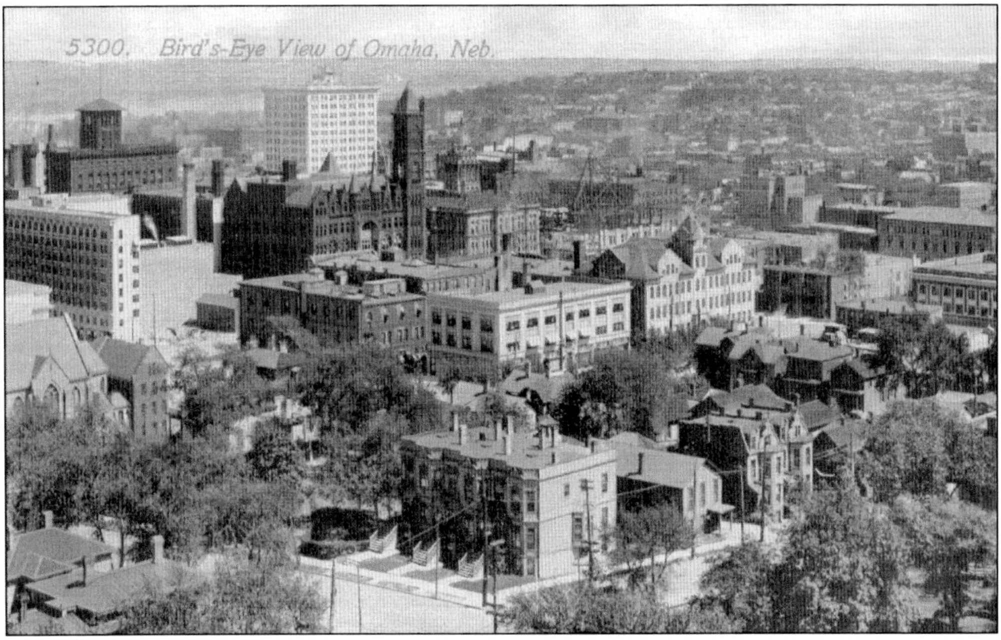

BIRD'S EYE VIEW OF OMAHA. In 1913 Omaha was a bustling center for railroads, livestock, and manufacturing with a population of approximately 140,000. Communications were cut by the tornado, and wild rumors spread across the country that Omaha's financial and retail district was destroyed, leaving 1,000 dead. Such rumors were completely untrue.

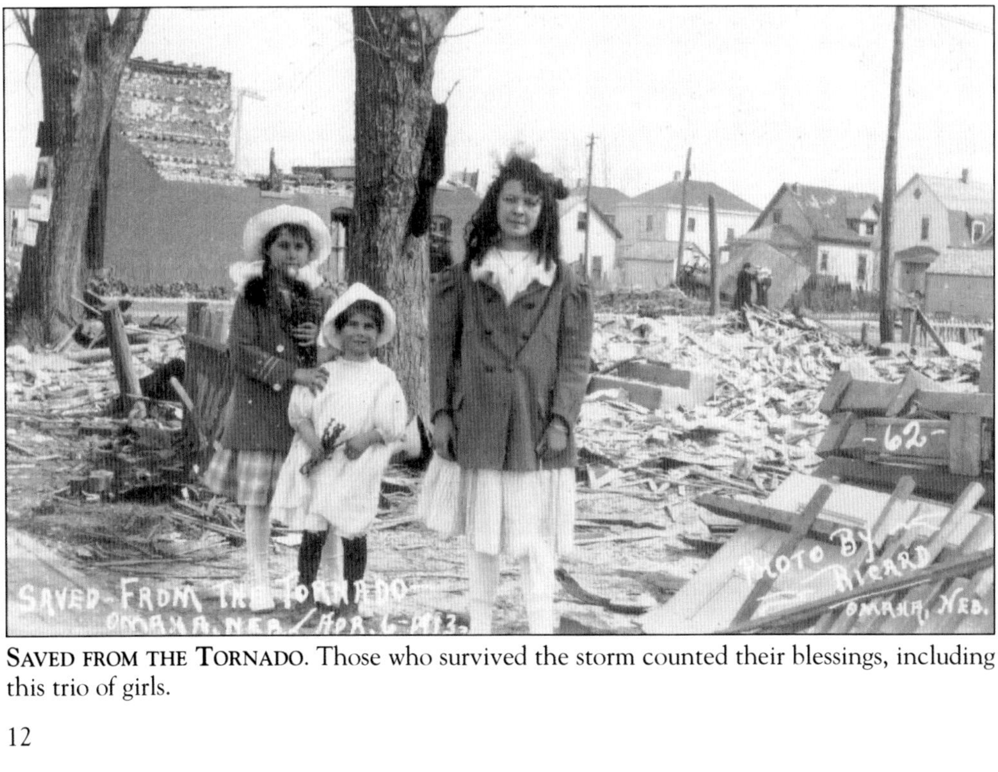

SAVED FROM THE TORNADO. Those who survived the storm counted their blessings, including this trio of girls.

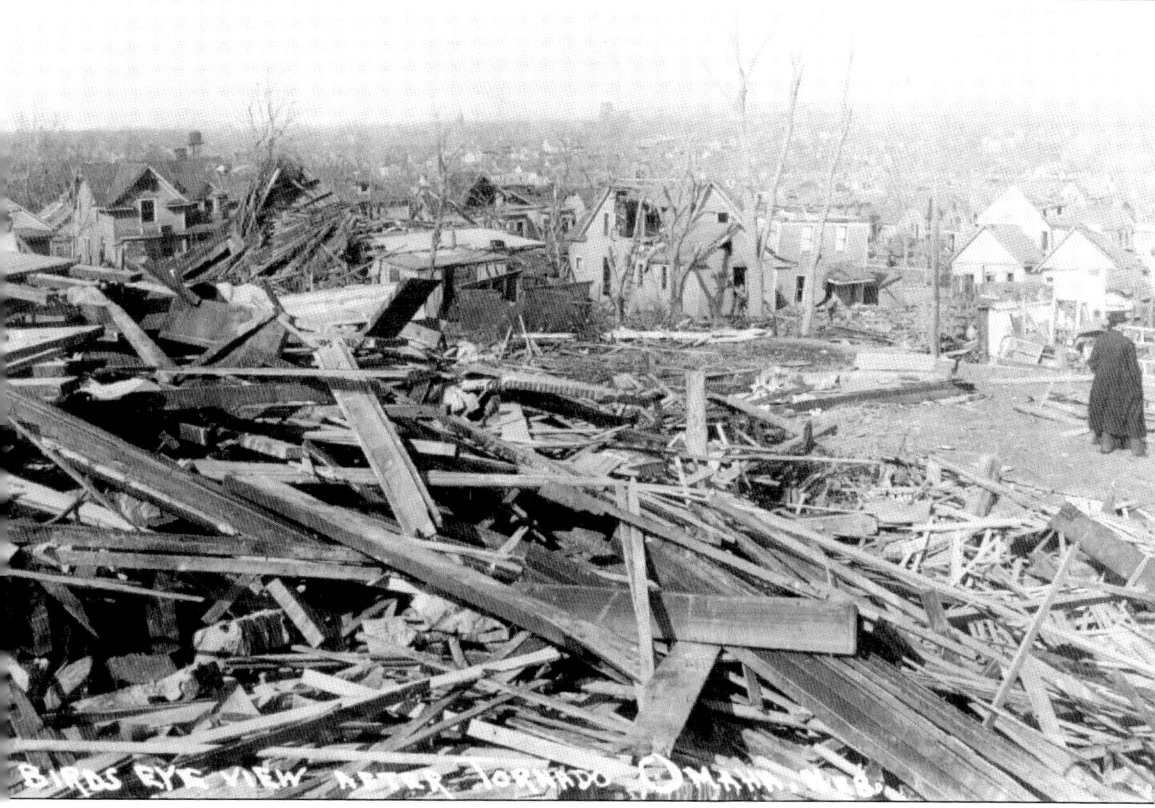

A BIRD'S EYE VIEW AFTER THE TORNADO. A lone figure surveys the path of wreckage left by the Easter tornado.

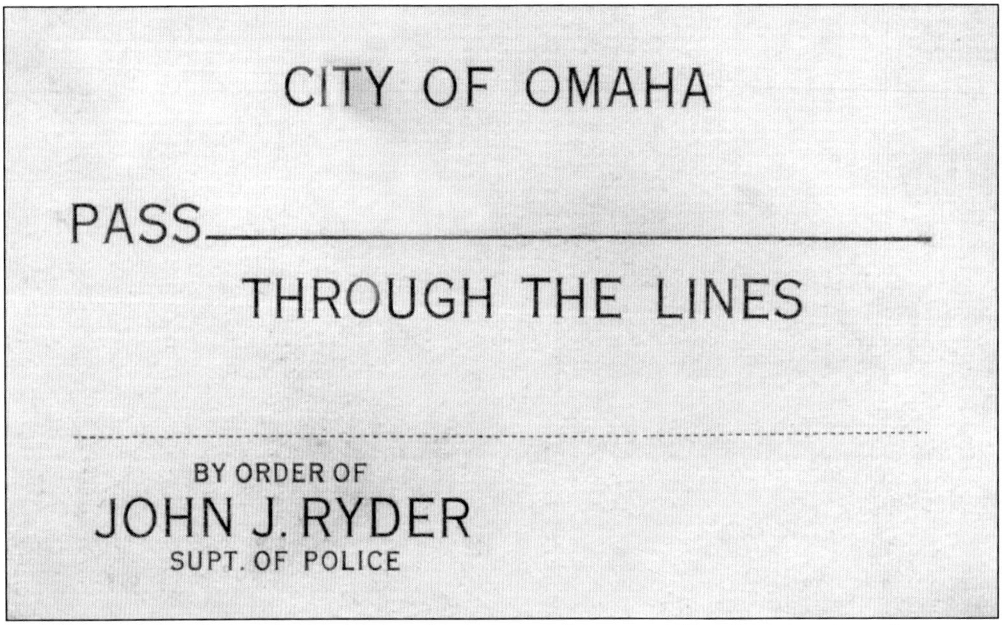

CITY OF OMAHA

PASS________________________________

THROUGH THE LINES

BY ORDER OF

JOHN J. RYDER

SUPT. OF POLICE

POLICE PASS. The tornado district quickly came under martial law. Passes such as these were required of anyone living in the area to gain access to their property. Major Carl F. Hartmann deployed 175 troops from Fort Omaha to assist the Omaha Police Department's 80 uniformed officers.

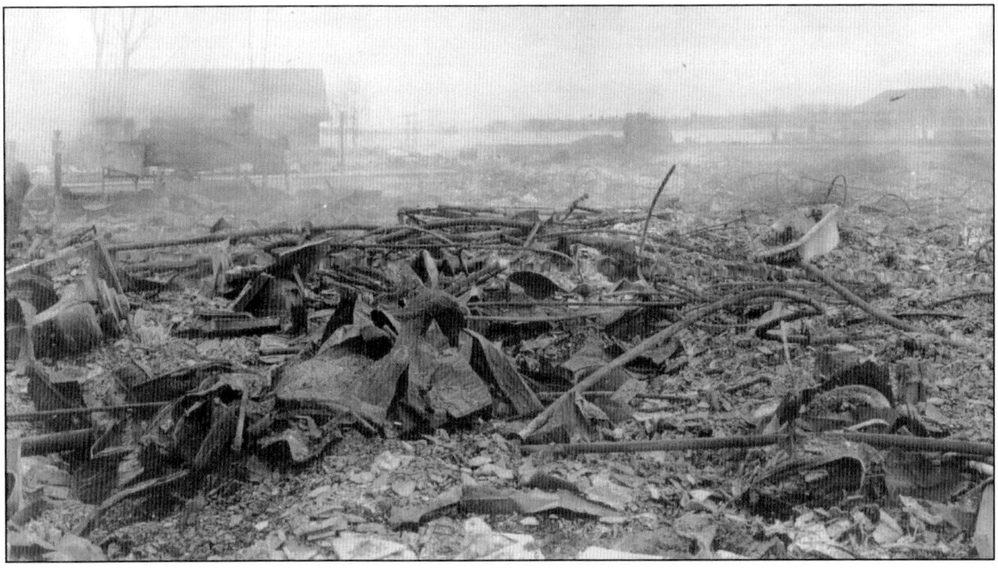

CHARRED REMAINS. Because of ruptured gas lines, approximately 20 fires of varying intensities broke out along the ravaged district. The fire departments of Omaha and Council Bluffs, Iowa, were summoned. Despite debris-filled streets that did not allow fire wagons to get close, most fires were extinguished within hours. This unfortunate building was completely consumed.

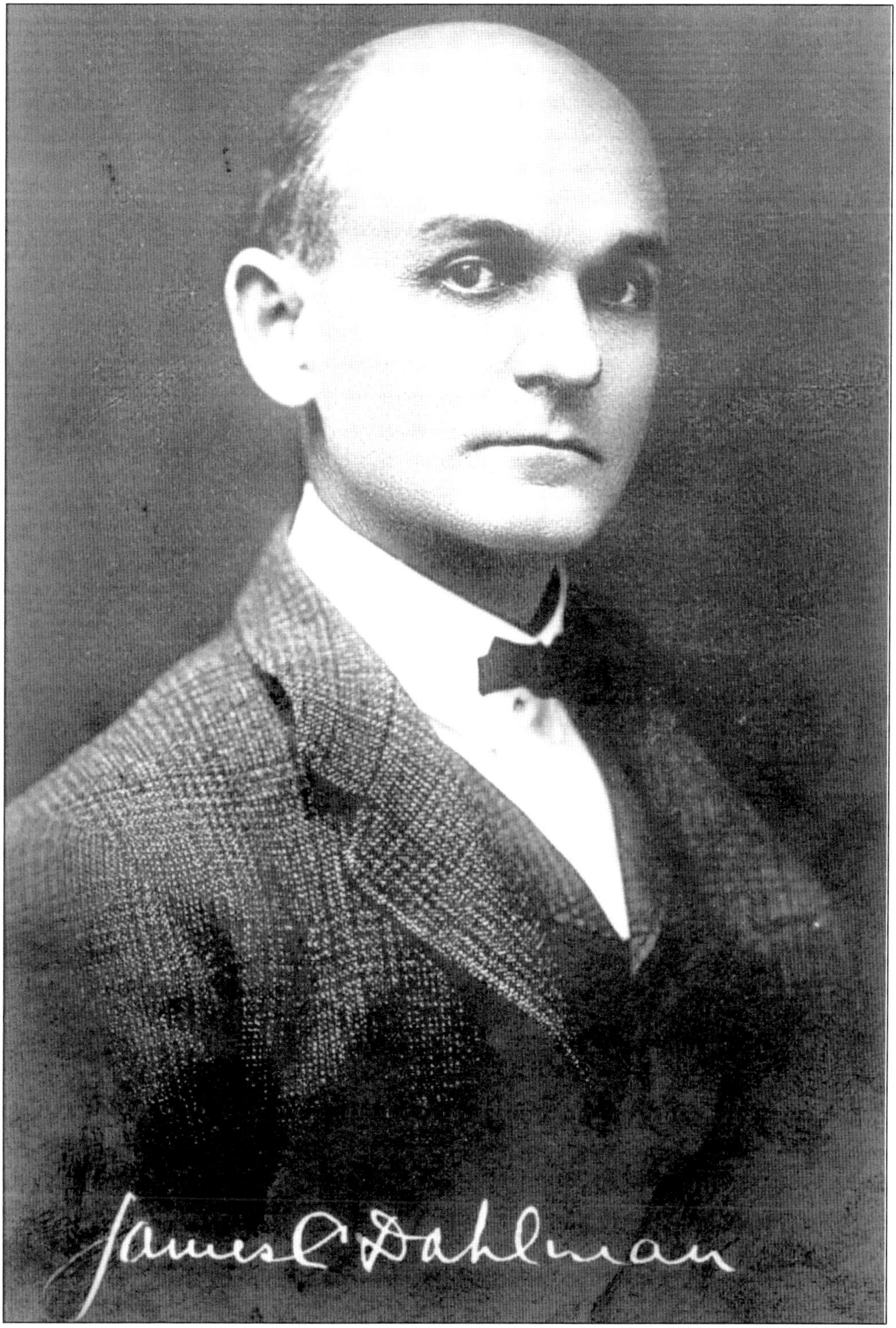

MAYOR DAHLMAN. Omaha Mayor James C. Dahlman (known as "Cowboy Jim") held the office for 23 years (1906–1918, 1921–1930), the longest in the city's history.

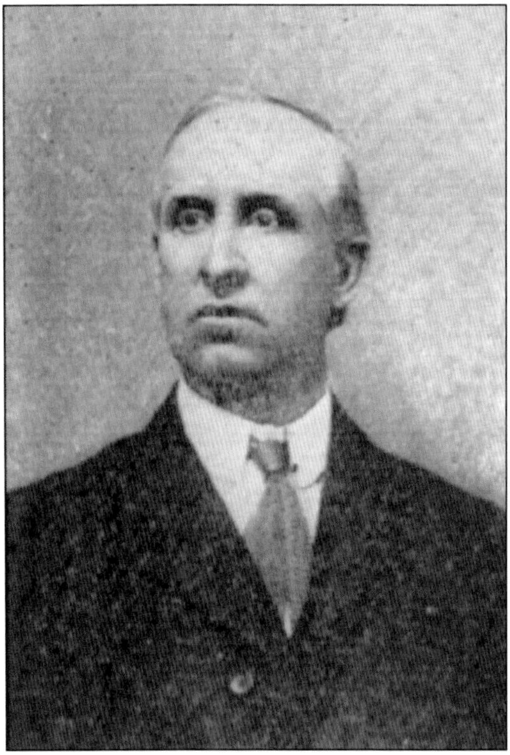

GOVERNOR MOREHEAD. John H. Morehead was Nebraska governor from 1913 through 1917. Morehead dispatched a special train from Lincoln after midnight to make Omaha by 3:45 a.m. on Monday. Upon viewing the ruin at dawn he uttered, "This is enough like my conception of hell to suit me." On April 2, Morehead approved House Bill 877, allotting $100,000 for tornado relief.

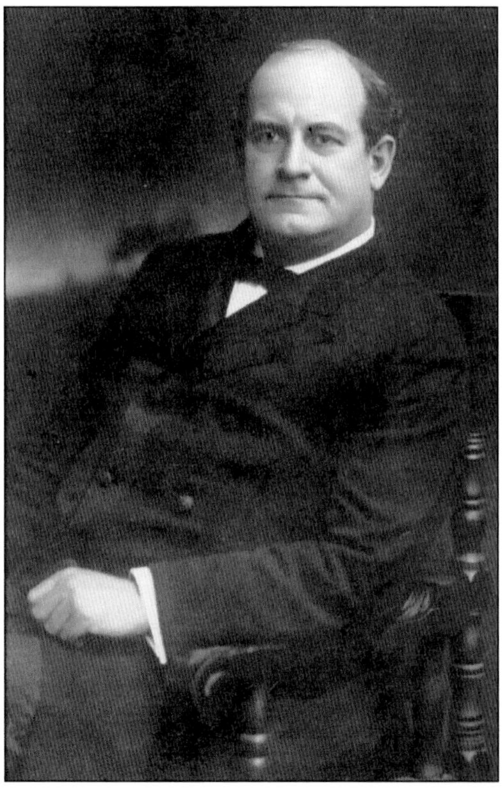

WILLIAM JENNINGS BRYAN. The "Great Commoner," serving as President Woodrow Wilson's Secretary of State, was in Omaha on a speaking engagement the day before the storm. He left Easter morning for his home, Fairview, in Lincoln. From his front porch, Bryan watched tornados pass through Lancaster County.

FR. WILLIAM F. RIGGE, S.J. Rigge was a renowned scientist, and one of the five Jesuits on the original faculty when Creighton College opened in 1878. When asked his opinion about the storm, Rigge made sharp distinction between tornado and cyclone. His conclusion was that it was a tornado which struck Omaha. (Creighton University Reinart/ Alumni Memorial Library.)

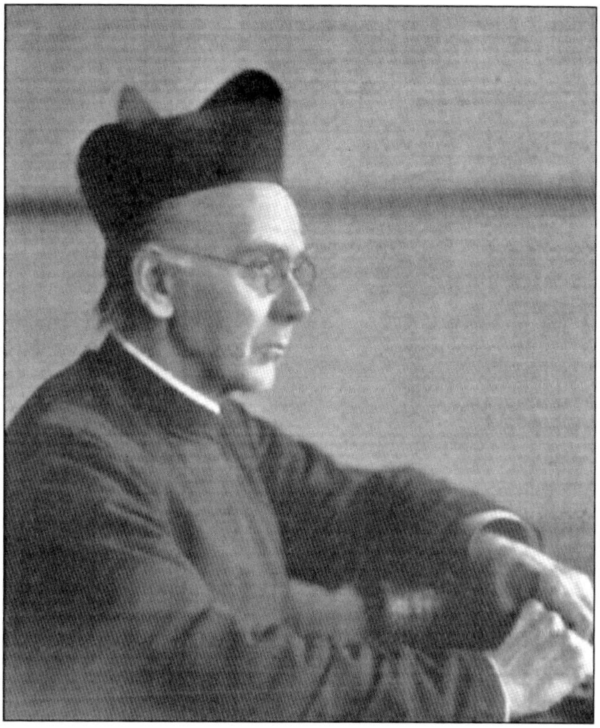

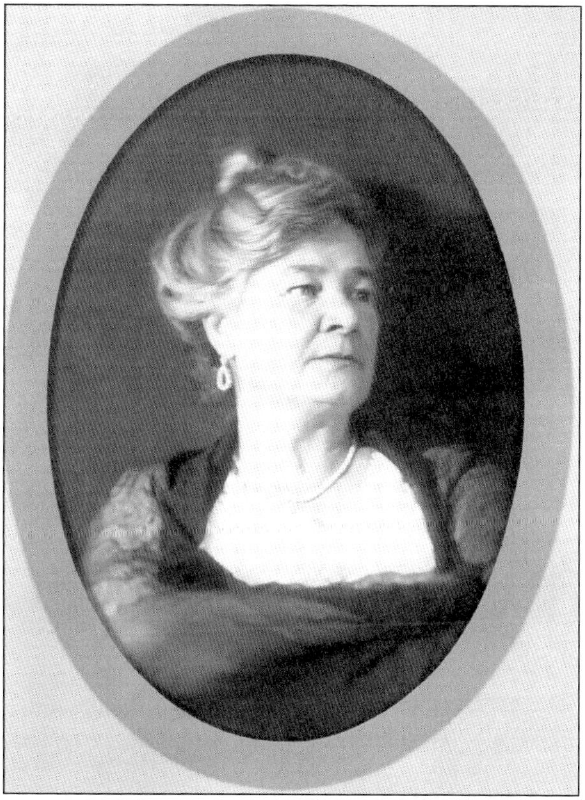

MADAME SCHUMANN-HEINK. The opera star had recently performed in Omaha, and canceled scheduled appearances upon hearing of the disaster. She wrote from Chicago, "I need one or two weeks' absolute rest. Gave up my concerts. I love Omaha special… so imagine my shock… I am heart and soul, Omaha's." (Ernestine Schumann-Heink Collection, Honnold/Mudd Library, Claremont College.)

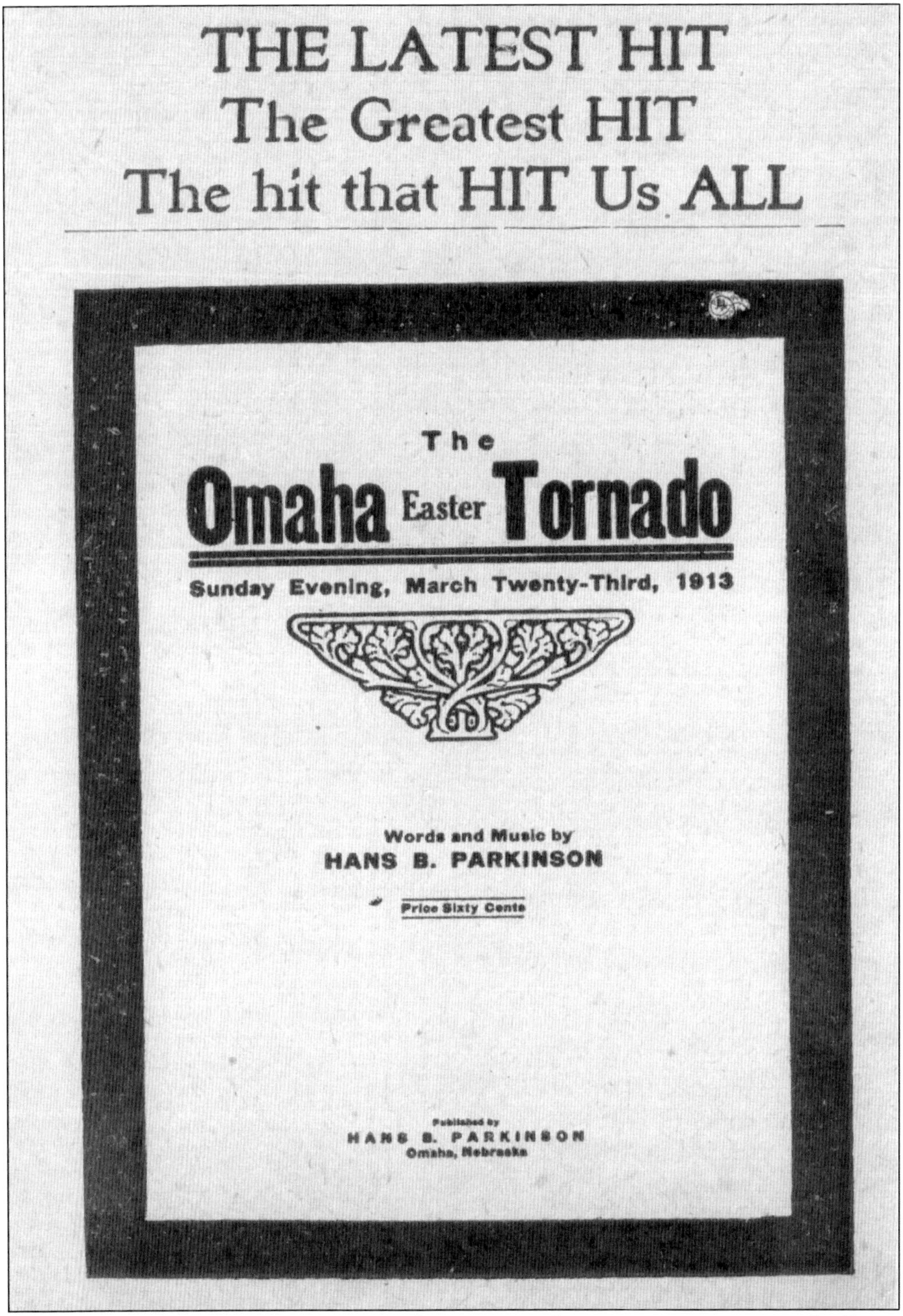

THE HIT THAT HIT US ALL. Hans B. Parkinson wrote this song to commemorate the Easter tornado. This advertisement postcard shows the front of the sheet music folio, and proclaims the song to be "the hit that hit us all."

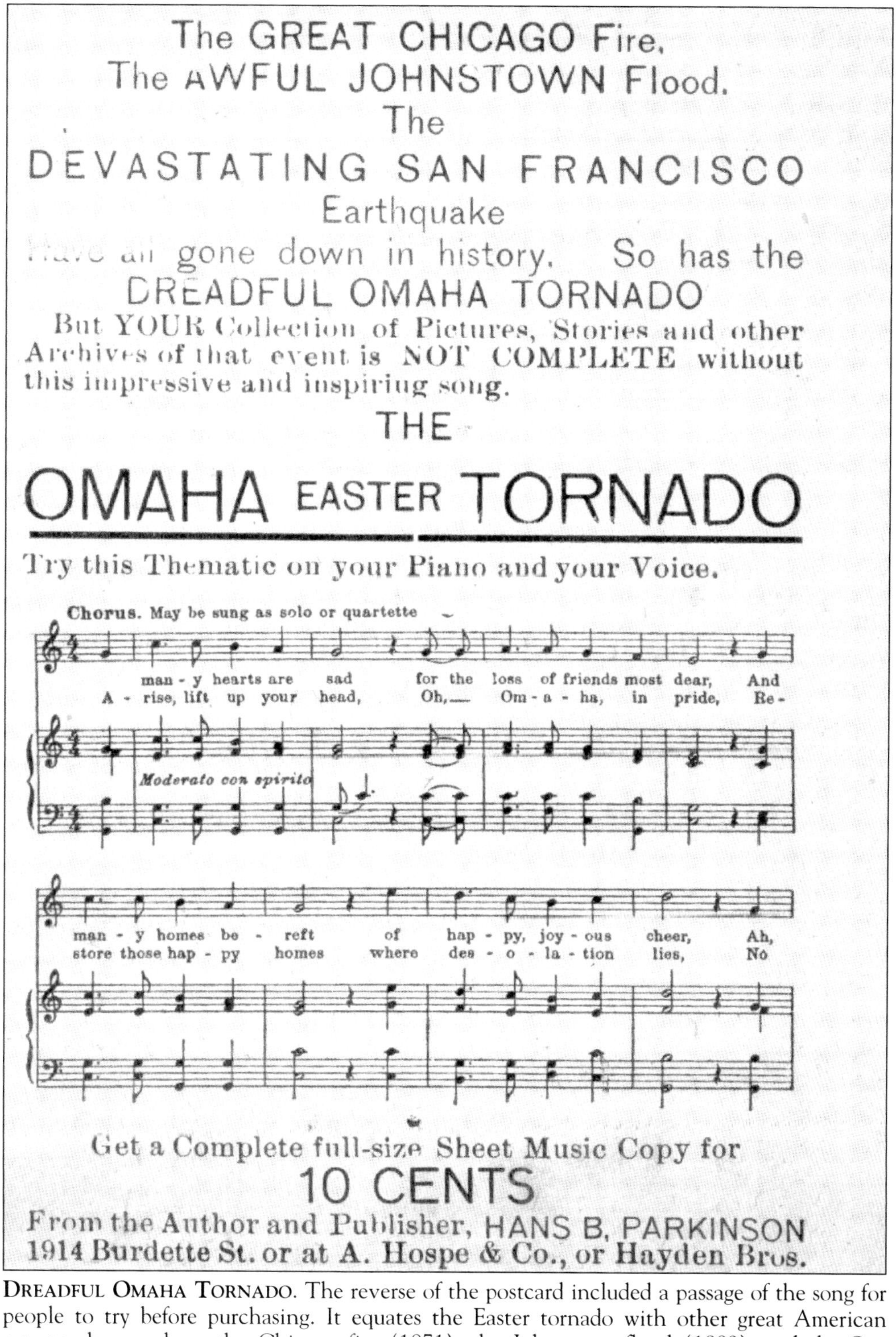

DREADFUL OMAHA TORNADO. The reverse of the postcard included a passage of the song for people to try before purchasing. It equates the Easter tornado with other great American catastrophes, such as the Chicago fire (1871), the Johnstown flood (1889), and the San Francisco earthquake (1906).

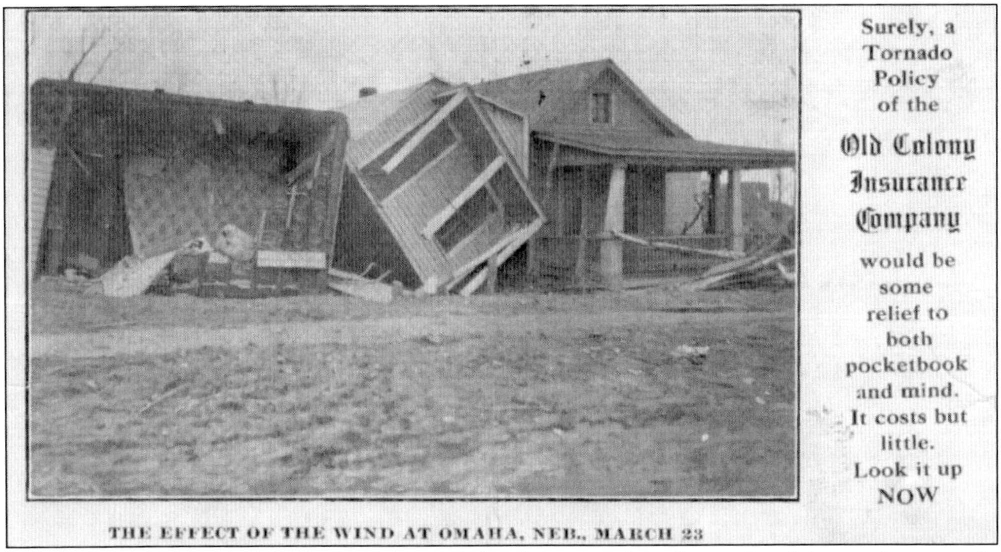

INSURANCE ADVERTISEMENT POSTCARD. The disaster ushered in a local boom for tornado insurers, as only a small percentage of the blighted buildings were covered by tornado insurance. Within two weeks of the storm, 12,000 Omahans signed tornado policies amounting to $10 million in coverage.

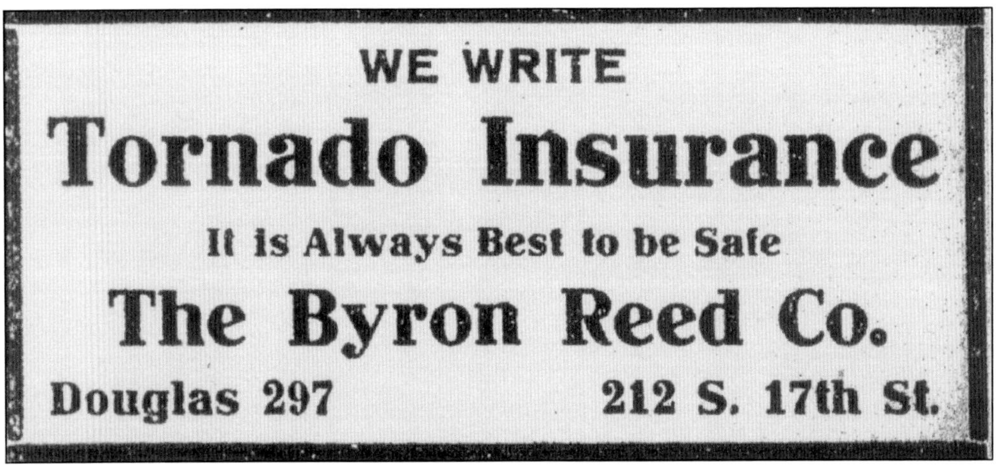

BYRON REED CO. ADVERTISEMENT. Omaha newspapers were soon filled with advertisements urging people to purchase tornado insurance. Byron Reed opened his real estate business in Omaha in 1856, and soon branched out to other capitalist ventures. By the time he passed away in 1891, Reed had amassed one of Omaha's greatest fortunes.

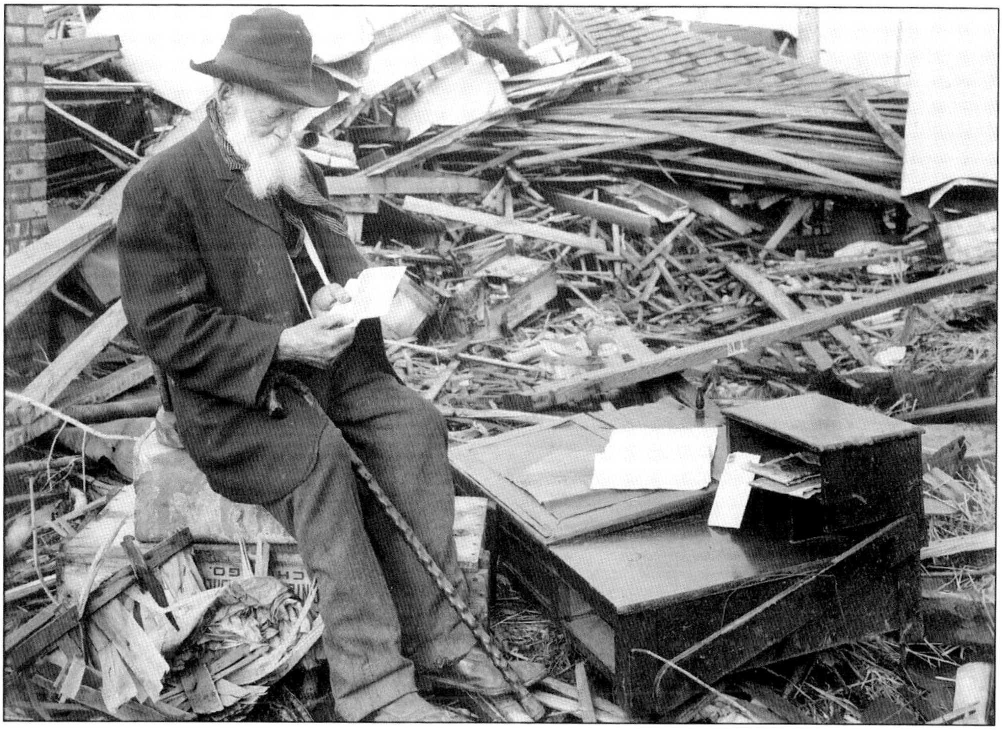

INSURANCE DOCUMENT. This elderly gentleman holds an insurance document amid the ruins of his former home. Only two percent of property owners carried tornado insurance at the time of the storm. (Bostwick-Frohardt Collection, Durham Western Heritage Museum.)

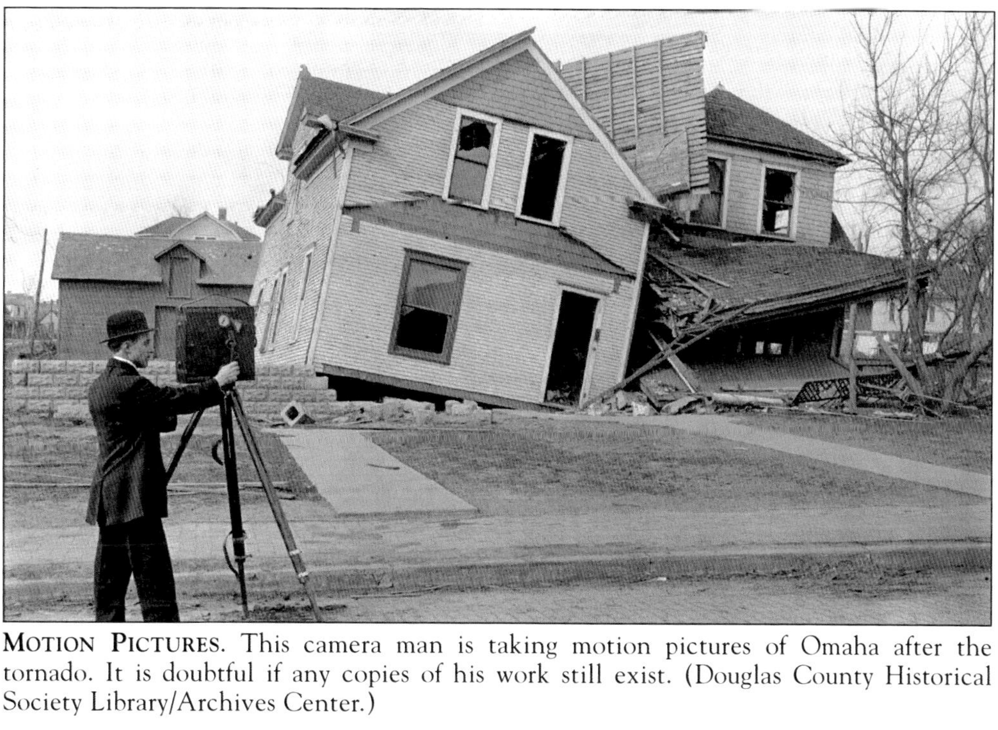

MOTION PICTURES. This camera man is taking motion pictures of Omaha after the tornado. It is doubtful if any copies of his work still exist. (Douglas County Historical Society Library/Archives Center.)

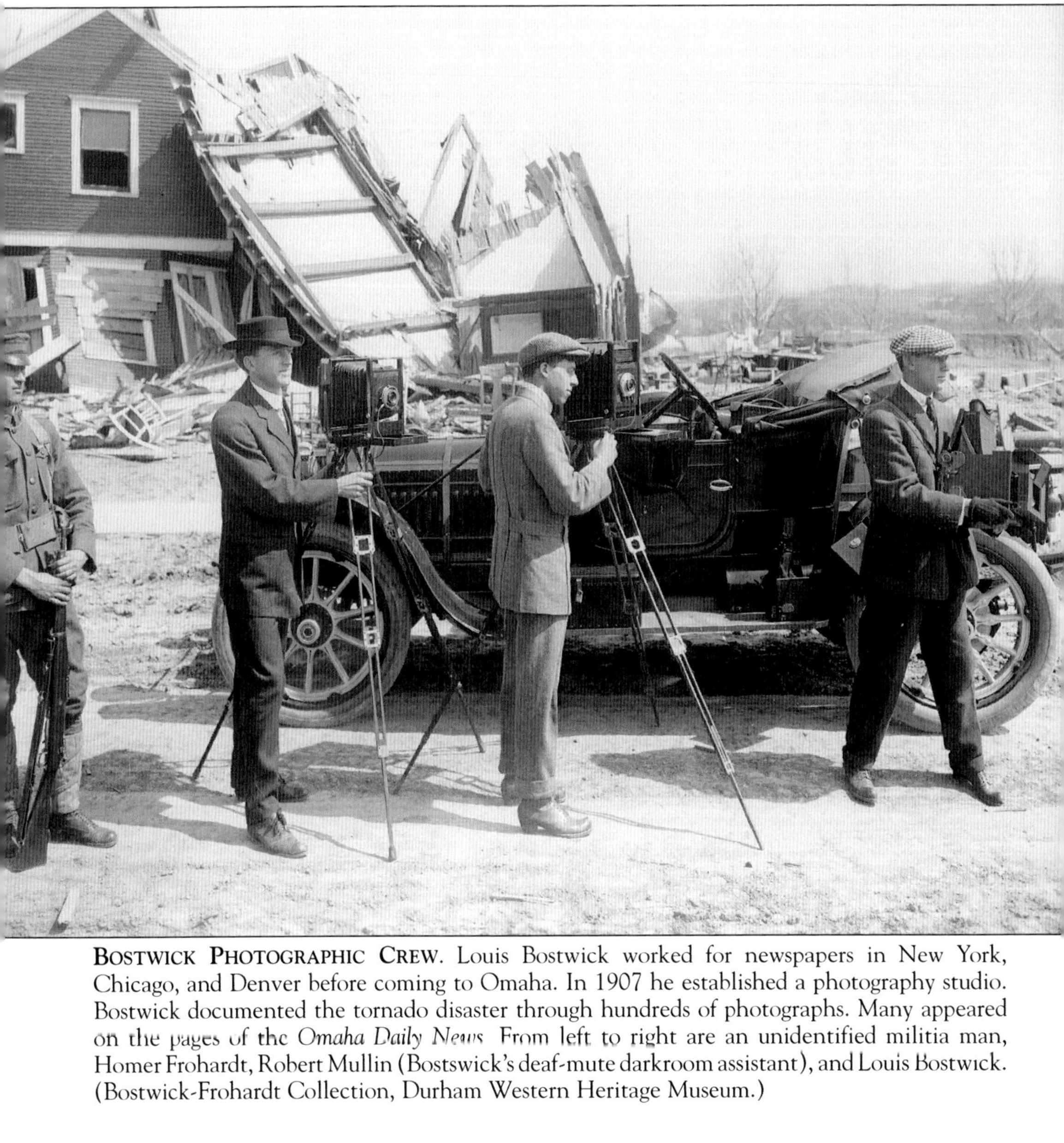

BOSTWICK PHOTOGRAPHIC CREW. Louis Bostwick worked for newspapers in New York, Chicago, and Denver before coming to Omaha. In 1907 he established a photography studio. Bostwick documented the tornado disaster through hundreds of photographs. Many appeared on the pages of the *Omaha Daily News*. From left to right are an unidentified militia man, Homer Frohardt, Robert Mullin (Bostswick's deaf-mute darkroom assistant), and Louis Bostwick. (Bostwick-Frohardt Collection, Durham Western Heritage Museum.)

Two

RALSTON

Ralston was just beginning to get on its feet and its factories had arrived at the point where they could see independence, when everything was swept away by the tornado... Omaha hopes to see Ralston speedily rebuilt. It was an independent little community the success of which some doubted for awhile, but which had proved itself worthy, and was beginning to attract the attention of men who have a dream of greater Omaha.

—Omaha Excelsior, *April 12, 1913*

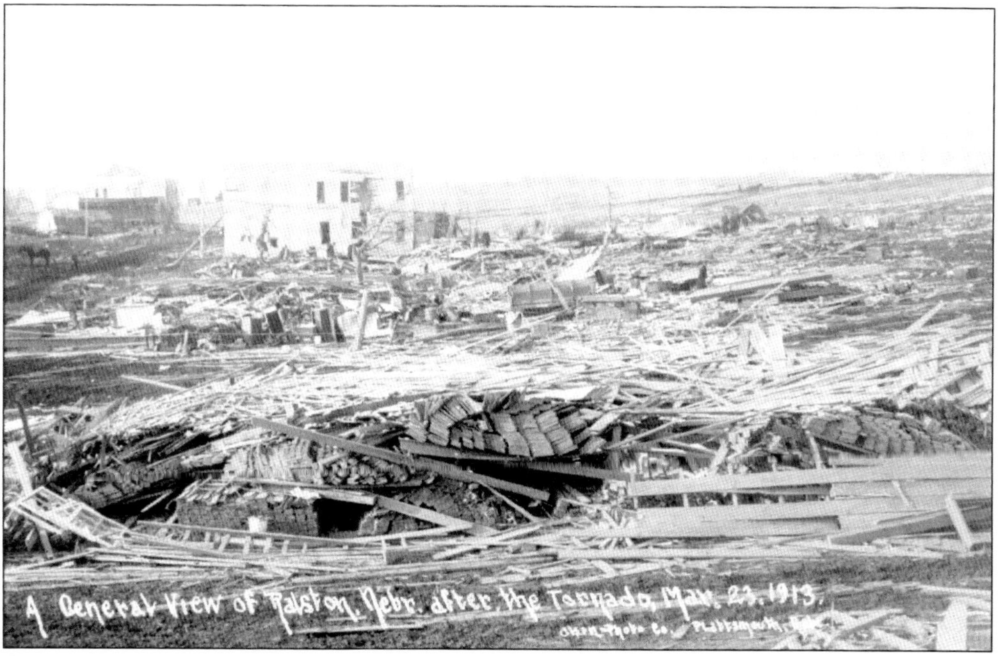

GENERAL VIEW OF RALSTON. Downtown Ralston is in the distance with the debris widely scattered. Before hitting Omaha, the twister first touched down in Ralston, destroying most of the village's downtown and manufacturing houses.

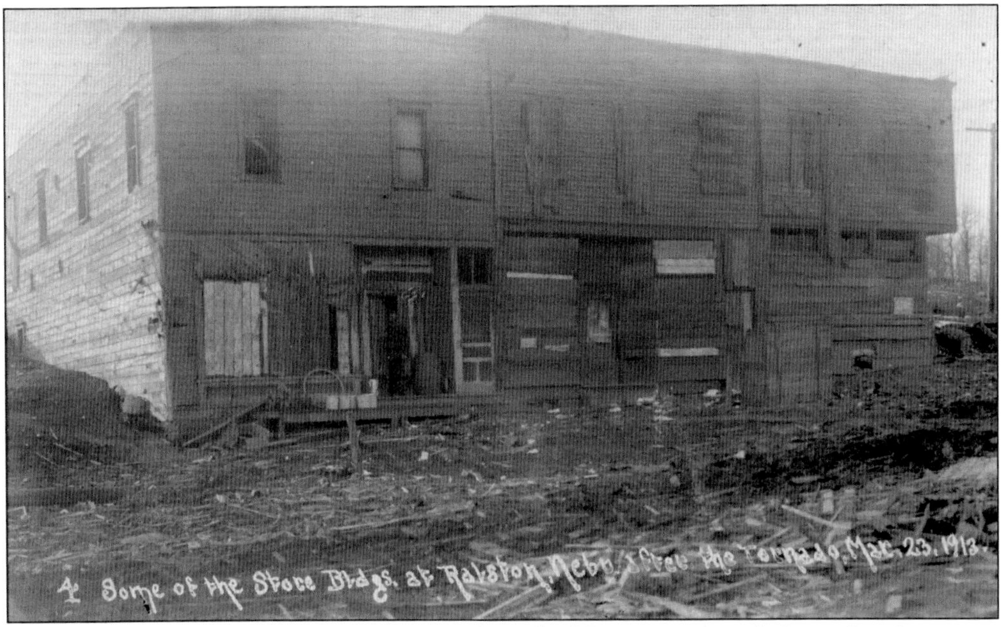

BOARDED-UP DOWNTOWN. Downtown Ralston buildings were boarded up after the storm, including the R.T. Propst Grocery Store at left. (The Frank & Velma Johnson Ralston Archives Museum.)

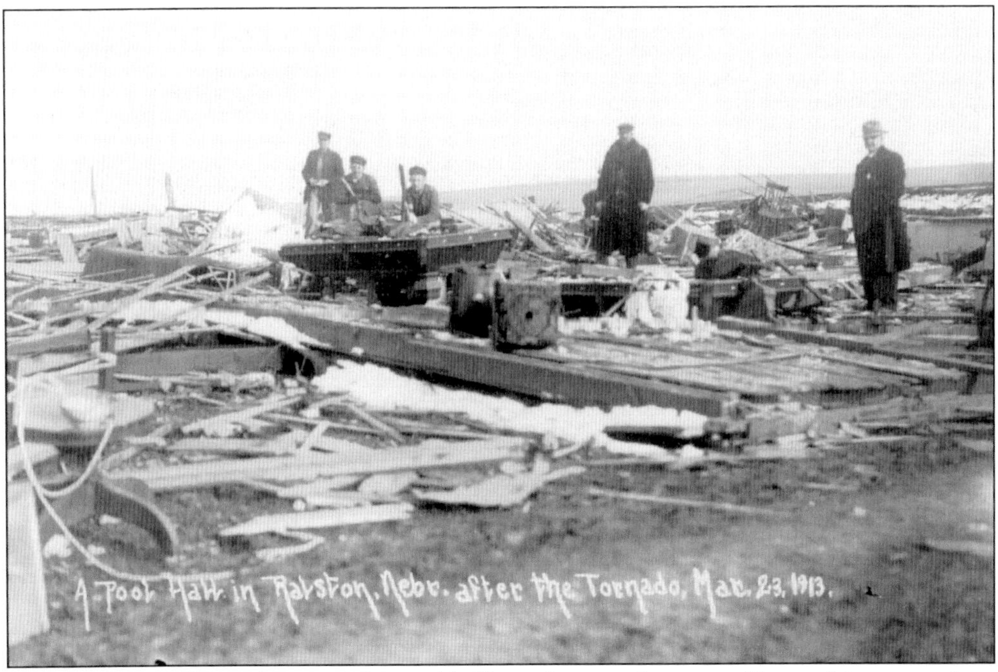

RALSTON POOL HALL. A view of the pool hall wreckage, with men and boys taking pause from sifting through rubble.

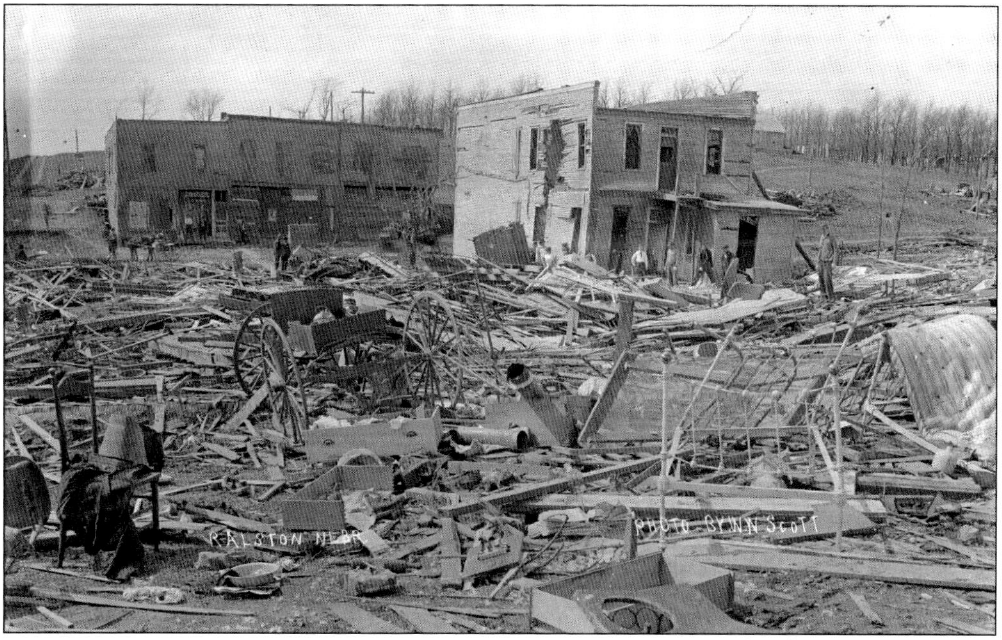

WRECKAGE AT RALSTON. The business district of Ralston was the hardest hit. Across the street, businesses are boarded up, and on this side, various items have been strewn by the storm. (Douglas County Historical Society Library/Archives Center.)

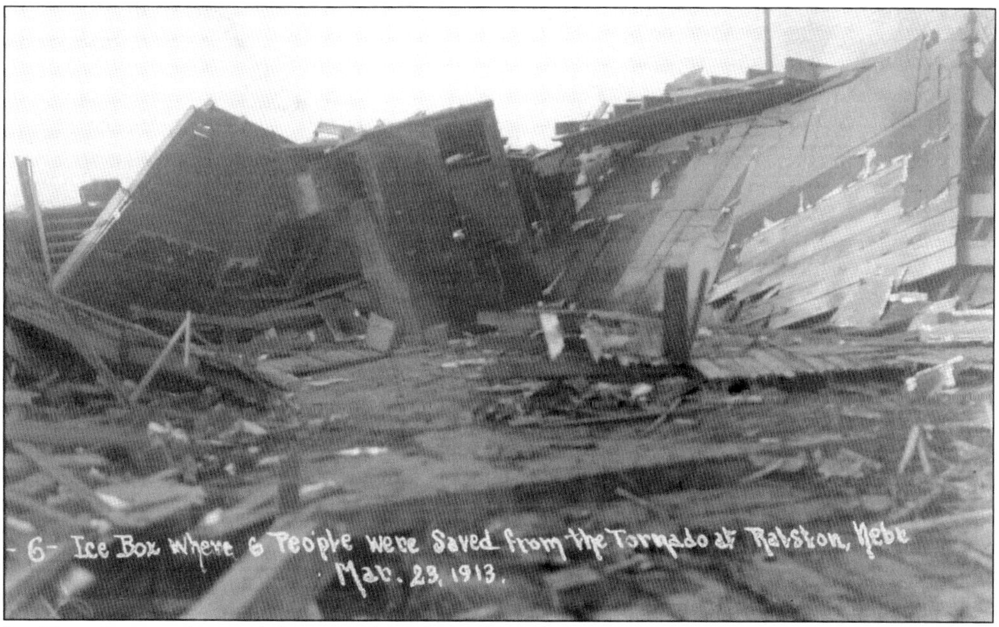

ICE BOX. Six people saved their own lives by seeking shelter inside an ice box. (The Frank & Velma Johnson Ralston Archives Museum.)

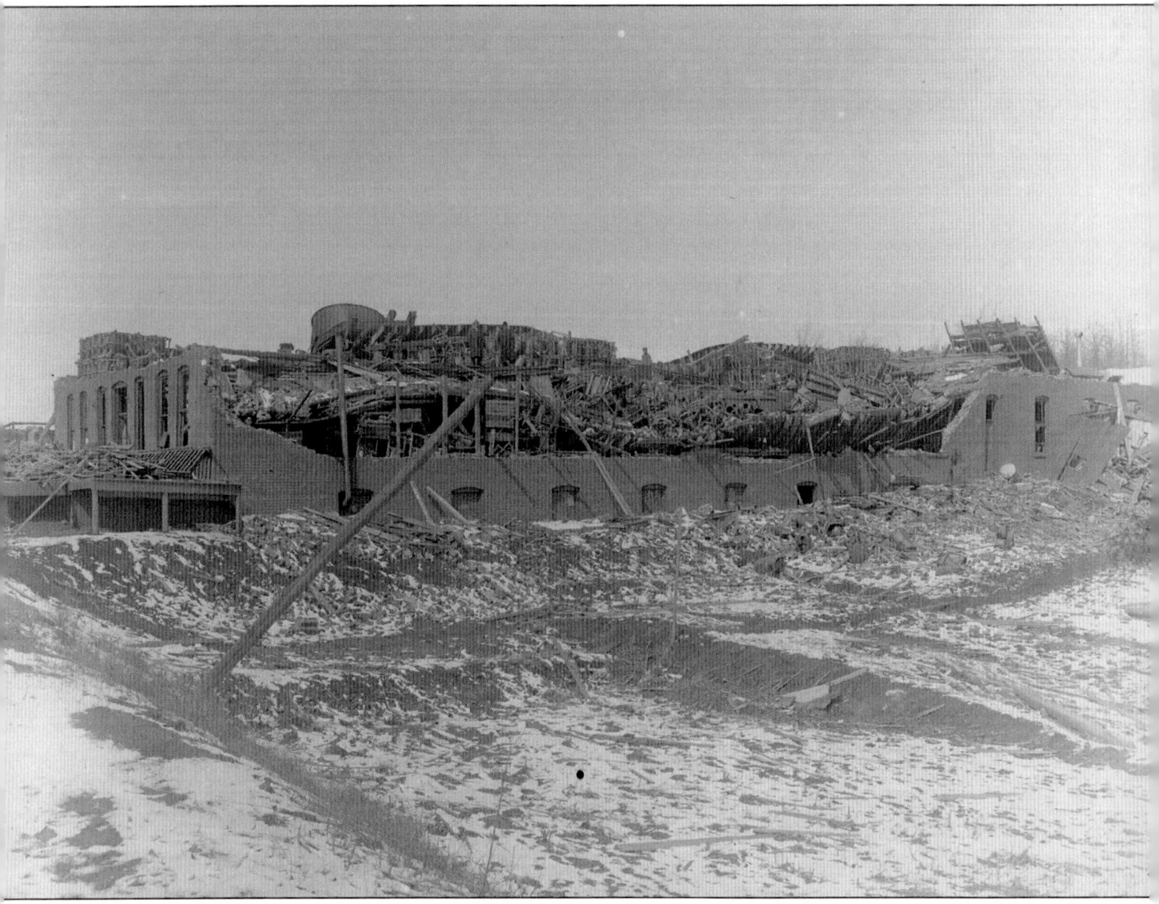

HOWARD STOVE WORKS. This view shows the full extent of the devastation inflicted on the impressive brick building. (The Frank & Velma Johnson Ralston Archives Museum.)

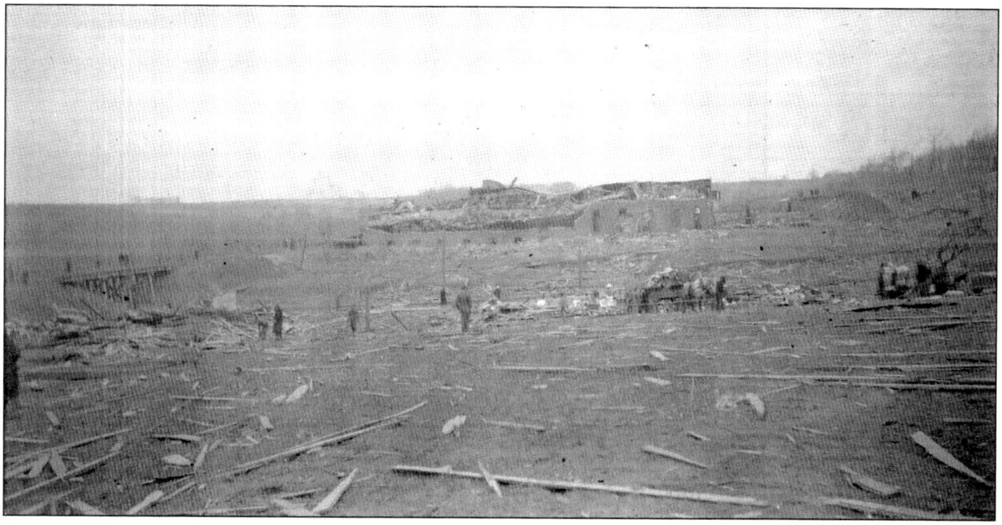

Stove Works. This wide view features the Howard Stove Works in the center. The rubble near the railroad trestle indicates where the depot had stood. (The Frank & Velma Johnson Ralston Archives Museum.)

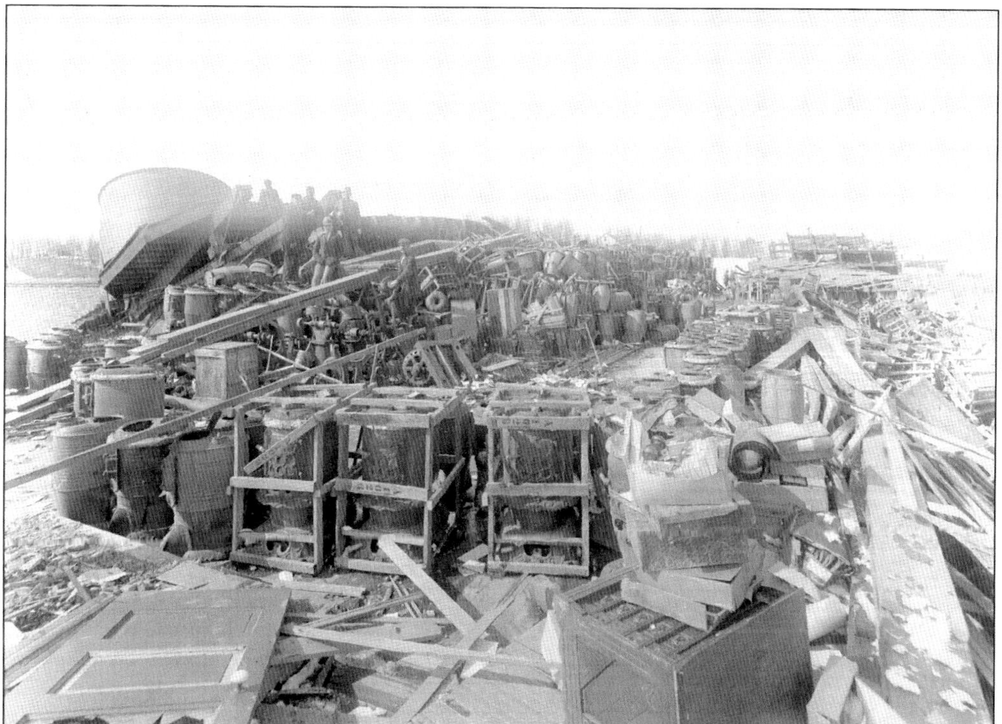

Stove Works Roof. These men are on top of the Howard Stove Works. Three stoves in shipping crates are in the center of the photo. (The Frank & Velma Johnson Ralston Archives Museum.)

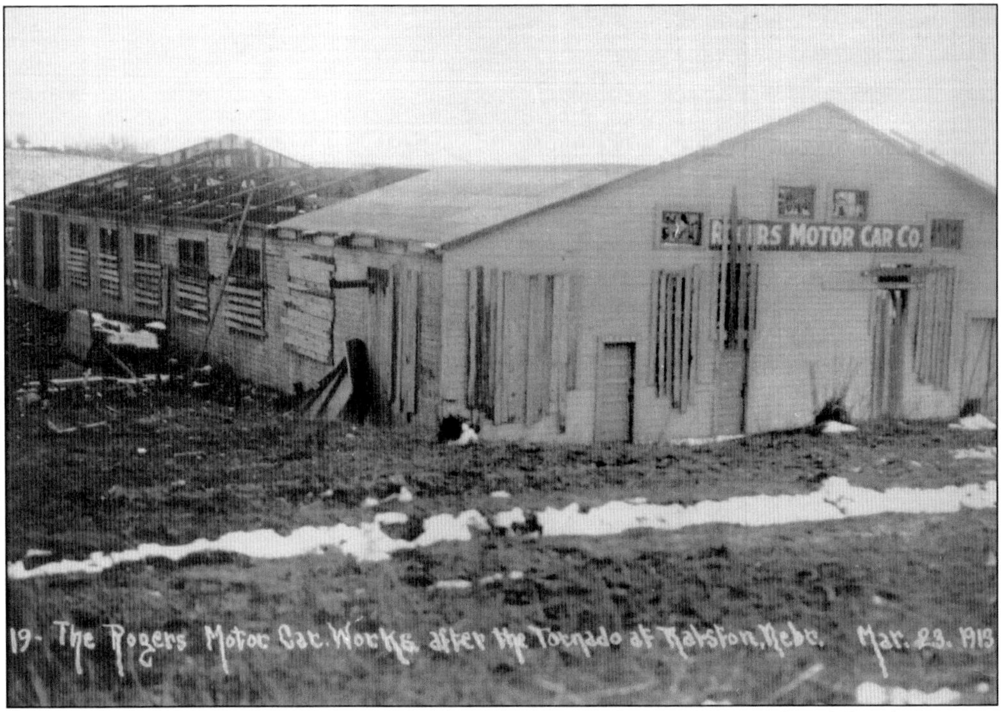

Rogers Motor Car Works. Only eight automobiles were ever produced by the Rogers Motor Car works. The Omaha Electric Company purchased the first Rogers auto. Despite the auto fever sweeping the nation, the building was repaired and sold to the Omaha Tub Factory, which manufactured butter tubs. (The Frank & Velma Johnson Ralston Archives Museum.)

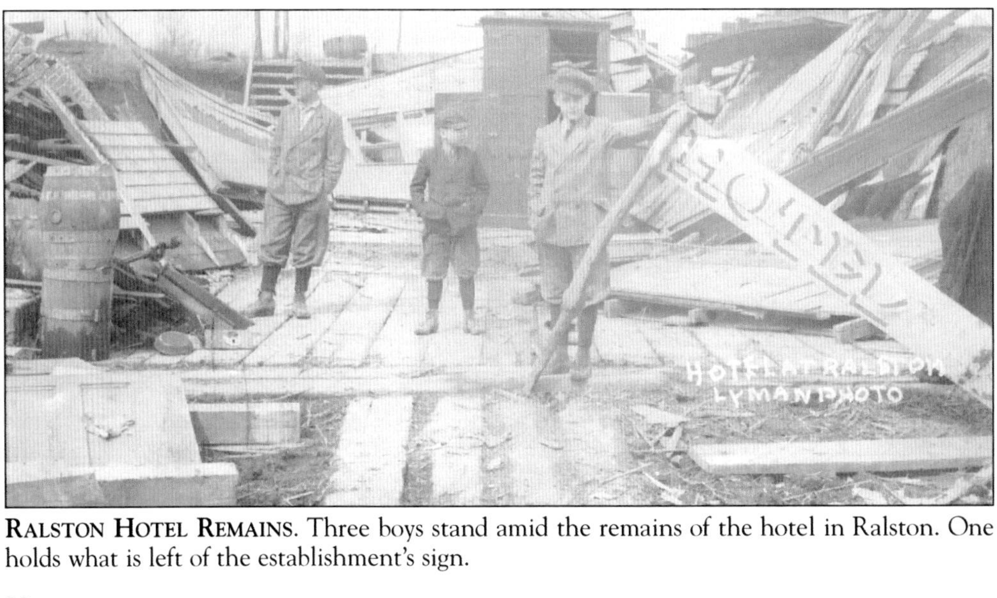

Ralston Hotel Remains. Three boys stand amid the remains of the hotel in Ralston. One holds what is left of the establishment's sign.

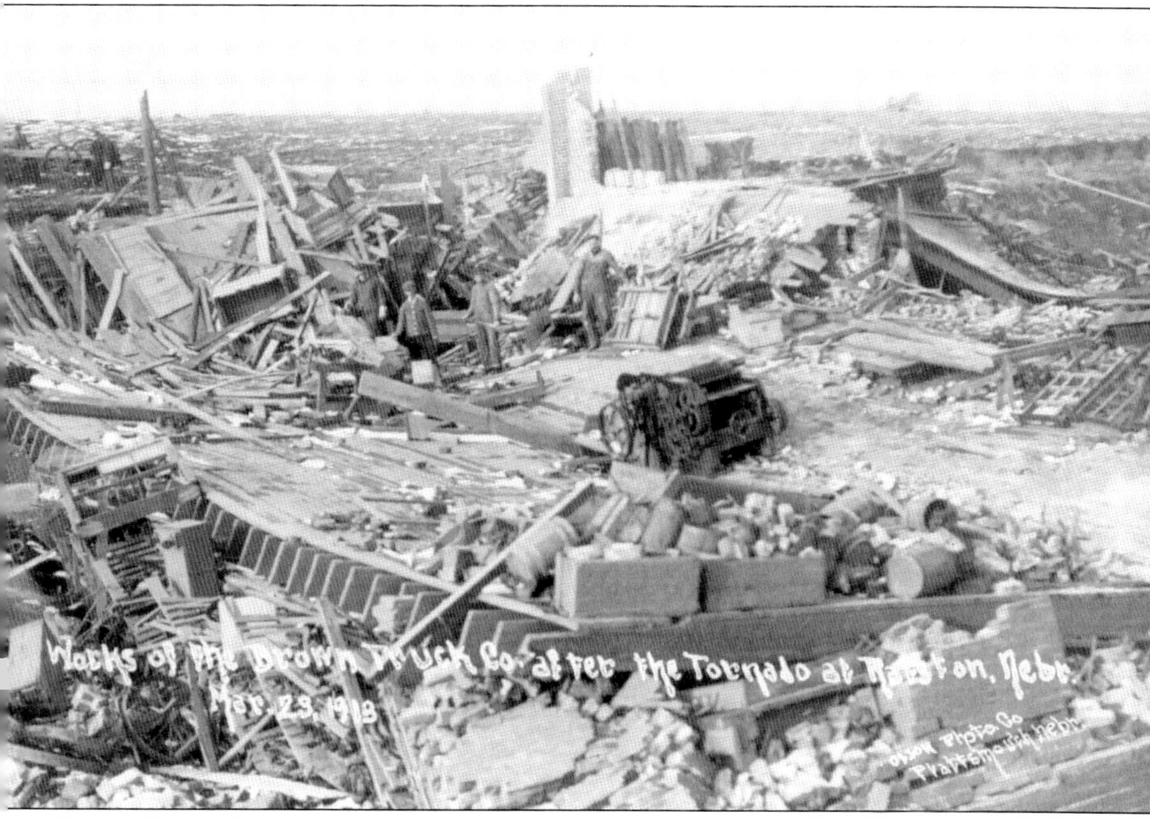

BROWN TRUCK COMPANY. The Brown Truck Company was just one of many factories vital to the local economy and heavily damaged by the tornado.

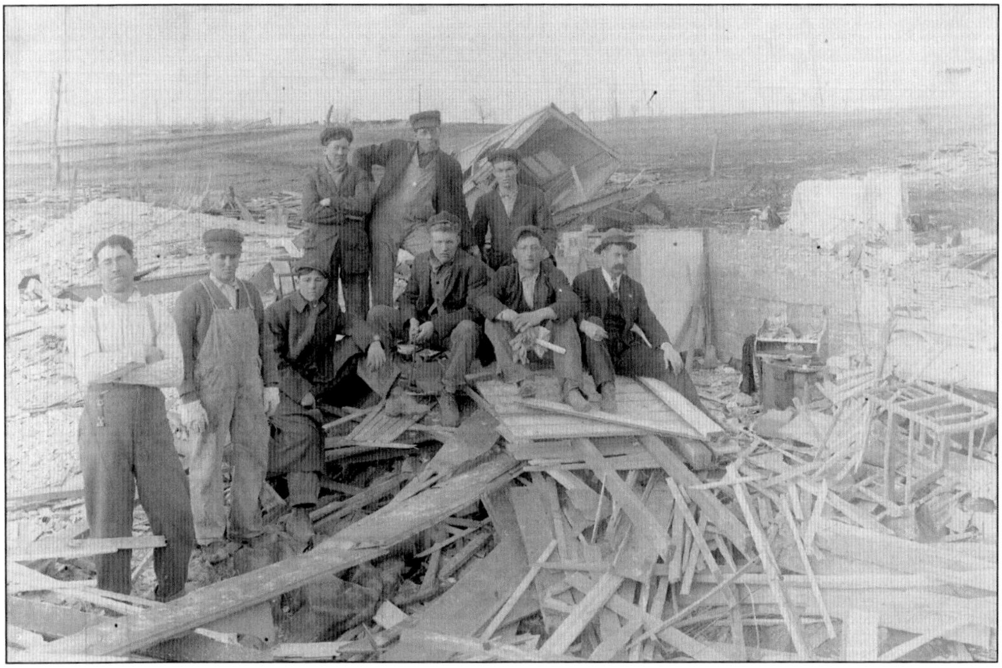

MILLER'S RESTAURANT SURVIVORS. The caption attached to this photograph of Miller's Restaurant patrons proclaimed: "All men shown in the picture except two crawled out of the wreckage without receiving a scratch." (The Frank & Velma Johnson Ralston Archives Museum.)

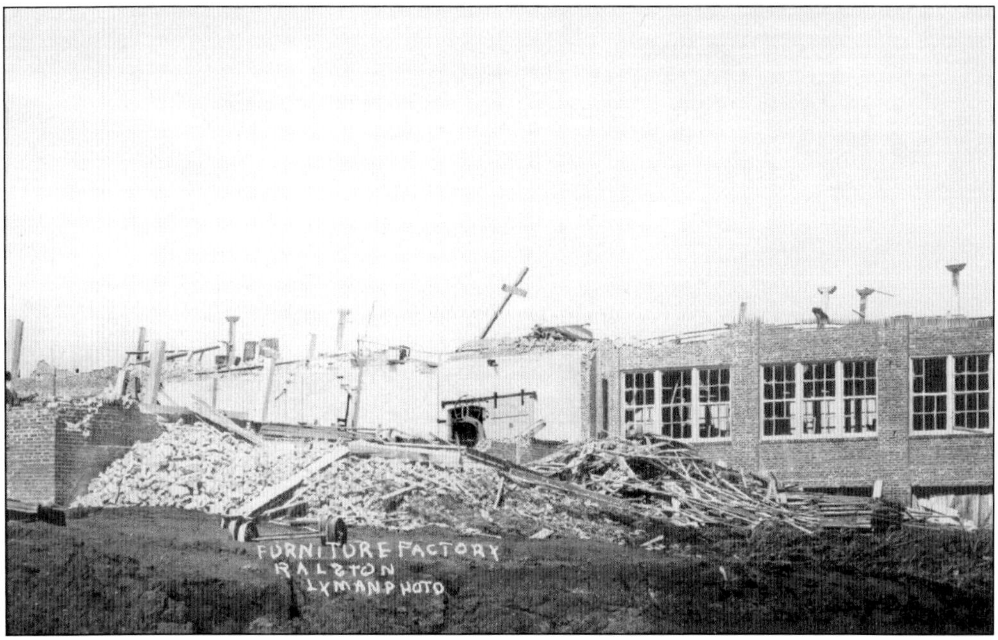

OMAHA FURNITURE FACTORY. The Omaha Furniture Factory (later Orchard & Wilhelm Furniture) was established in 1910, and crafted home furnishings for dining rooms and kitchens, as well as upholstered living room furniture.

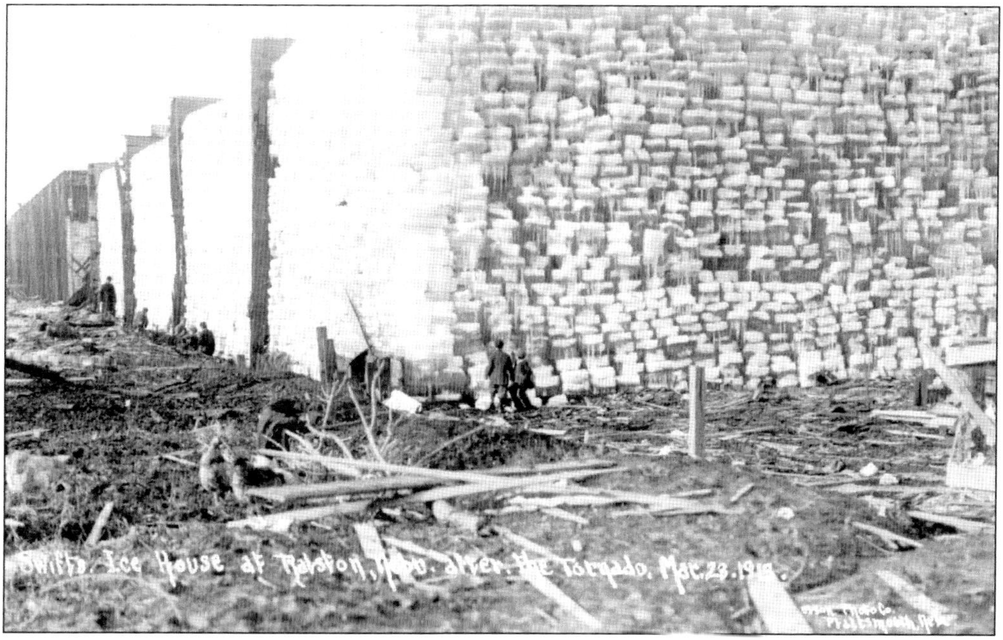

SURVEYING THE CUDAHY ICE HOUSE. Men and boys survey the Cudahy Ice House, which had its outer walls stripped away, leaving $500,000 worth of ice exposed. Colder weather prevailed after the storm, which ultimately spared about half of the ice. The card is mislabeled as the Swift & Company Ice House.

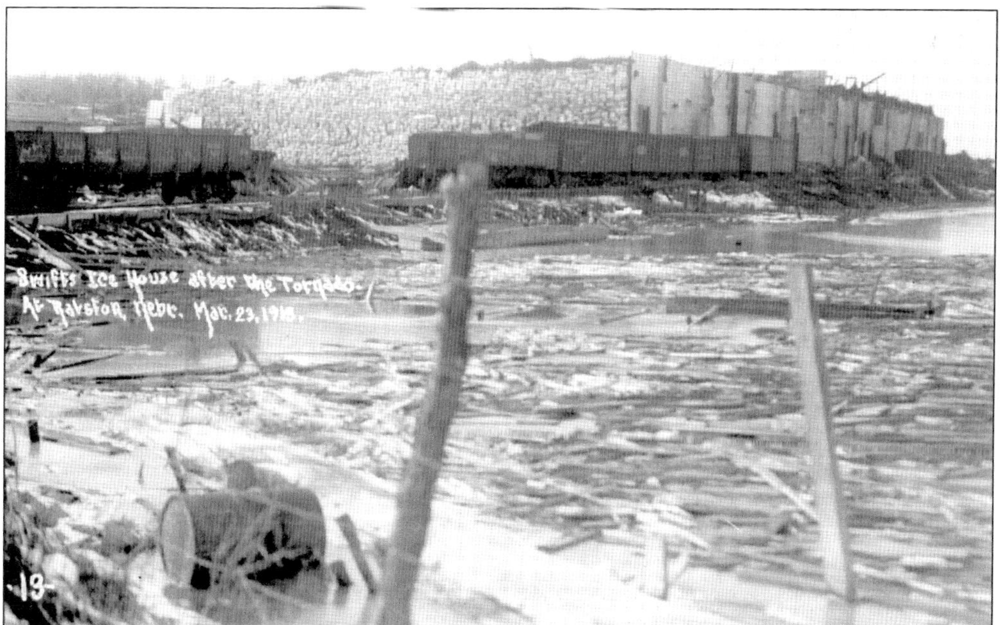

DEBRIS ON SEYMOUR LAKE. Ice was harvested during the winter from Seymour Lake. The ice house was connected by rail to the Cudahy Packing plant in South Omaha. Debris at the bottom of the image is floating on Seymour Lake. The card is mislabeled as the Swift & Company Ice House.

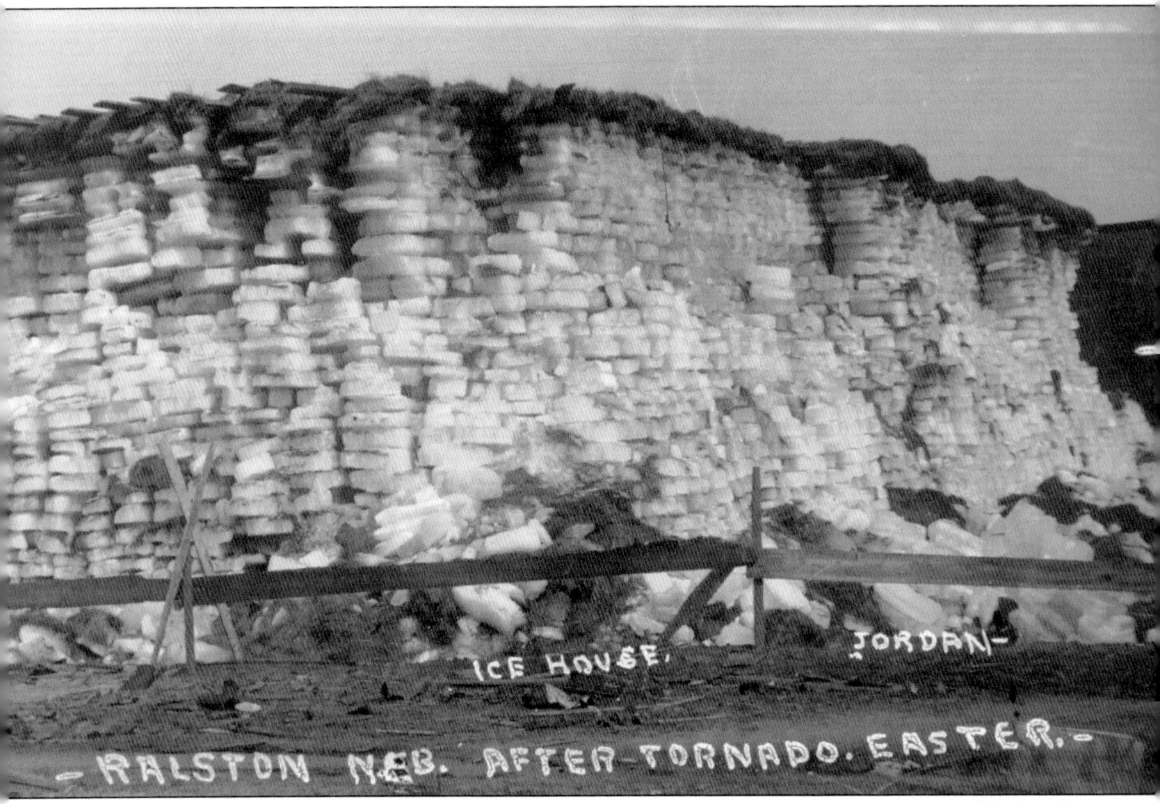

CUDAHY ICE HOUSE. This close-up view of the ice house details the massive blocks that were stored there.

Three

WEST FARNAM

It veering mounted the beautiful heights of Thirty-eighth street, crowned the costly dwellings, mostly new and built of solid material. Into their midst it dipped as in fiendish mockery of the magnificence puny man had wrought. And it tore through the region of wealth and beauty as if it were a canebreak, hurling houses, or parts of houses, high into the air and far down the slope of the hill to the east.

—*James B. Wootan, the* Omaha Bee*, March 30, 1913*

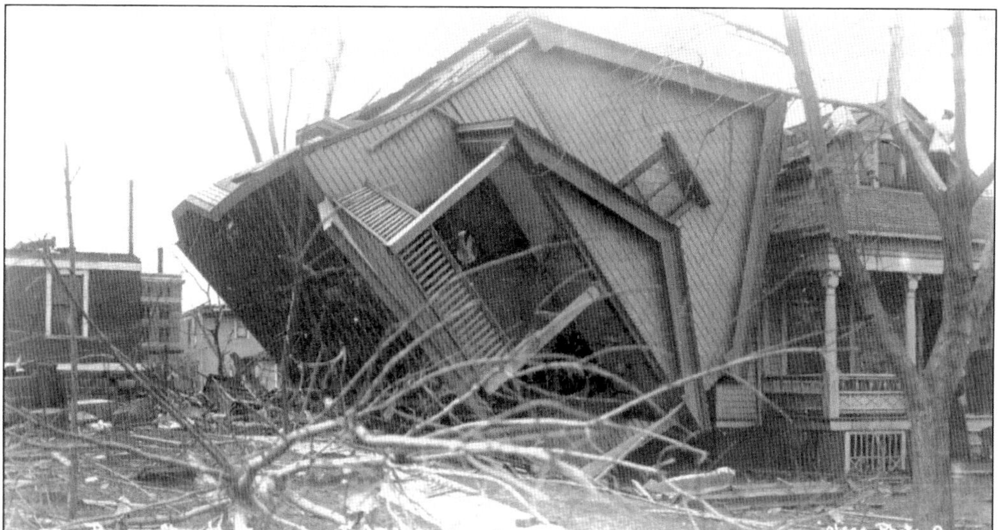

FREAK DAMAGE. These homes on Farnam Street demonstrate some of the freak damage inflicted by the tornado. The house of C.F. Hopper was blown onto the neighboring house, which suffered little damage.

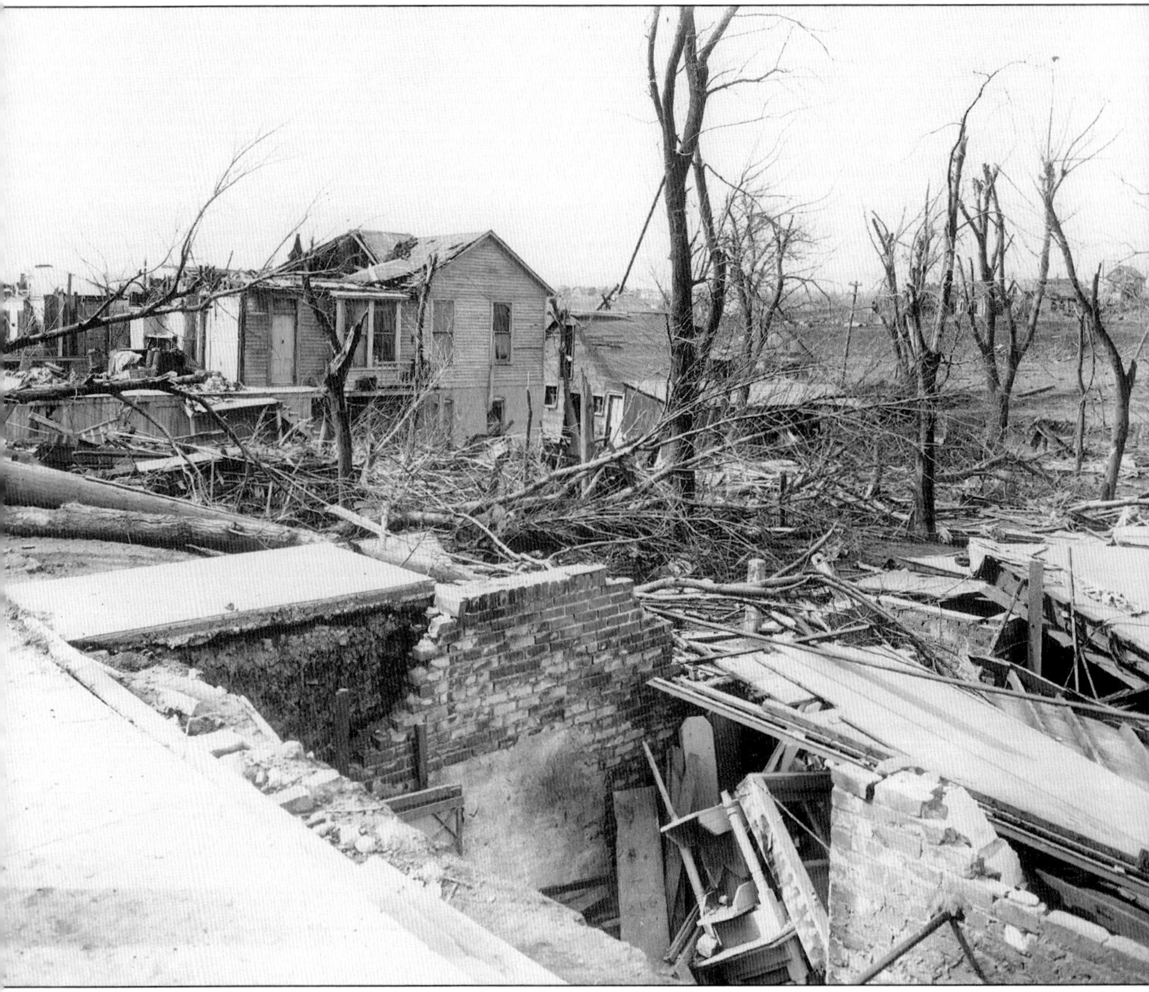

FORTY-NINTH AND LEAVENWORTH STREETS. This panoramic photo shows homes at the southwestern edge of Omaha along Leavenworth Street, including this one blown from its foundation. Twelve people lost their lives in this vicinity. On the hill at right is the

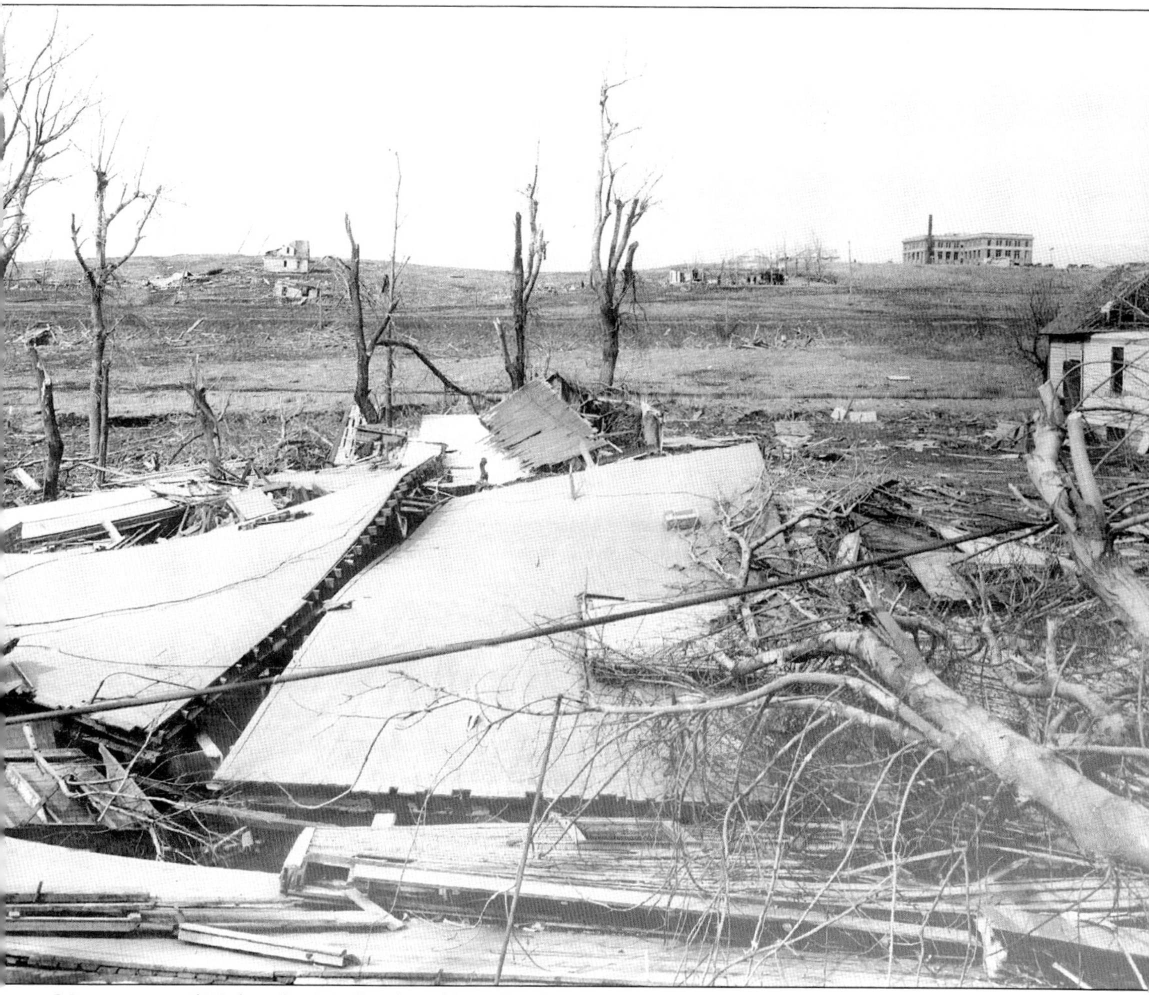

University of Nebraska Medical College building. (Bostwick-Frohardt Collection, Durham Western Heritage Museum.)

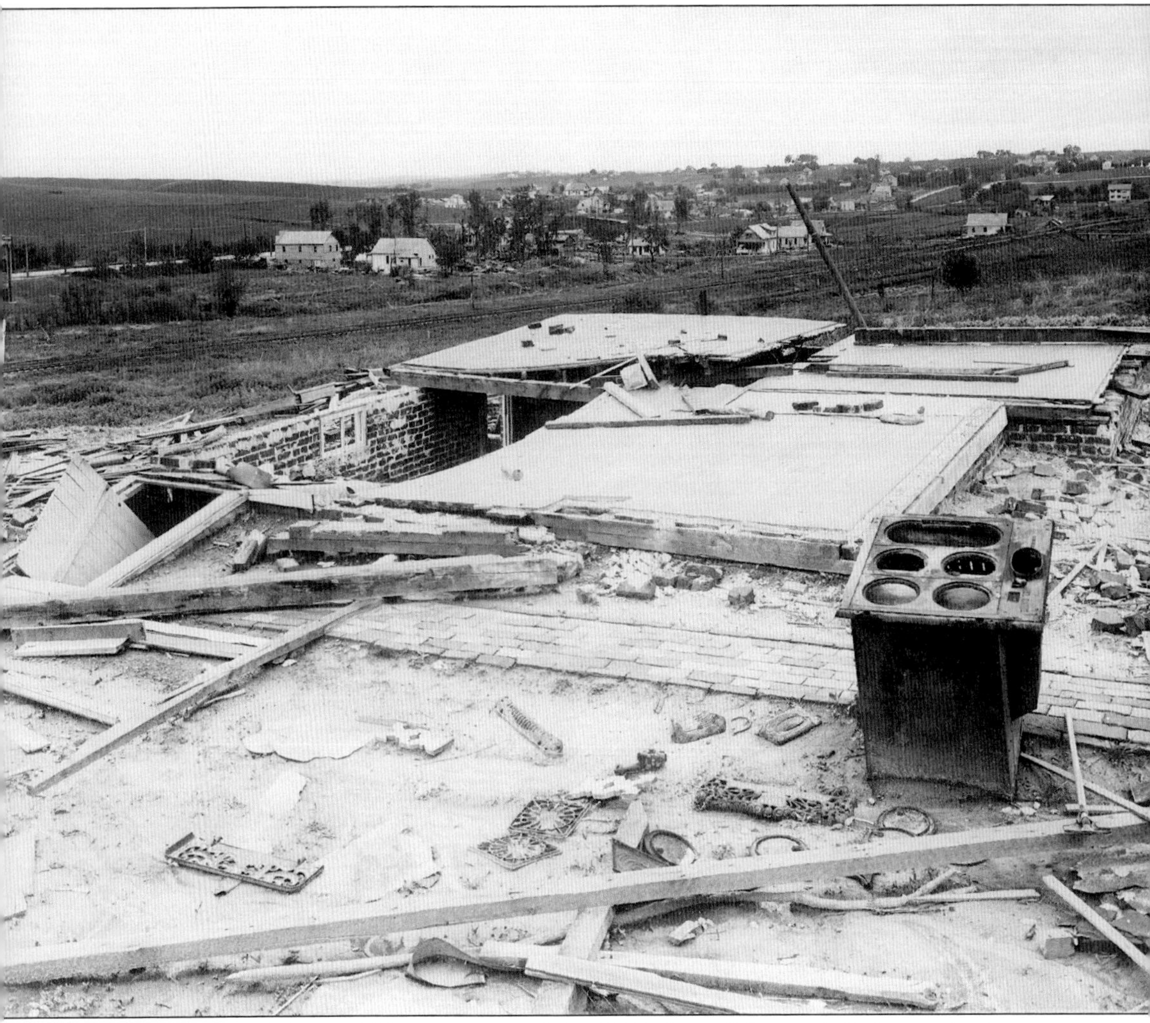

W.H. Russell House. What remains of the W.H. Russell house is little, as the home was wiped from its foundation, and only the stove was left standing. (Bostwick-Frohardt Collection, Durham Western Heritage Museum.)

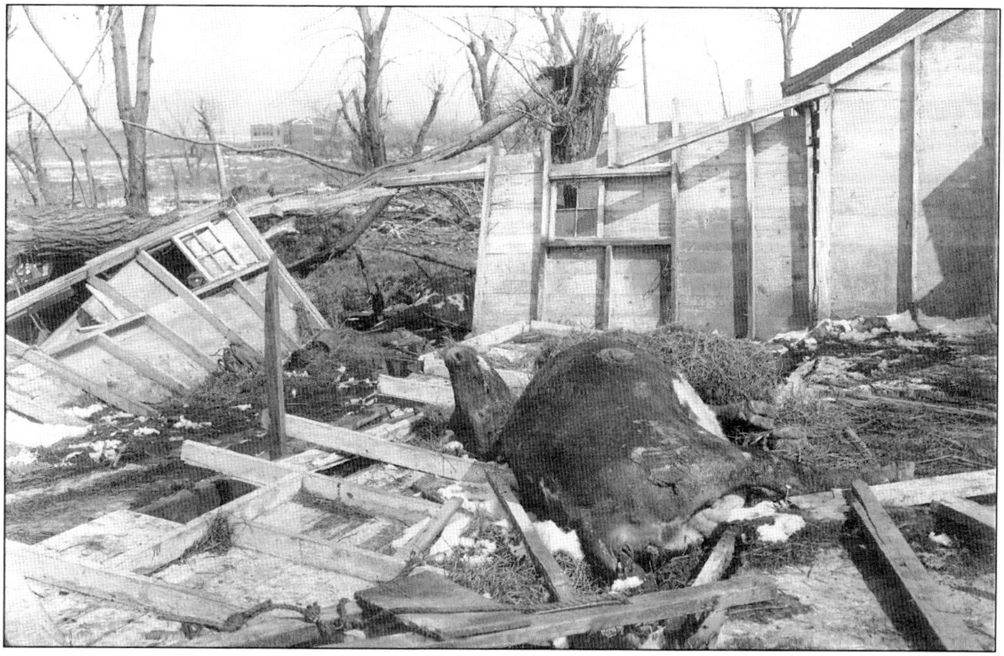

DEAD LIVESTOCK. On the path between Ralston and Omaha were many farms. Livestock such as chickens, horses, and cattle were all lost in the storm. Here a dead cow lies in the debris near 56th and Center Streets. (Bostwick-Frohardt Collection, Durham Western Heritage Museum.)

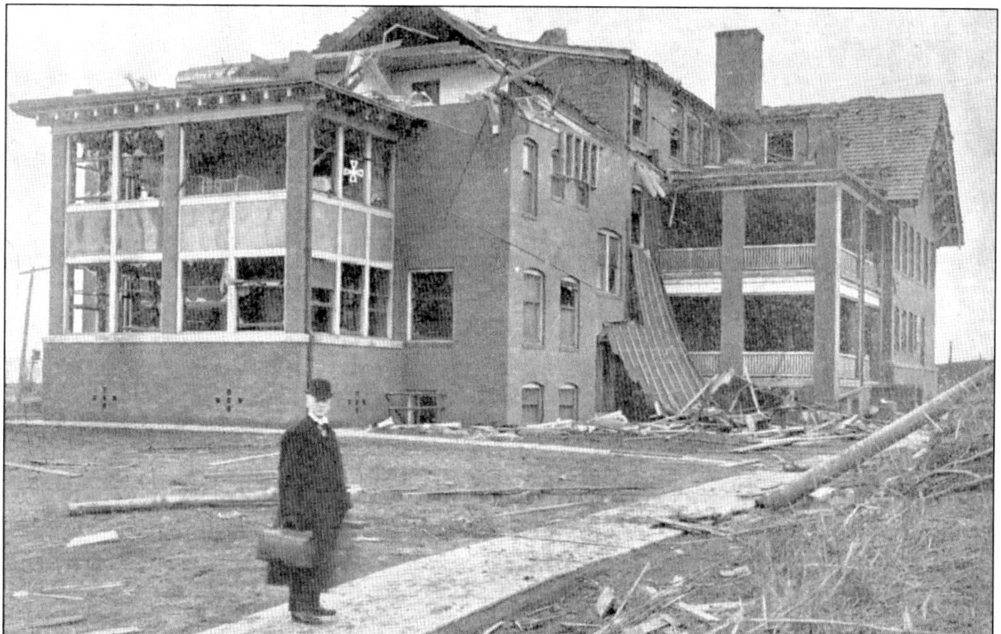

CHILD SAVING INSTITUTE. The Child Saving Institute building at 42nd and Jackson Streets was only a few years old. While half of the home's 50 children were rushed to the basement, several children were injured, and a few were swept from the building not to be found. The cross marks the window from which one child was blown. (Child Saving Institute.)

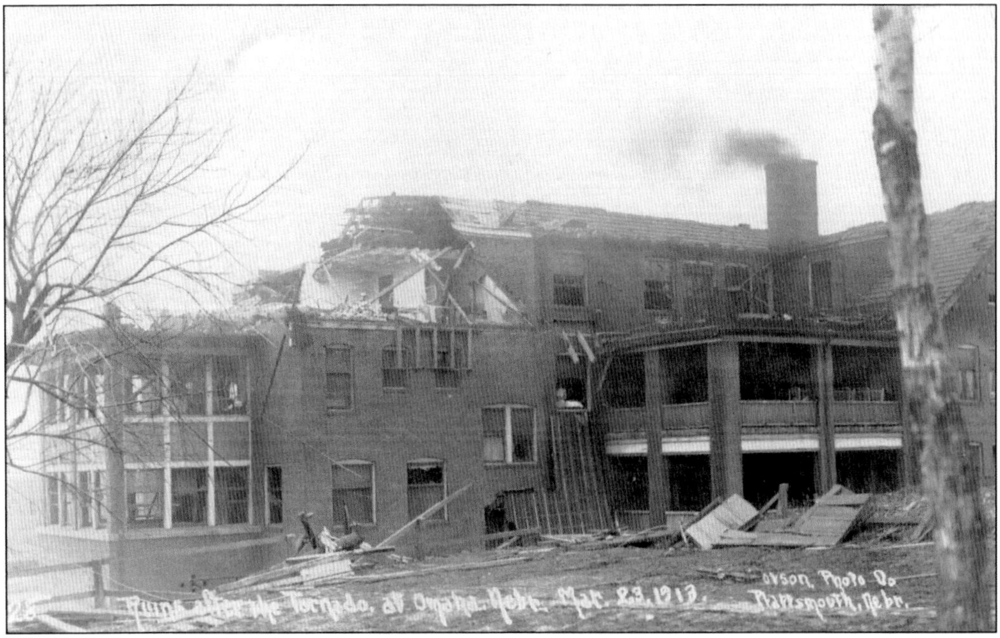

CHILD SAVING INSTITUTE, REAR VIEW. The Child Saving Institute acted as a makeshift hospital, as it was stocked with medical supplies for the children. About 50 neighborhood residents were treated here.

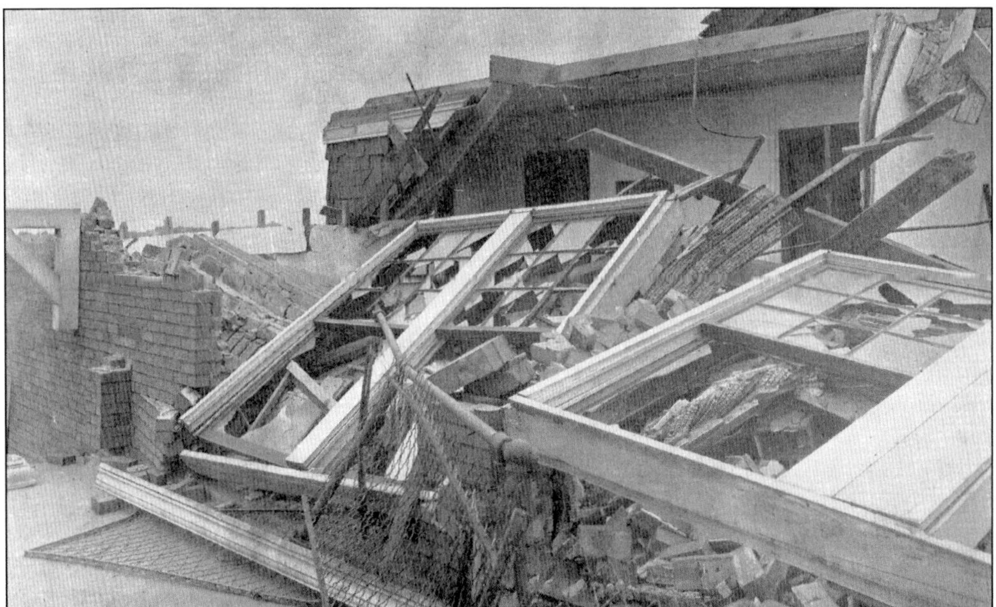

CHILD SAVING INSTITUTE ROOF. This photograph shows the damage to the roof of the building. (Child Saving Institute.)

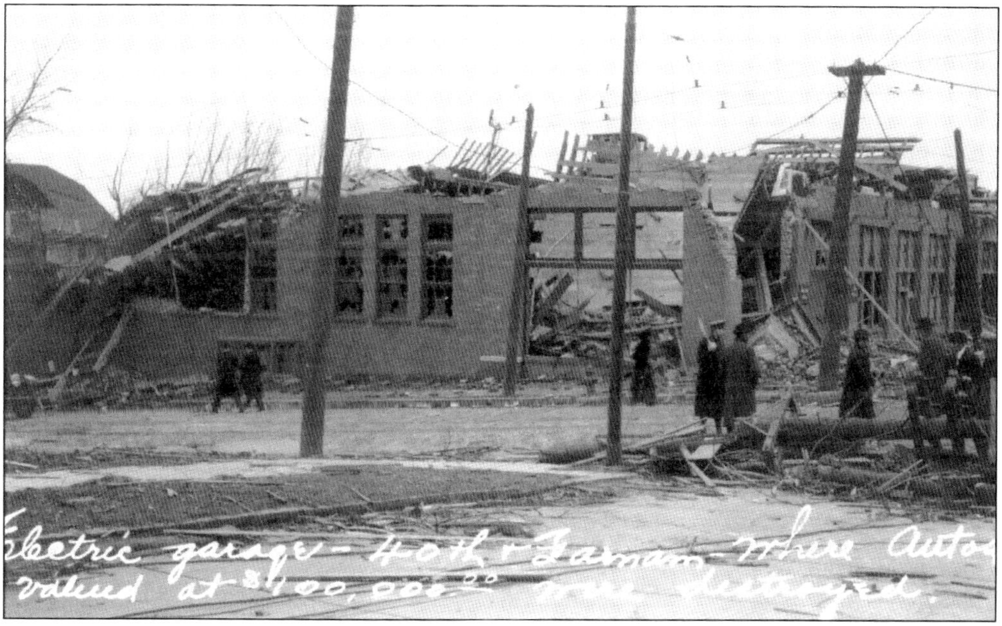

BAKER ELECTRIC GARAGE. Only six months earlier, the Baker Electric Garage at 40th and Farnam Streets had been damaged by a runaway streetcar. Two men died at this location.

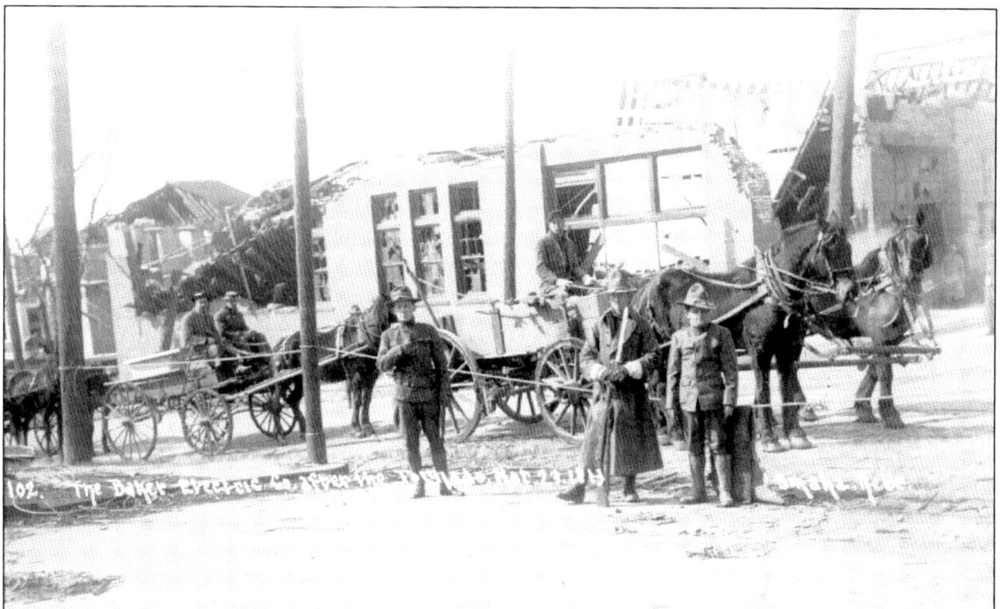

MILITIA AT 40TH AND FARNAM. The militia keeps watch over the wreckage of the Baker Electric Garage. The garage was known for its work on Studebakers. Photographer Louis Bostwick's Studebaker was inside, yet somehow escaped damage.

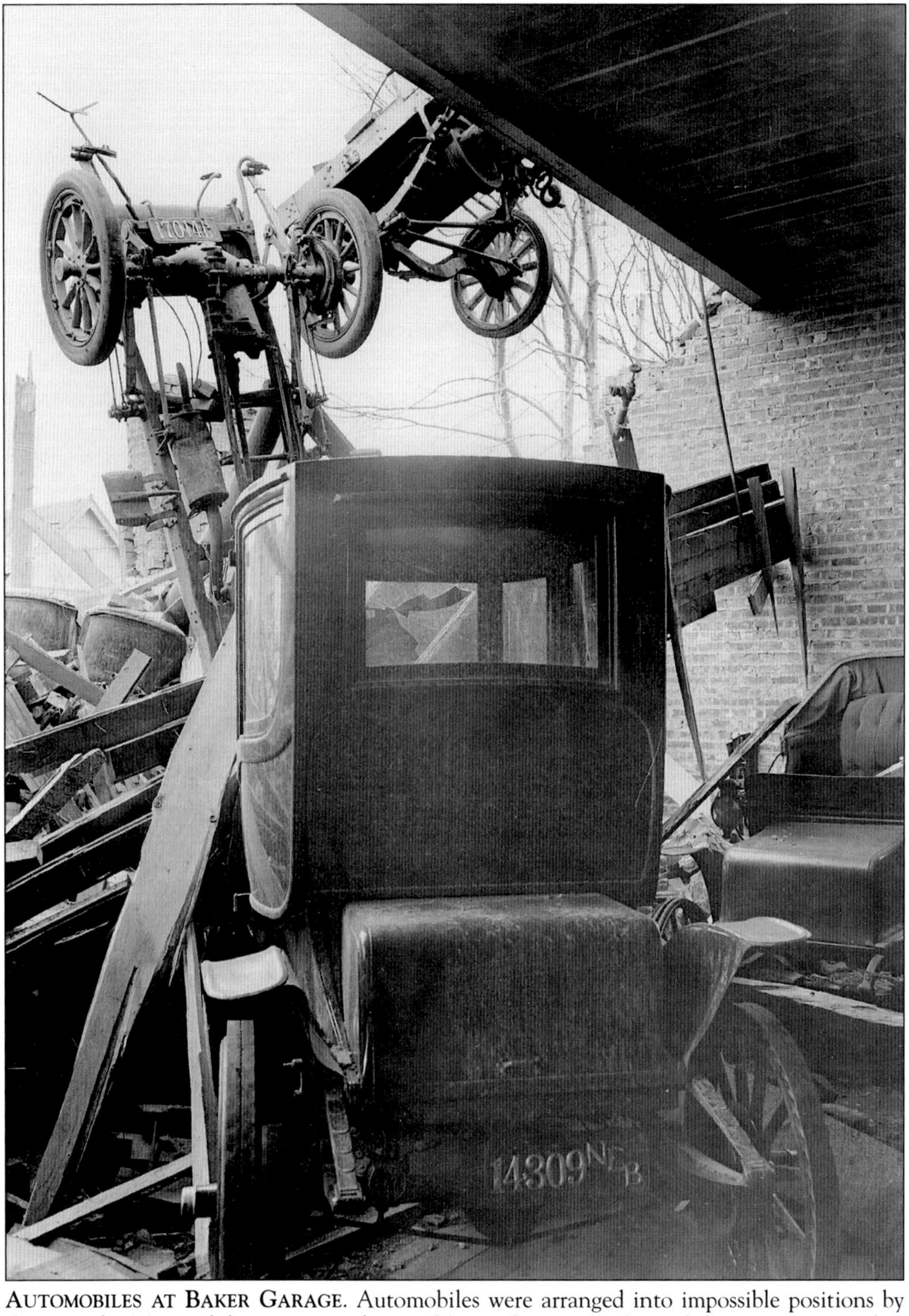

AUTOMOBILES AT BAKER GARAGE. Automobiles were arranged into impossible positions by the tornado. Many of the cars were damaged beyond repair, with total damages estimated at $100,000. (Bostwick-Frohardt Collection, Durham Western Heritage Museum.)

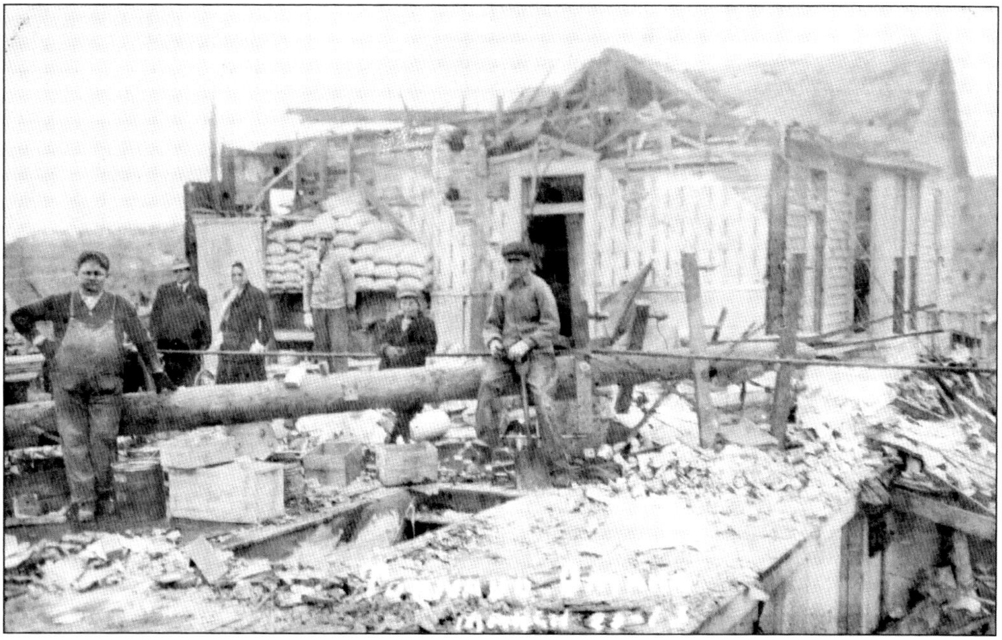

SCHULTZ GROCERY. The Schultz Grocery at 43rd and Leavenworth Streets was hit hard. Little of the store remained, yet against one wall some bags can be seen undisturbed.

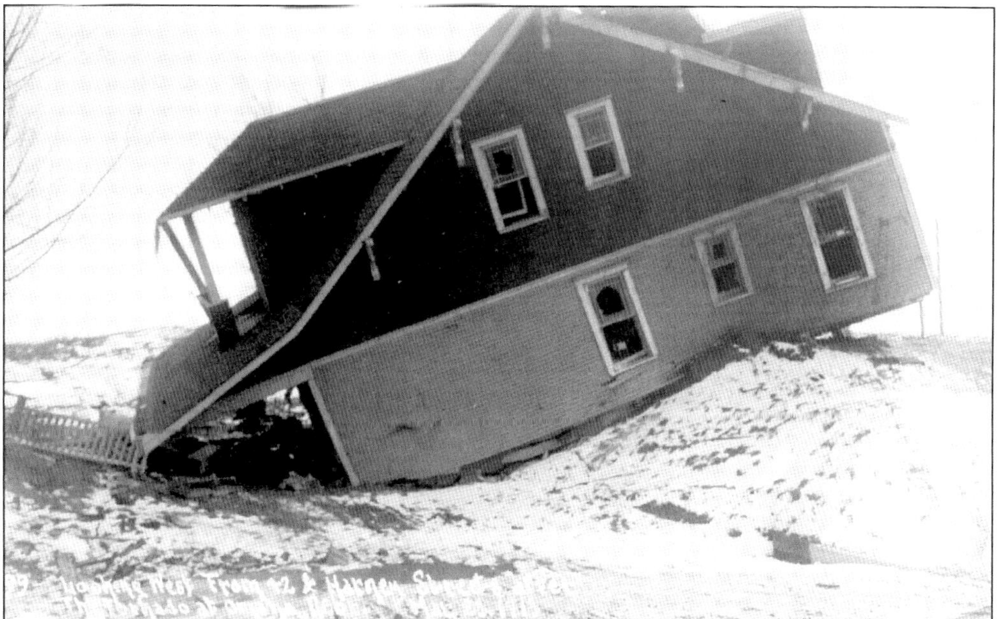

BAYSDORFER HOME. The home of Otto Baysdorfer at 44th and Harney Streets sat on a terrace facing Harney Street. It was blown around to face 44th Street.

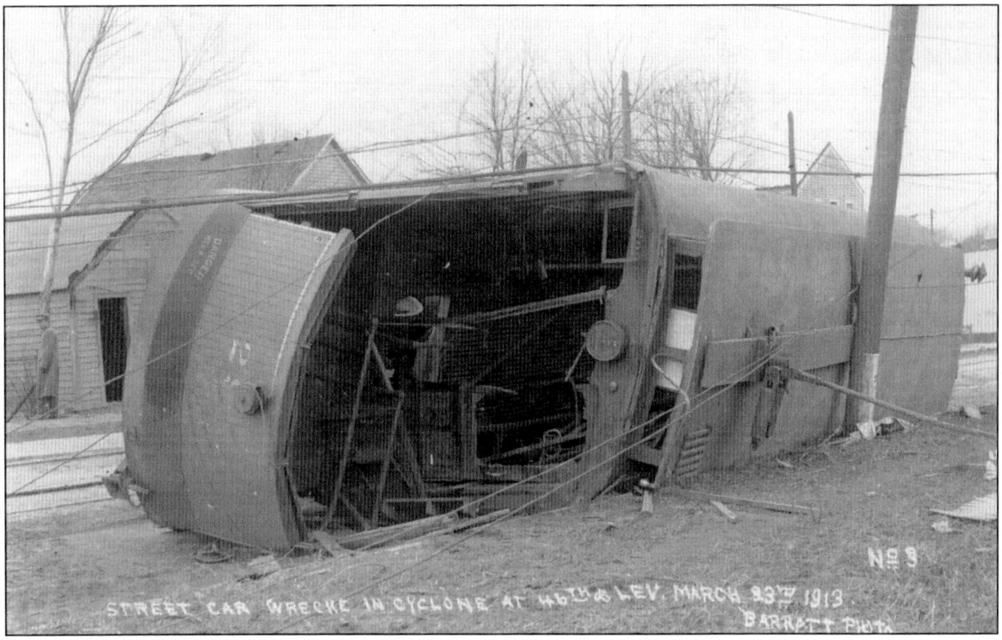

Leavenworth Trolley. These two views of streetcar #293 on the Leavenworth Street line near 46th Street reveal that it was picked up and turned on its side by the storm. The three passengers who were aboard when the tornado hit sustained only minor injuries.

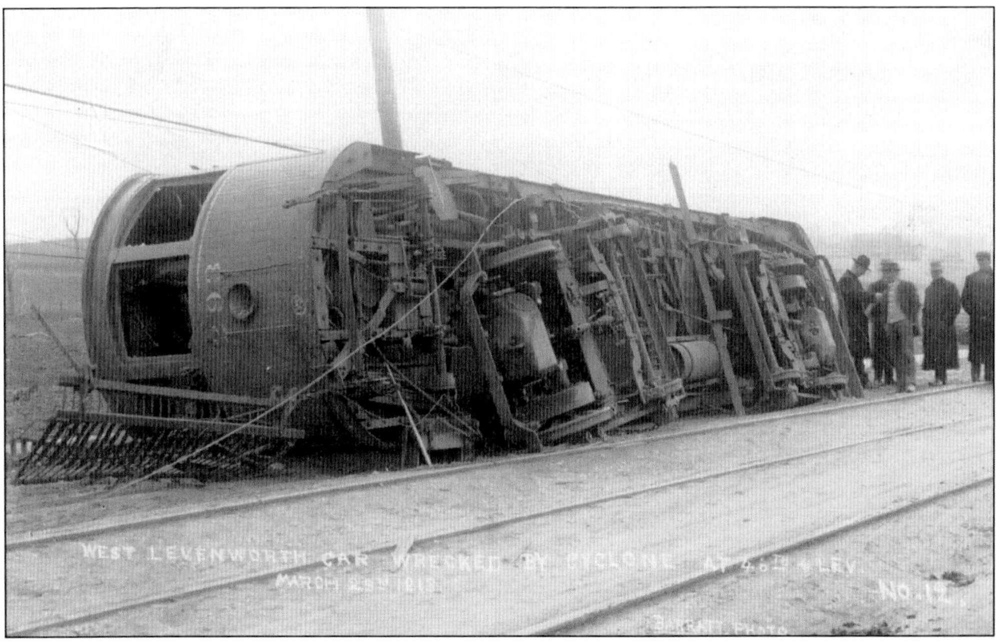

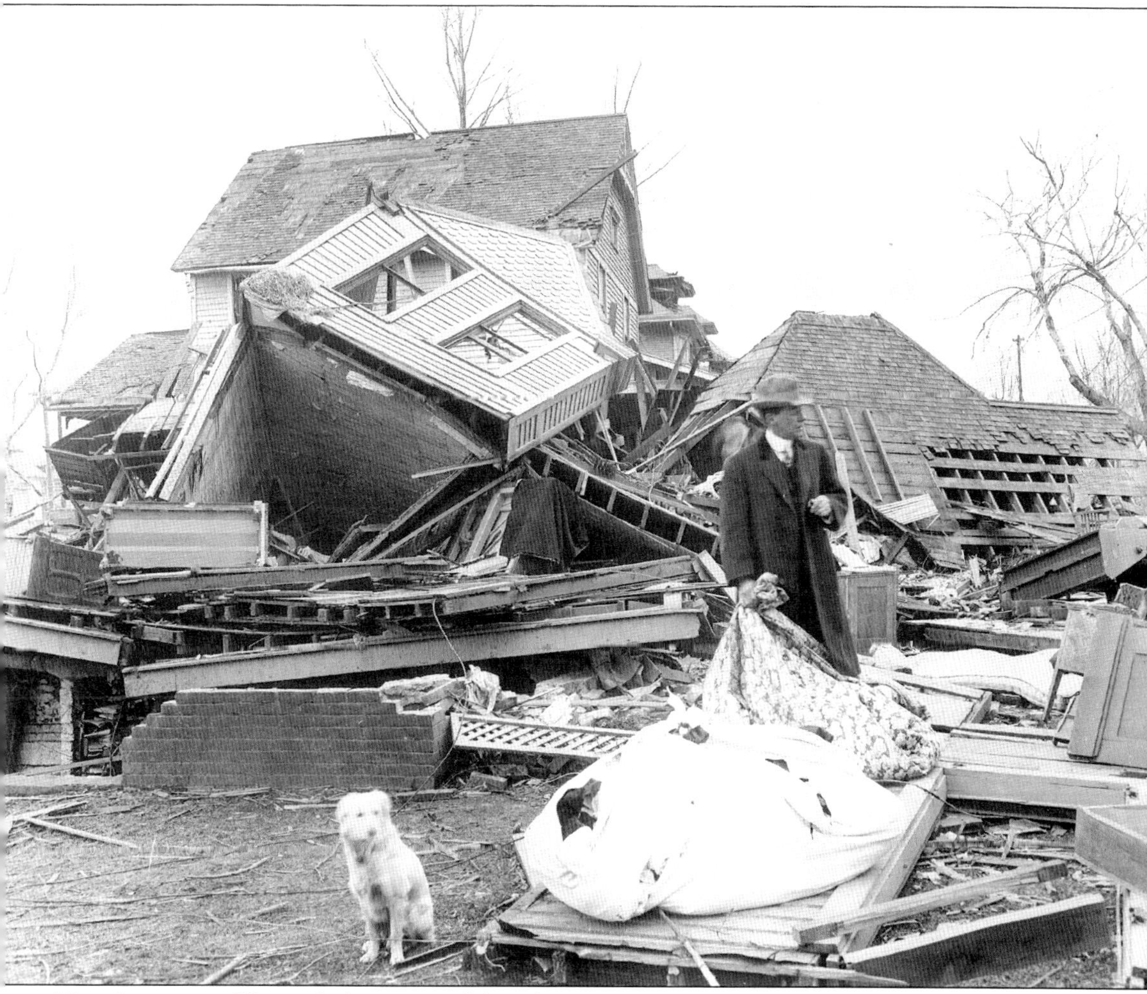

The Slabaugh Home. Judge W.W. Slabaugh is pictured here attempting to find salvageable items among the ruin. His faithful dog stayed with him all day. Slabaugh's daughter, Grace, was a talented pianist, and suffered a severe injury to her right wrist. (Bostwick-Frohardt Collection, Durham Western Heritage Museum.)

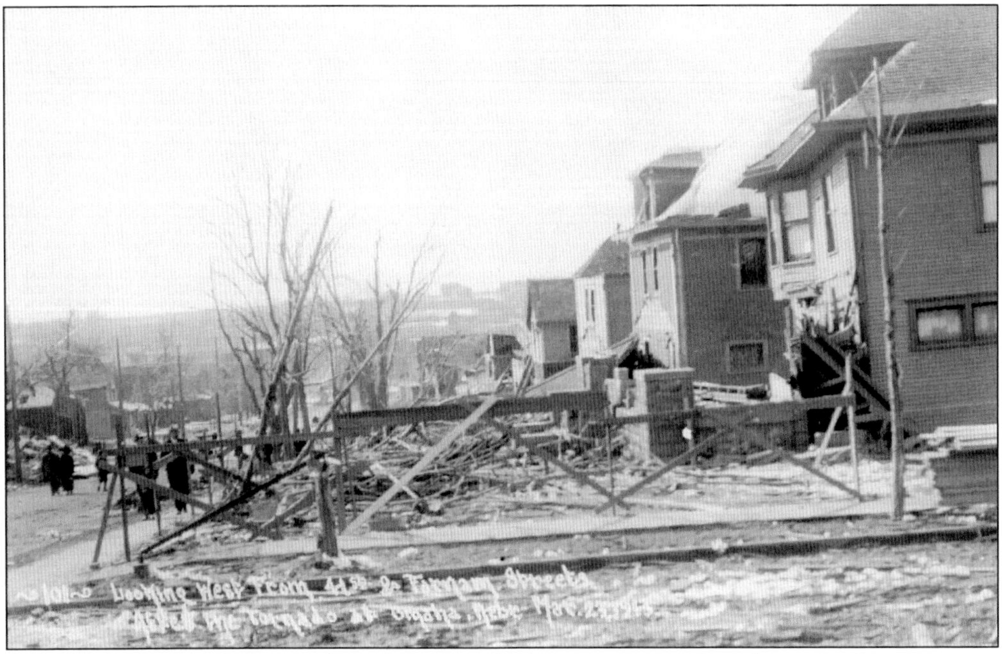

FARNAM STREET. This view of Farnam Street looking west was taken from 41st Street.

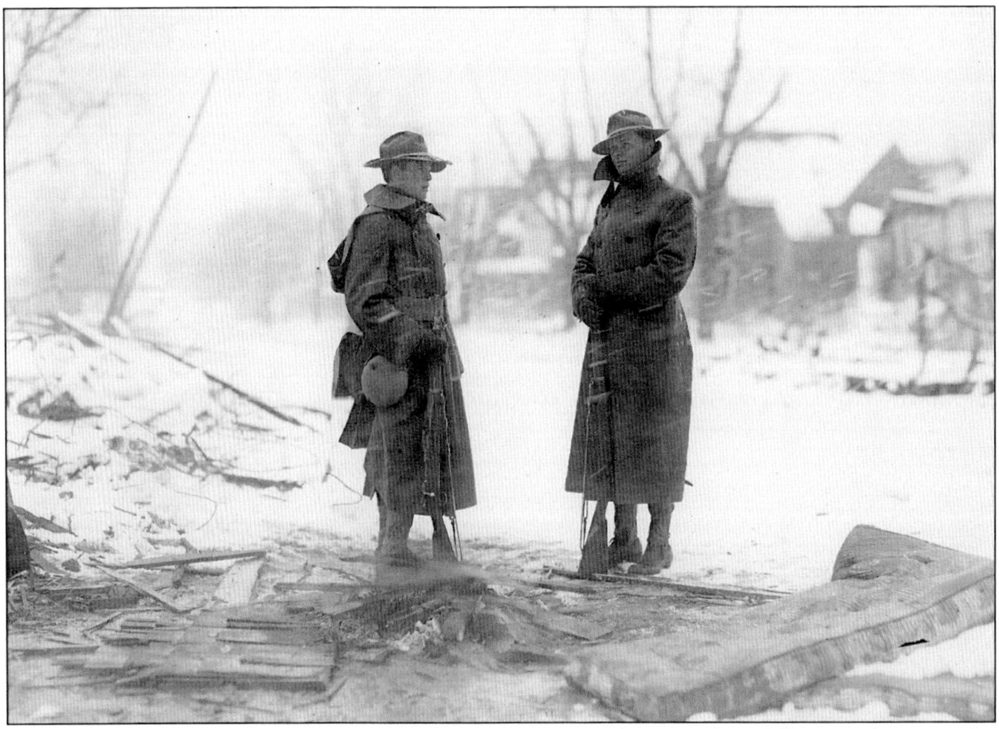

GUARDSMEN IN SNOW. More seasonable weather returned in the days following the tornado. These militia men stand near a small fire during a snowstorm on March 25th. (Bostwick-Frohardt Collection, Durham Western Heritage Museum.)

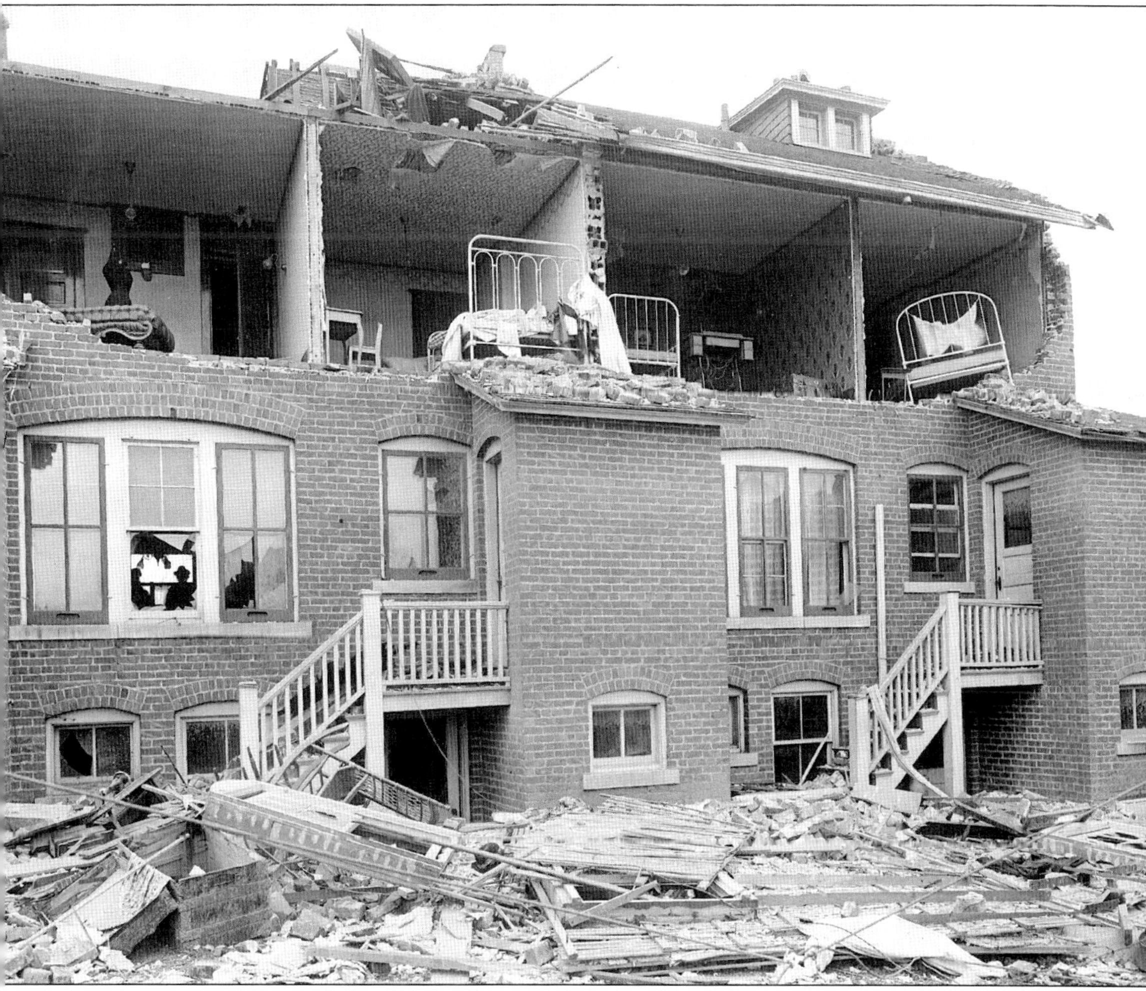

HIGHLAND TERRACE. Beds hang from the rear of the Highland Terrace apartments at 40th and Dewey Streets. (Bostwick-Frohardt Collection, Durham Western Heritage Museum.)

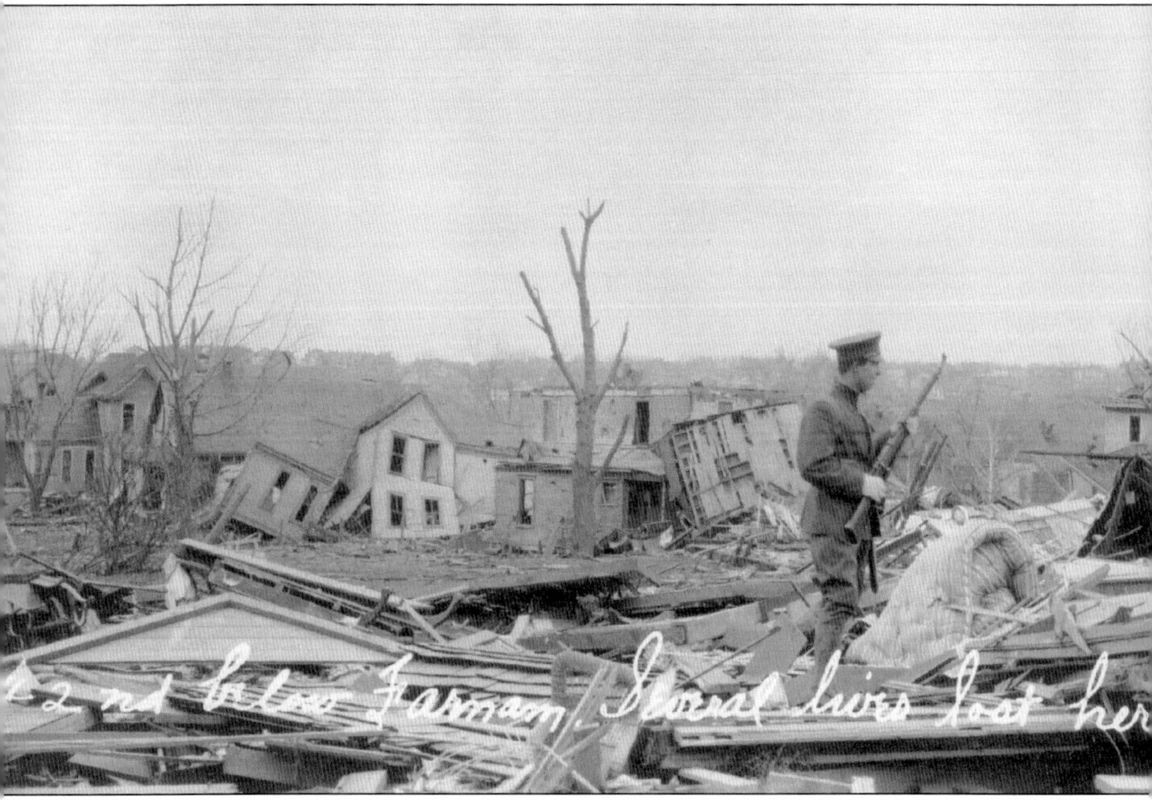

POLICE ON GUARD. An armed militia man keeps watch over the area of 42nd and Farnam Streets.

Soldier. This soldier at 42nd and Farnam Streets poses with his rifle. Each rifle was loaded with ball cartridges of five rounds of ammunition, and police orders against looters were "shoot to kill," if necessary. (Bostwick-Frohardt Collection, Durham Western Heritage Museum.)

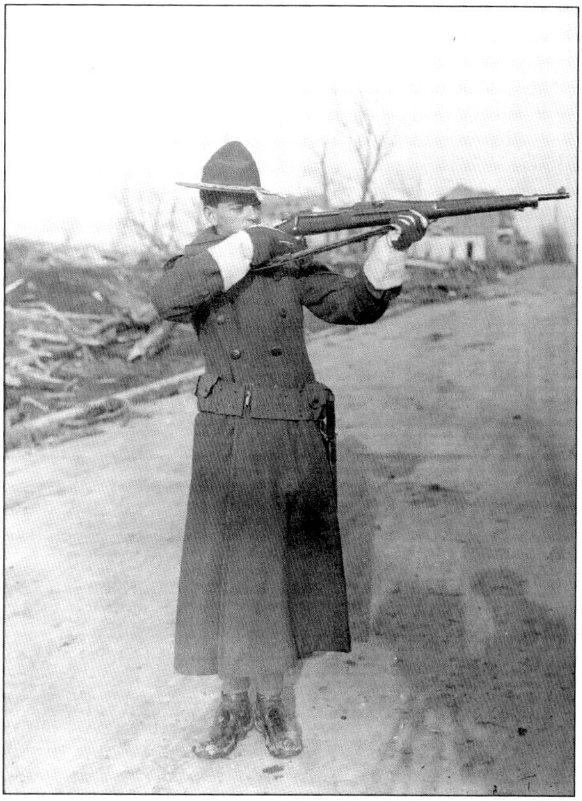

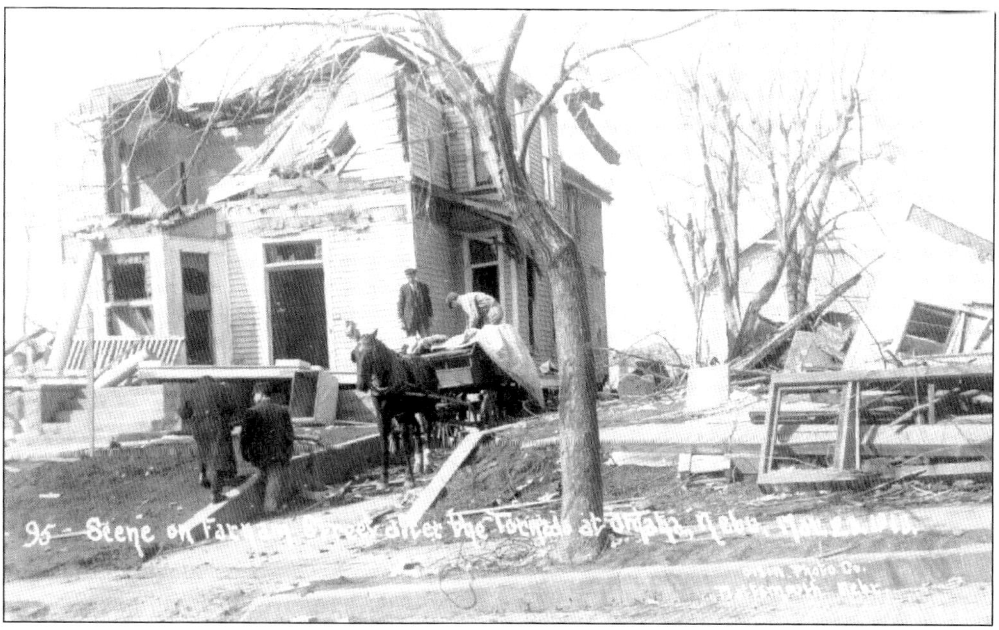

Scene on Farnam Street. People along Farnam Street are piling what belongings they can salvage into a wagon. The men in front of the house, one seen writing, could possibly be from the relief office checking on the validity of the claim.

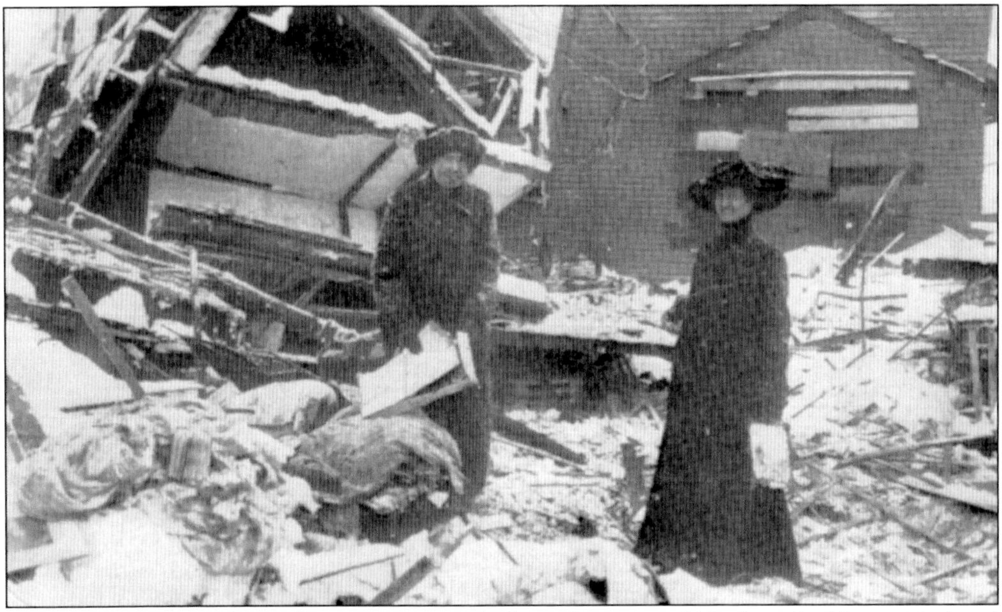

SULLIVAN SISTERS. The Sullivan sisters search through snowy rubble for valuables at 42nd and Harney Streets. Their mother was killed, and another sister was pulled alive from the ruins.

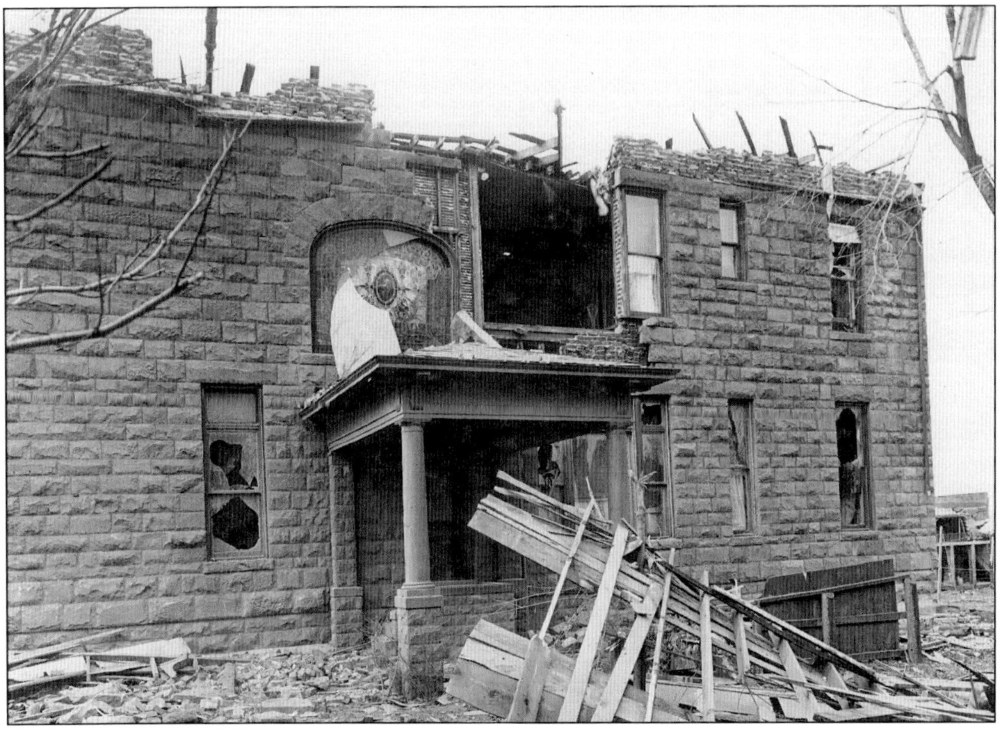

BALDRIDGE HOME. The roof collapsed and most windows were shattered at the Howard H. Baldridge home at 39th and Douglas Streets. (Bostwick-Frohardt Collection, Durham Western Heritage Museum.)

Four

CATHEDRAL

The chapel windows fell in with a crash, the statues of our Lady and St. Joseph were hurled to the floor together with all the candelabra and the flowers we had received in such abundance for this great feast. Benches and priedieux were thrown helter skelter and broken to pieces as if made of china. Several of the Religious were pinned down by the debris, while the majority, who had made some effort to escape were blown down the corridor like leaves in an autumn wind.

—*from the day journal of one of the Sisters at Sacred Heart Convent*

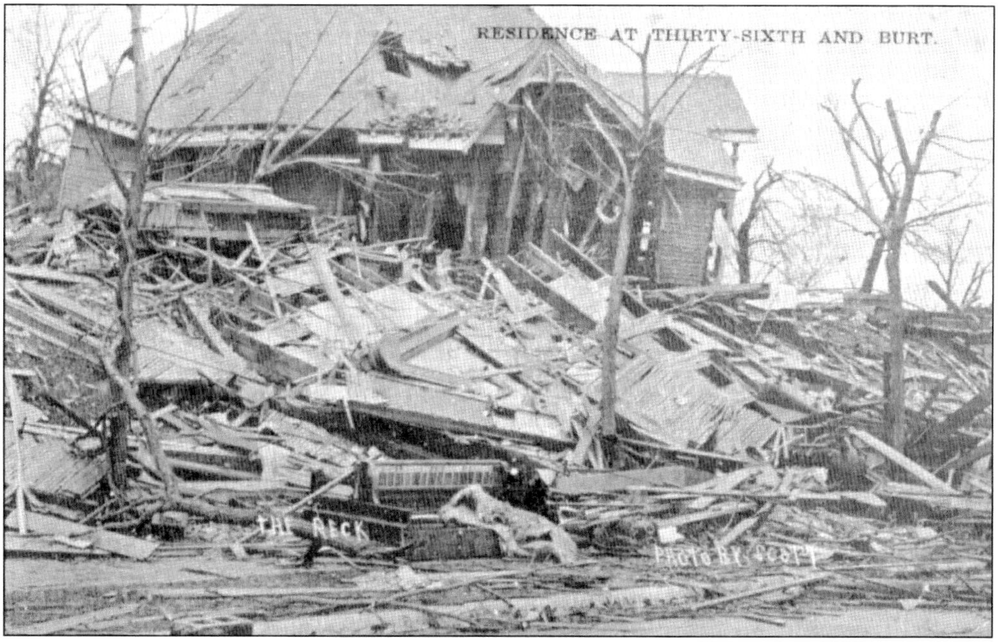

THE RECK. The piano from a demolished home at 36th and Burt Streets lies across the sidewalk.

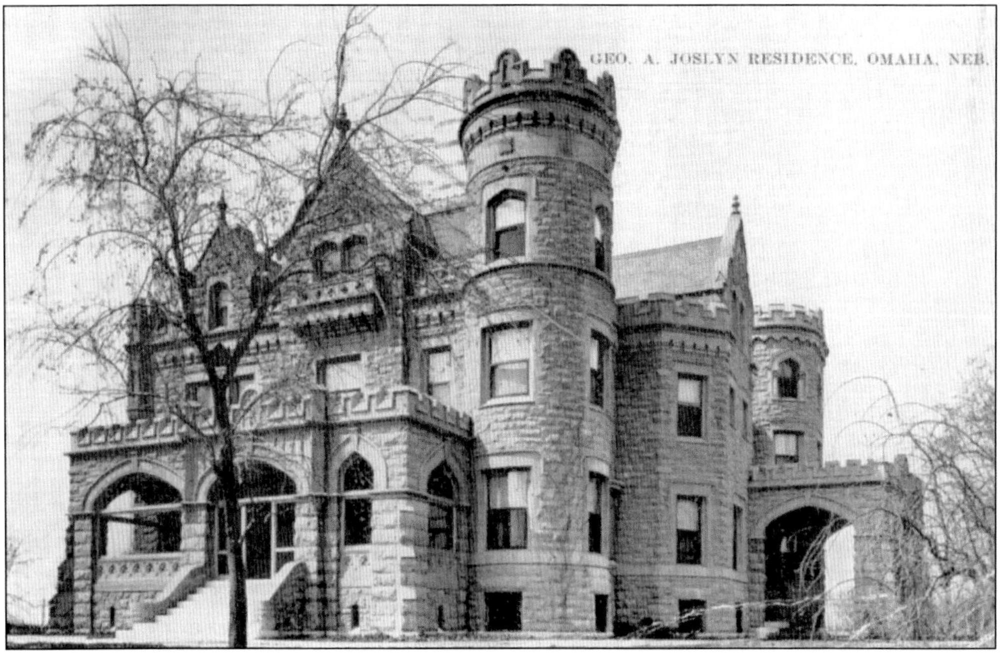

LYNHURST. The $250,000 home of George and Sarah Joslyn was scarcely a decade old in 1913. George Joslyn made his fortune through the Western Newspaper Union, selling boilerplates to newspapers throughout the western United States. The Joslyns knew their home as "Lynhurst," but to the chagrin of George, most Omahans called it "The Castle."

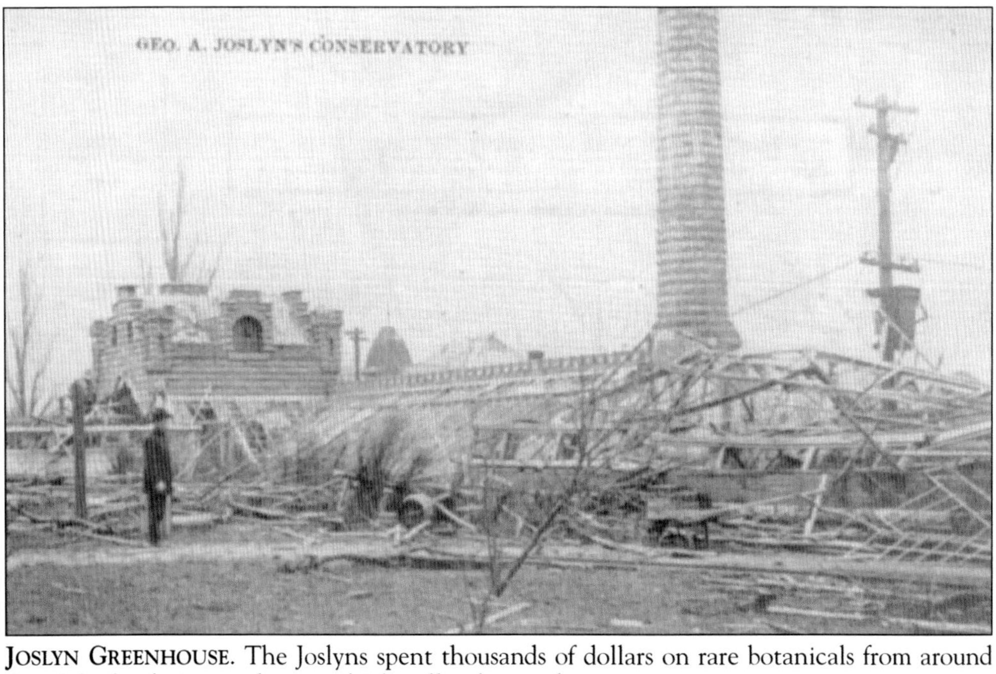

JOSLYN GREENHOUSE. The Joslyns spent thousands of dollars on rare botanicals from around the globe for their greenhouse, which suffered great damage.

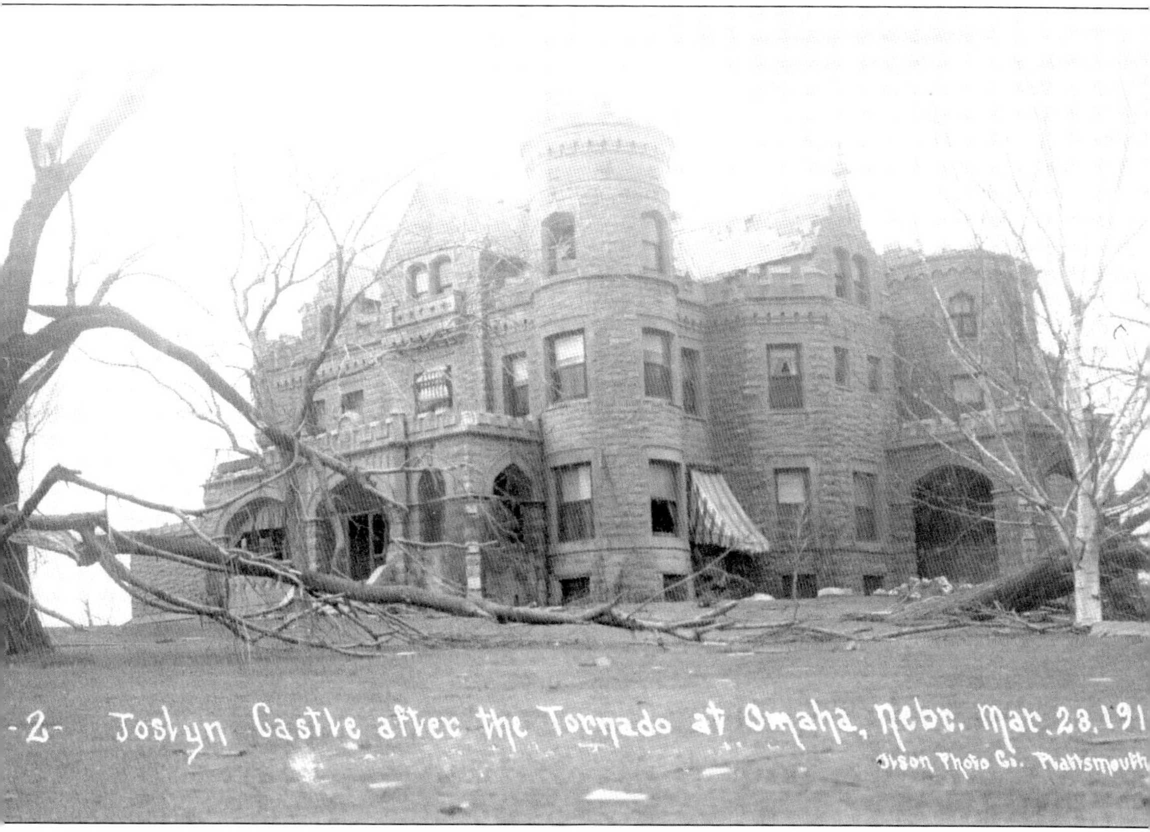

JOSLYN CASTLE AFTER THE STORM. While the finest home in Omaha was slightly damaged, the grounds and the greenhouse suffered much worse. On the interior of the home, some furniture, artwork, etchings, and a statuary were ruined.

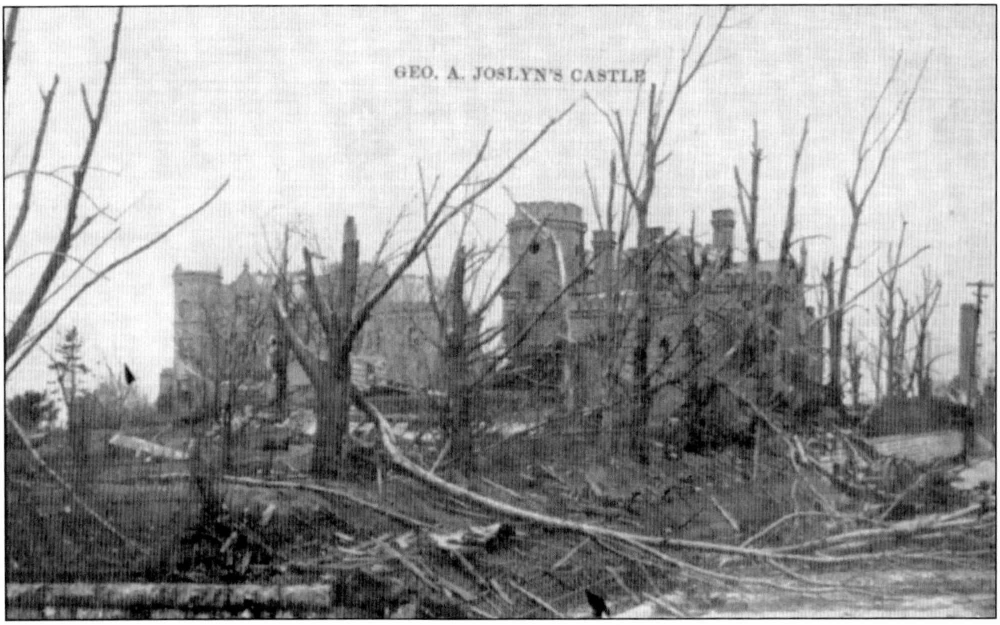

JOSLYN GROUNDS. George Joslyn spared little expense planting mature trees on his acreage. A distraught Joslyn declared that it would take 15 years to restore the 5.5 acres of estate grounds to their previous state. Joslyn eerily stated that he did "not expect to live that long." He passed away in 1916.

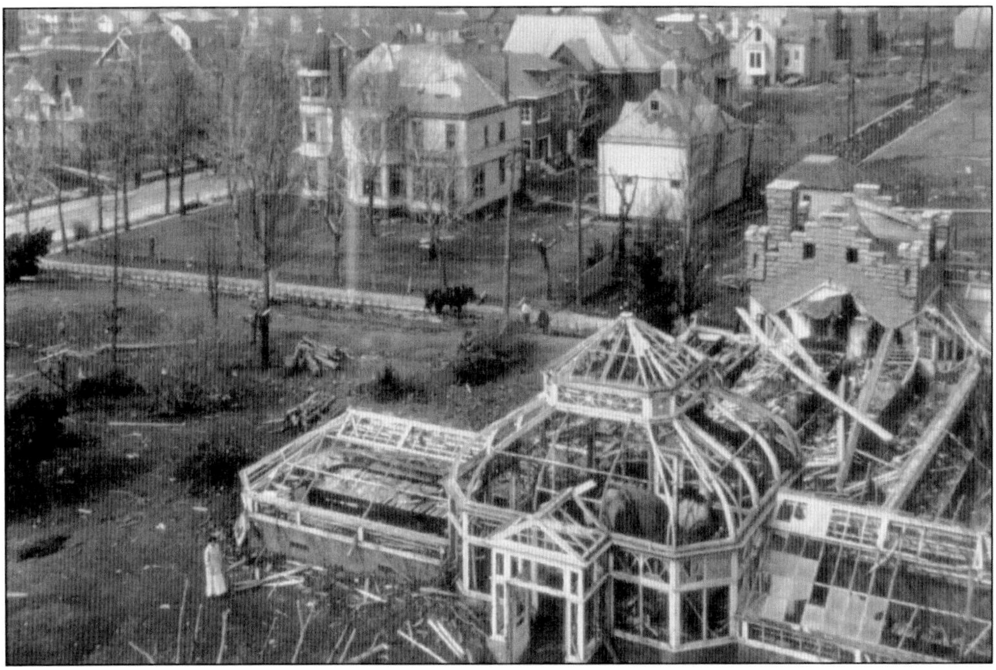

JOSLYN PALM HOUSE. This photograph from the top of the Joslyn home shows the wreckage of the greenhouse, with its main section called the "palm house." The Joslyns decided not to rebuild, so they donated the frame to Hanscom Park, where it was used as a greenhouse for 50 years. (Nebraska State Historical Society Photograph Collections RG 3654.)

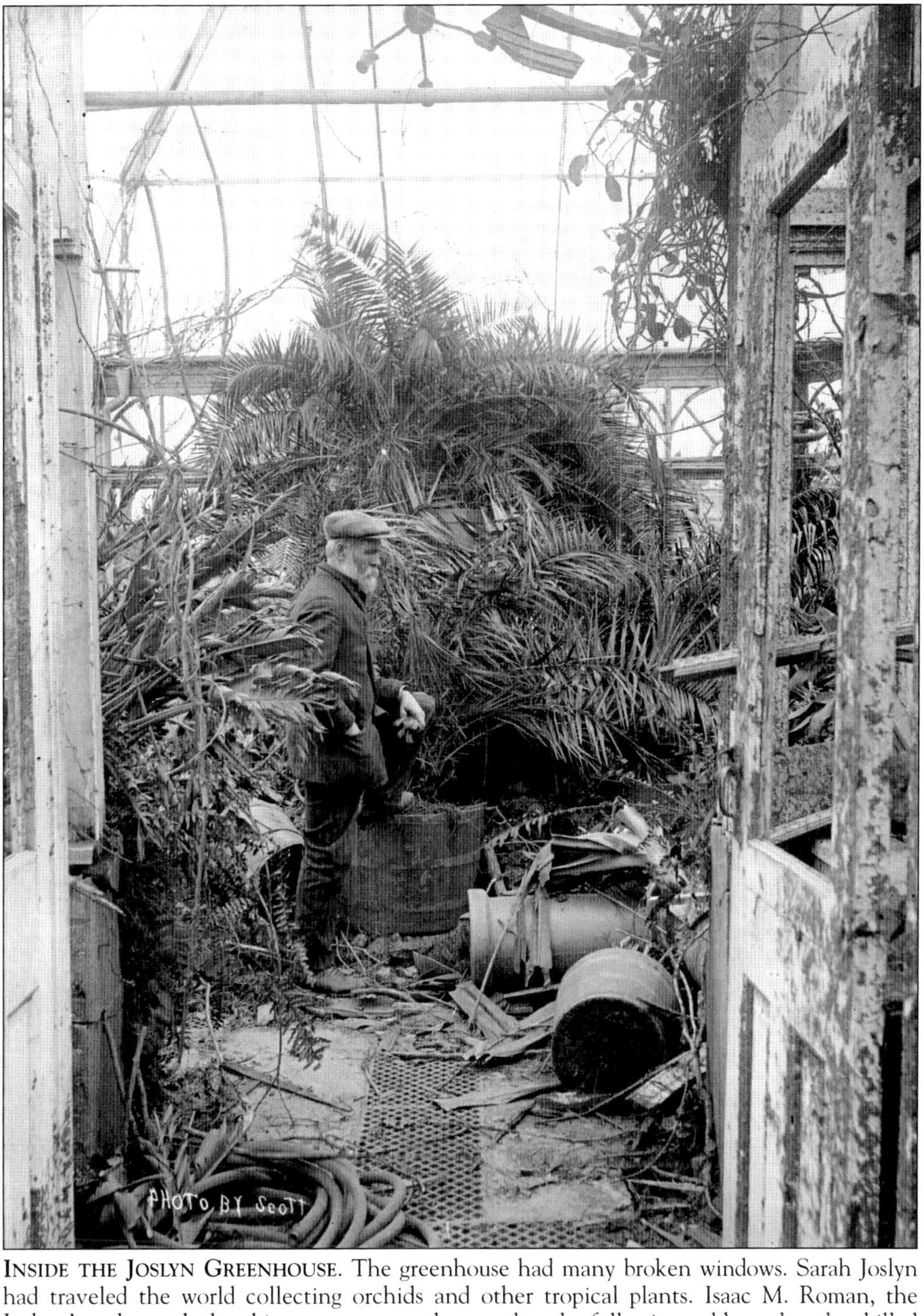

Inside the Joslyn Greenhouse. The greenhouse had many broken windows. Sarah Joslyn had traveled the world collecting orchids and other tropical plants. Isaac M. Roman, the Joslyns' gardener, declared it was not storm damage, but the following cold weather that killed the delicate plants. (Douglas County Historical Society Library/Archives Center.)

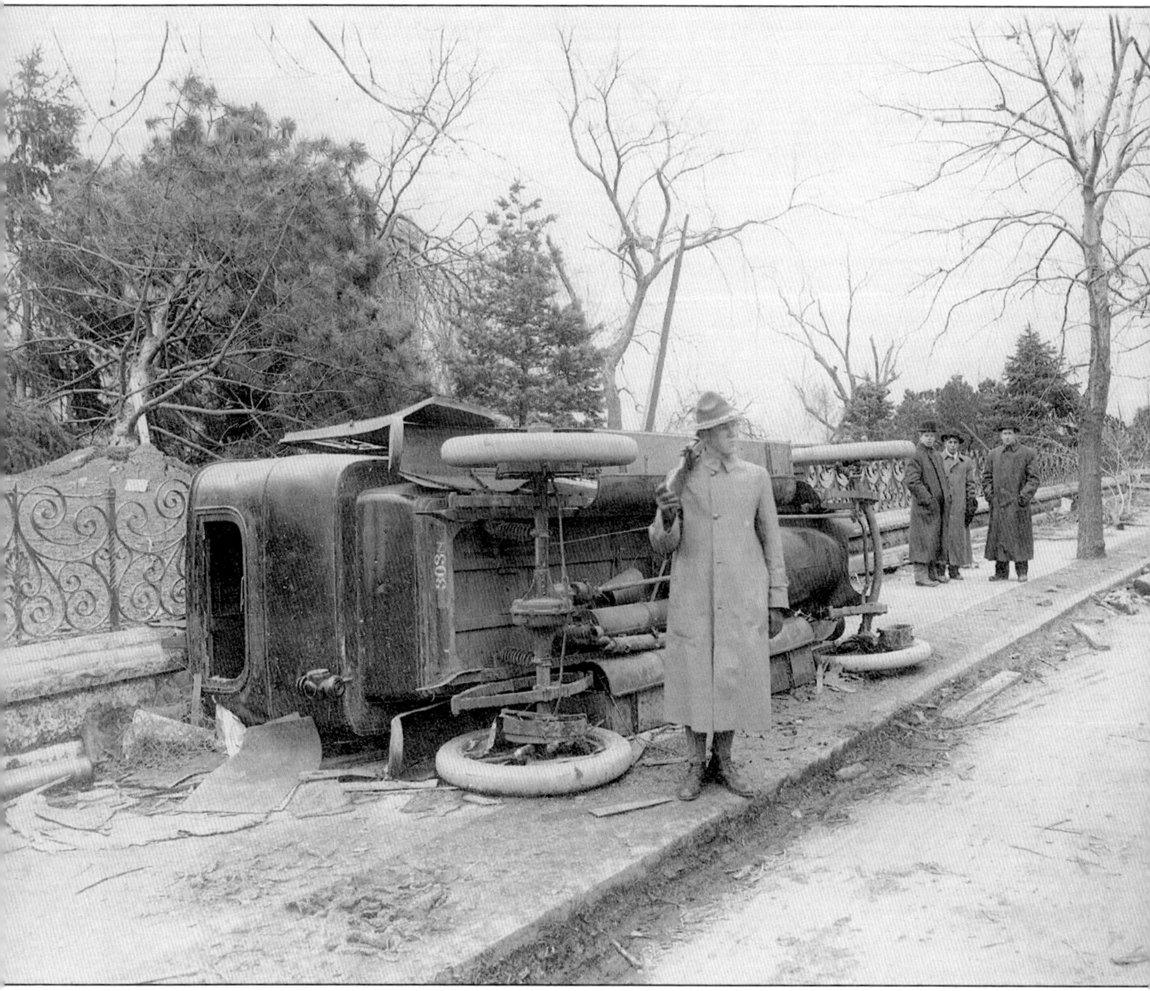

OUTSIDE THE JOSLYN ESTATE. A soldier is at watch on the perimeter of the Joslyn estate. Onlookers view the Nelson E. Updike limousine turned on its side. Updike's chauffeur was in the car when it turned over, but was unharmed. (Bostwick-Frohardt Collection, Durham Western Heritage Museum.)

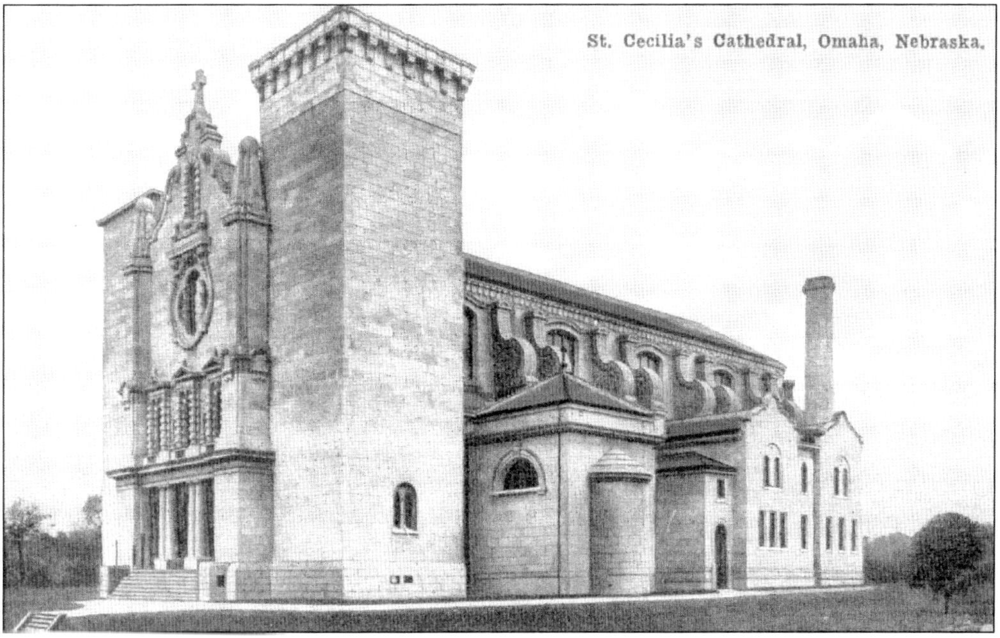

ST. CECILIA'S CATHEDRAL. St. Cecilia's had been under construction for eight years when the tornado passed. It was reported that the cathedral (which was under construction for 54 years, from 1905 to 1959) "did not suffer the loss of a brick," but the nearby parochial school and Bishop Scannell's residence were damaged.

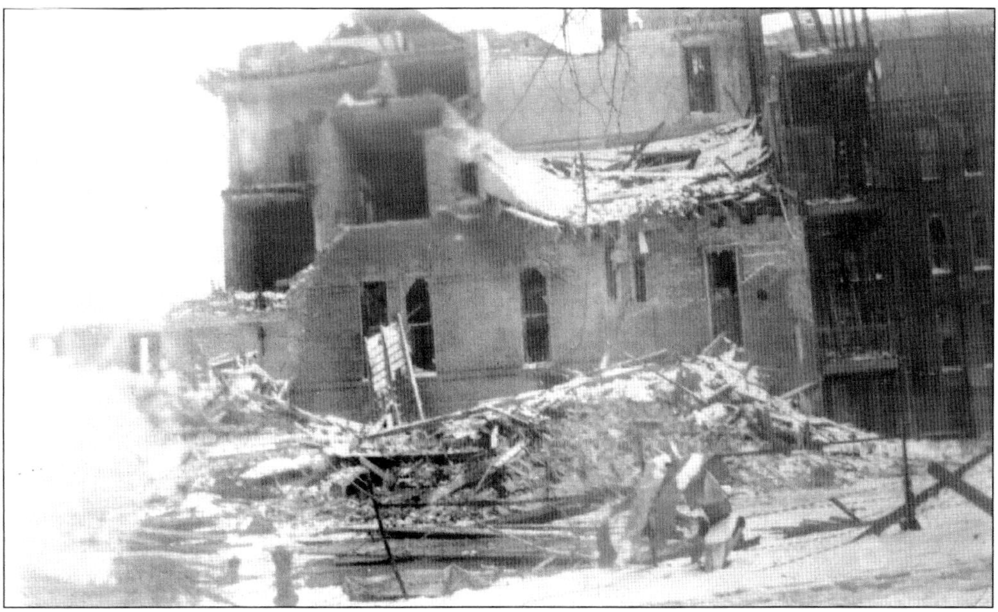

SACRED HEART CONVENT UPPER FLOORS. This view shows the damage done to the upper floors of the convent. Although the walls ranged from 13 to 17 inches thick, weak lime mortar did not sufficiently bind the bricks, making the building susceptible to the tornado's force. (Duchesne Academy of the Sacred Heart Archives.)

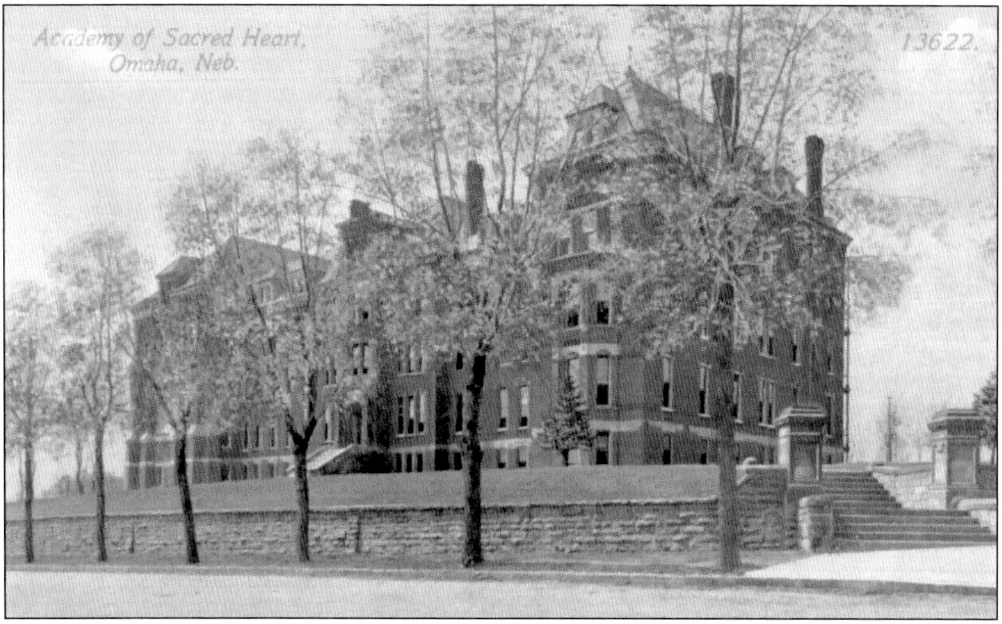

SACRED HEART. This is the Sacred Heart Convent and Academy as it looked before it was heavily damaged in 1913.

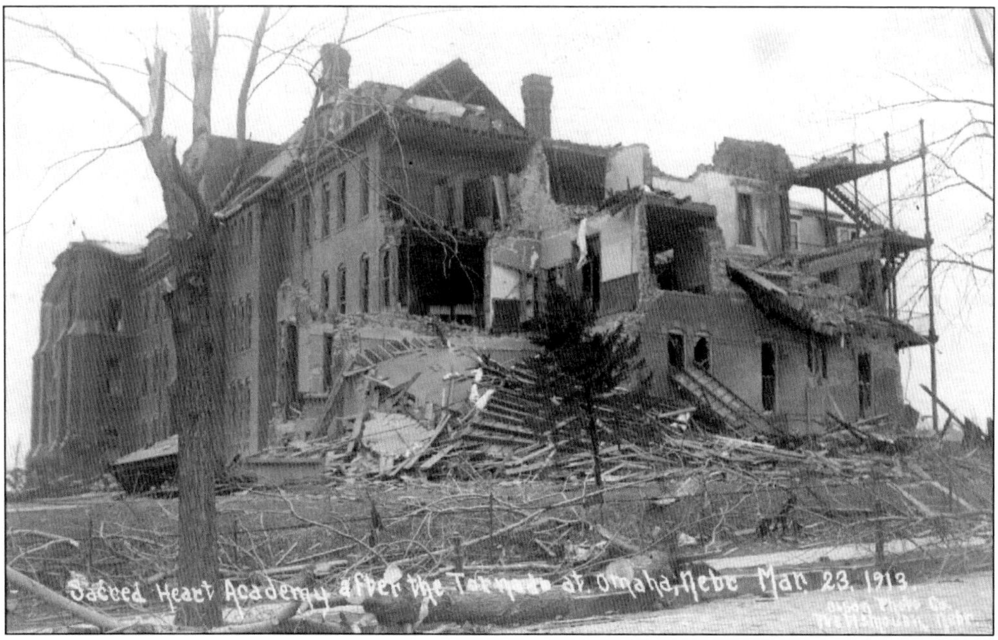

SACRED HEART CONVENT. The storm struck the Sacred Heart Convent soon after Easter evening services had commenced. This view is of the north side of the impressive 1882 building along Burt Street. (Duchesne Academy of the Sacred Heart Archives.)

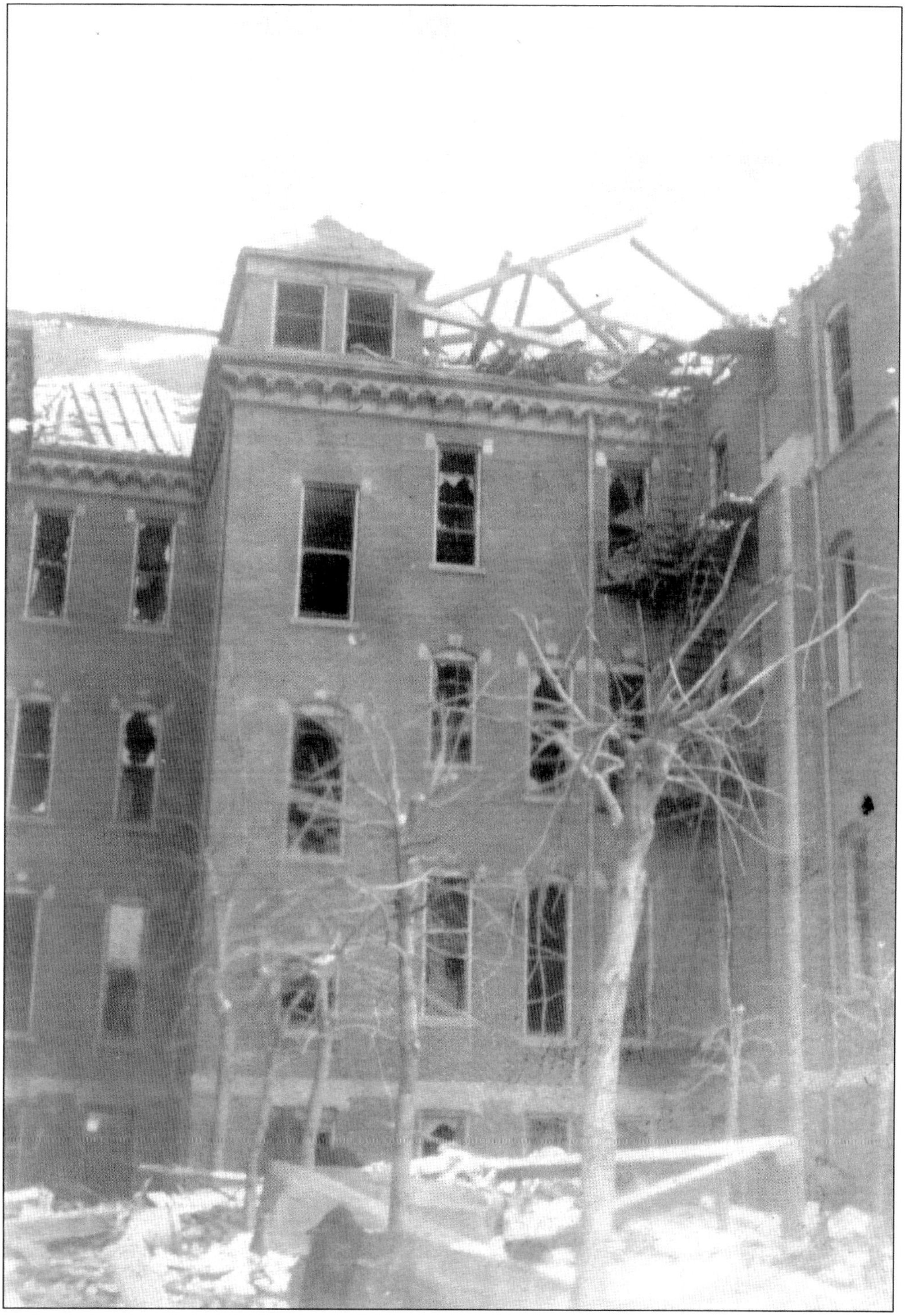

SACRED HEART WINDOWS. Many of the windows were broken by hailstones that preceded the tornado. Total damages to the building were estimated at $40,000. (Duchesne Academy of the Sacred Heart Archives.)

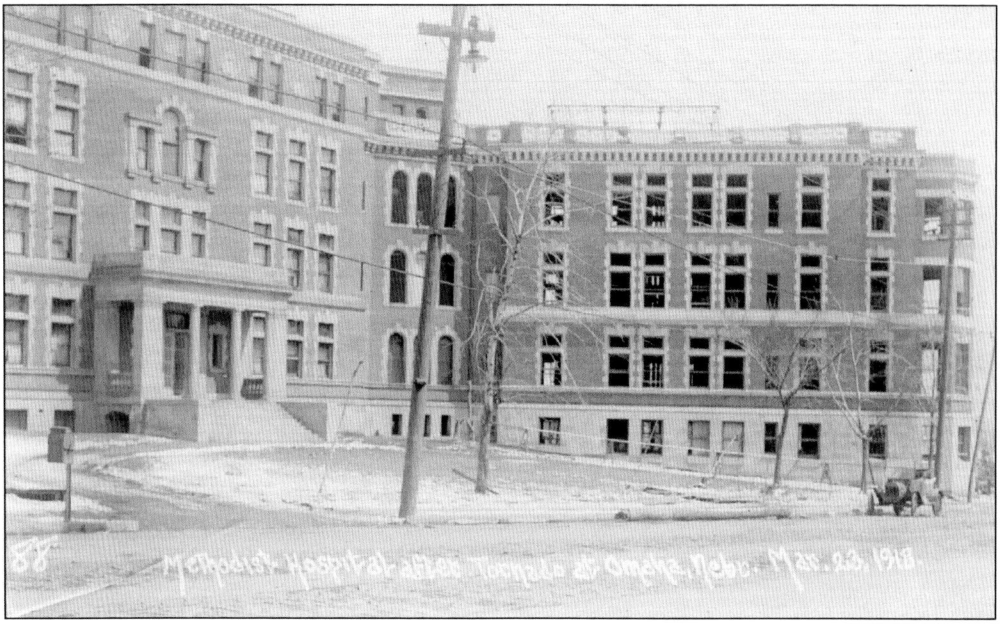

METHODIST HOSPITAL. The hospital at 36th and Cuming Streets had many windows blown out. It was overflowing with victims "because a hospital with the windows broken out was considered better than the open roadside." Some non-critical patients were transferred downtown to the Henshaw Hotel.

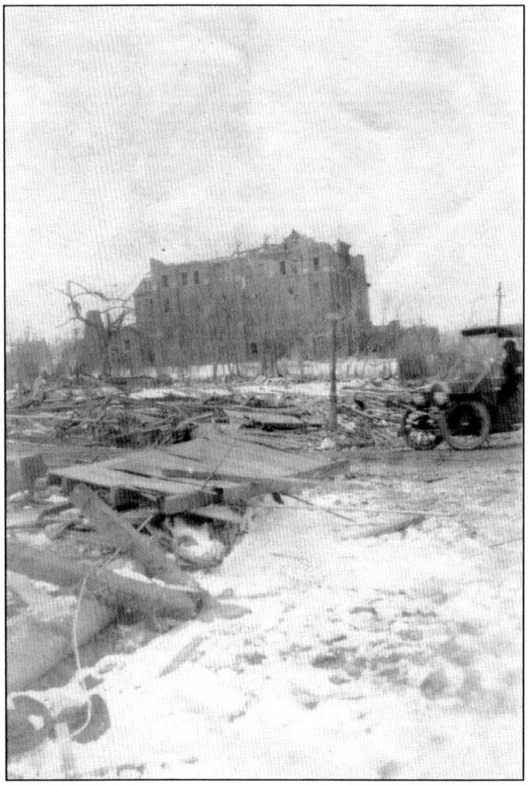

AUTOMOBILE NEAR SACRED HEART CONVENT. Traversing tornado district streets was a dicey proposition. One newspaper reported, "Automobile drivers, once so careful of punctures and rough roads now sent their machines over broken glass, nails and even a telegraph pole when necessary without the least hesitation." (Duchesne Academy of the Sacred Heart Archives.)

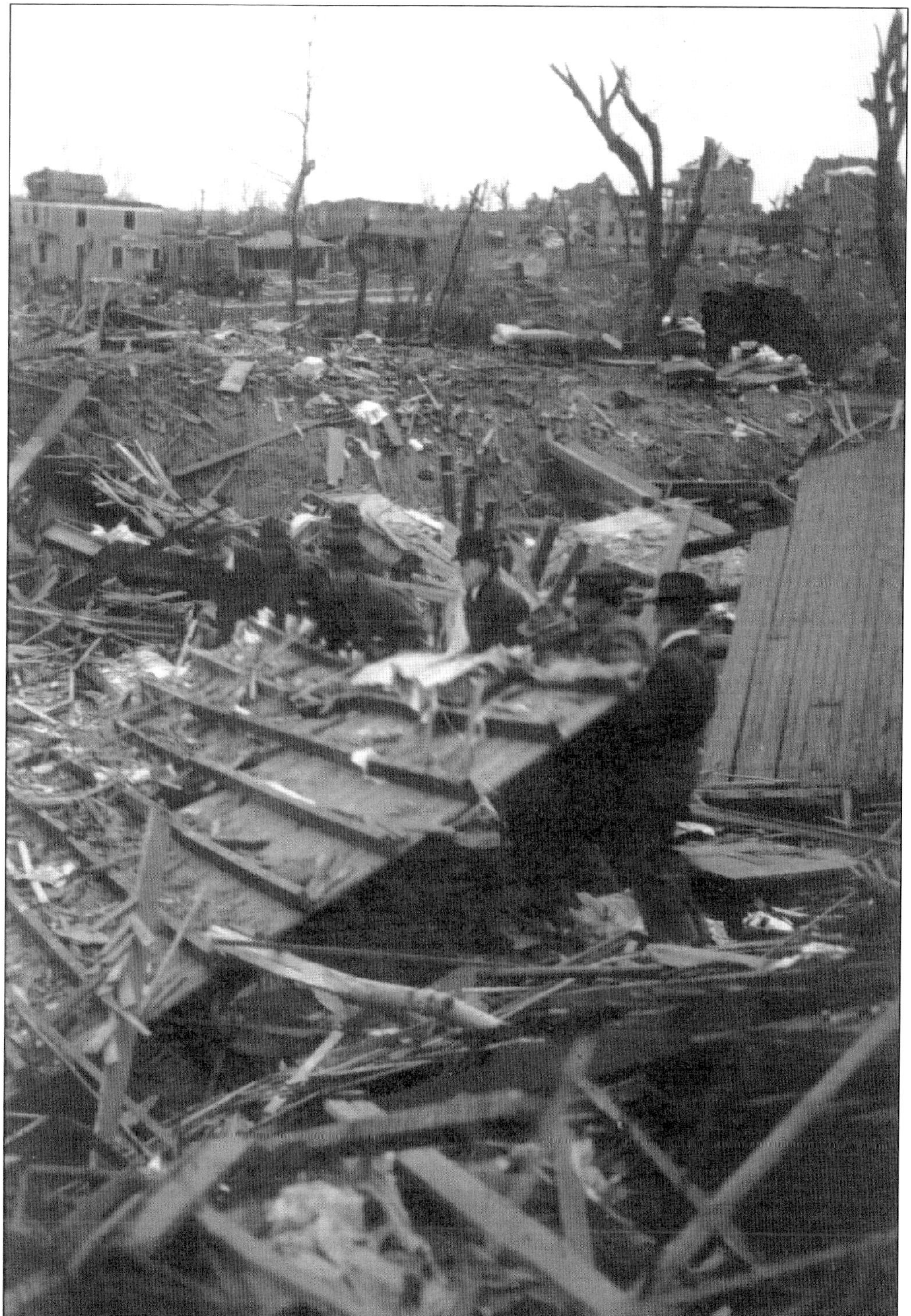

SEARCHING FOR BODIES. Several men attempt to lift a large piece of debris in the search for bodies near 36th and Webster Streets. (Duchesne Academy of the Sacred Heart Archives.)

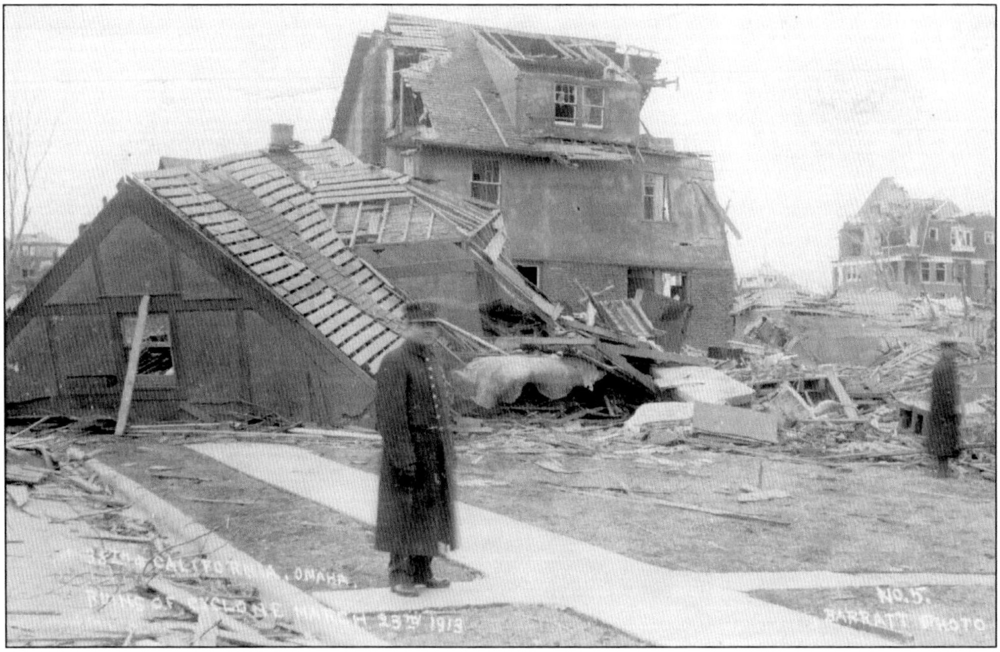

AT 38TH AND CALIFORNIA. Two Omaha policemen patrol the area at 38th and California Streets.

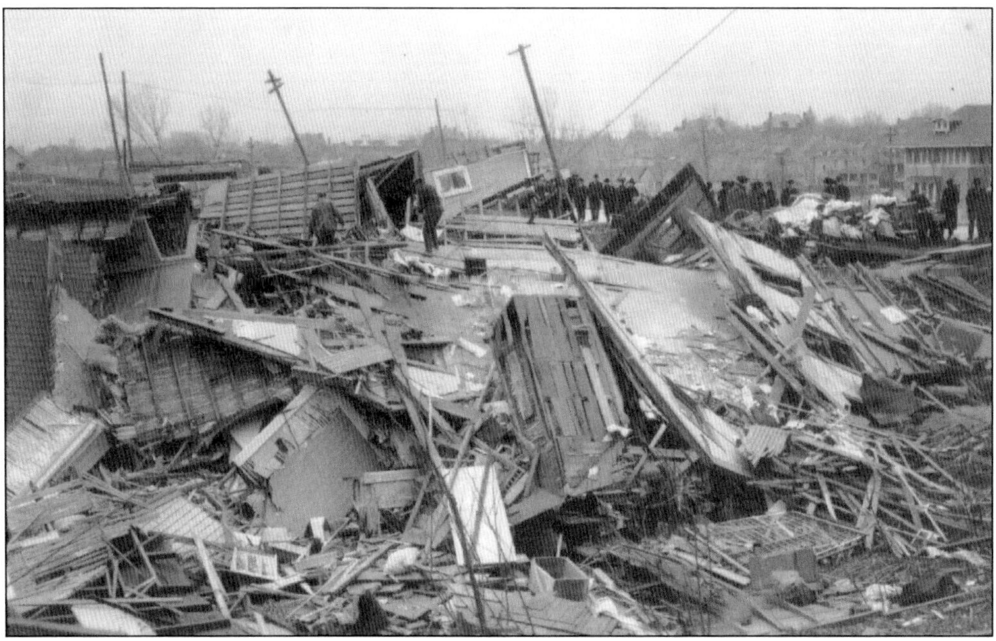

REMAINS OF THREE HOUSES. The wreckage of three houses on Davenport Street commingle into one indistinguishable pile of rubble.

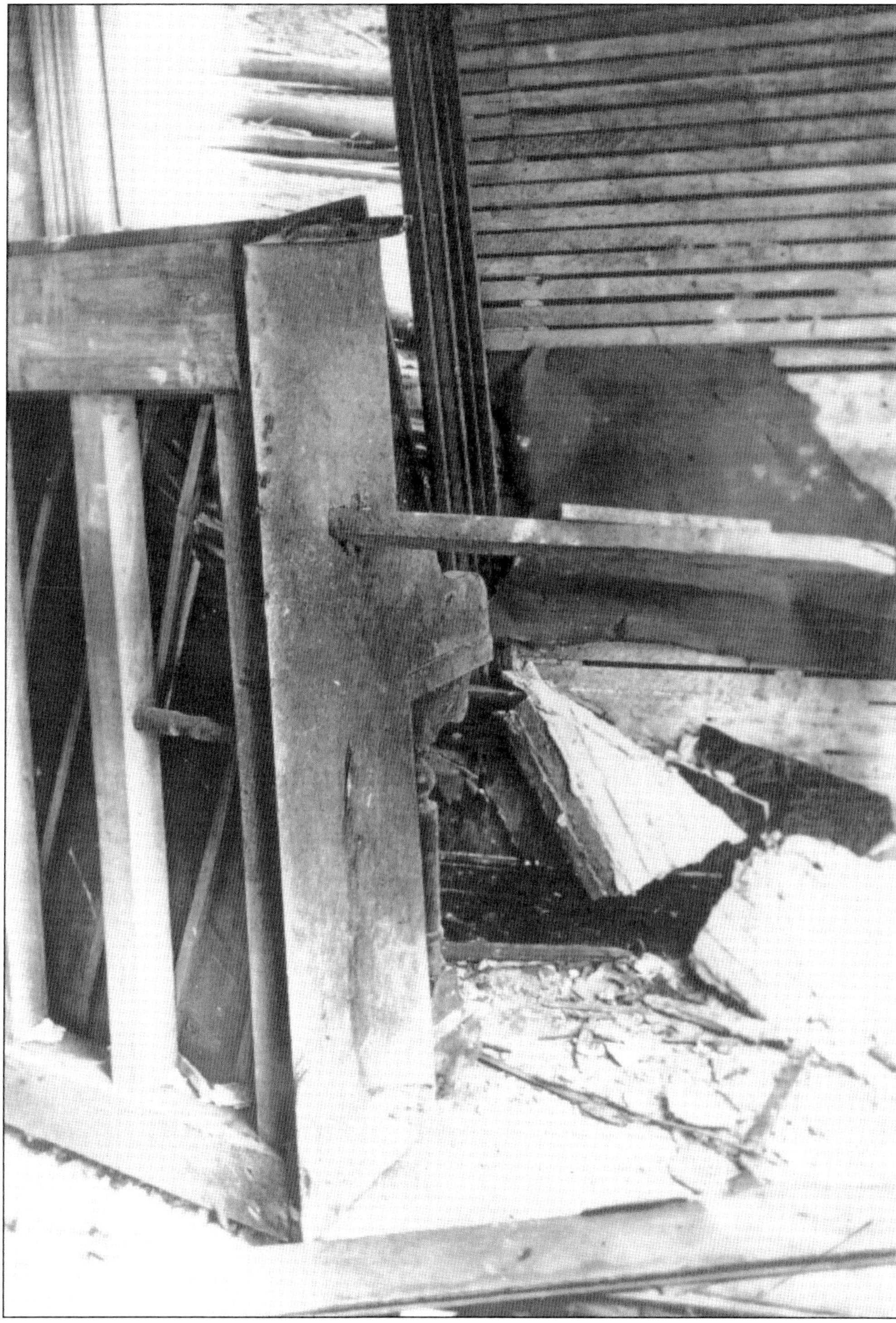

Piano Speared by Timber. Just one of the freak accidents caused by the storm is this piano skewered by debris in a home near 35th and Chicago Streets. This piano and nine others that went through the storm were later on display downtown at Orkin Brothers department store.

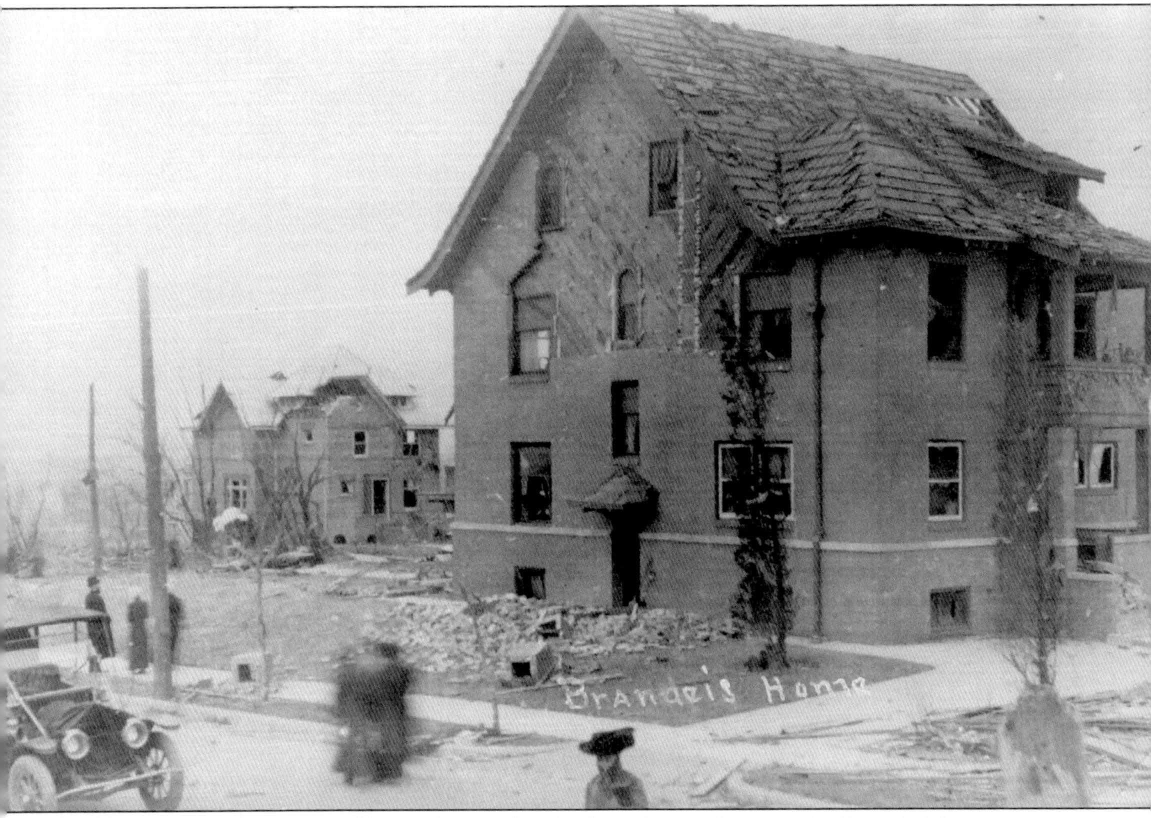

Arthur D. Brandeis Home. Located at 38th and Cass Streets, the Brandeis home was one of the finer residences struck by the tornado. The family was in New York City during the storm, and hurried back to Omaha. Brandeis was relieved that damages were no worse, as New York newspapers he read claimed that the tornado and ensuing fires had left 1,200 dead. A grateful Brandeis donated $2,500 to the local relief fund.

Five

Bemis Park

*I heard a distant roaring—such a noise as I can hardly describe like a large lumber wagon coming toward one on a cobble stone street and drawn by runaway horses. The noise kept getting louder and louder and coming right at me—it was very bewildering.... [t]he heavy blackness in the southwest assumed a funnel shape. . . . I was looking into the mouth of the funnel [***sic***] and could feel the force of the wind.*

—*tornado survivor Beulah Adams in a letter to her mother*

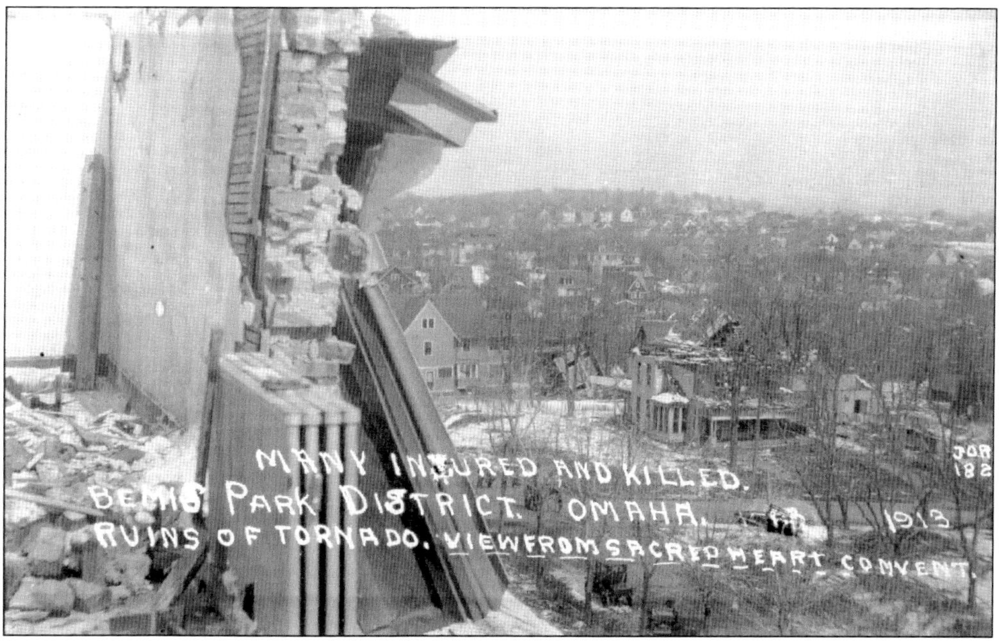

MANY INJURED AND KILLED. This view looks northeast towards Bemis Park from the damaged upper floor of Sacred Heart Convent.

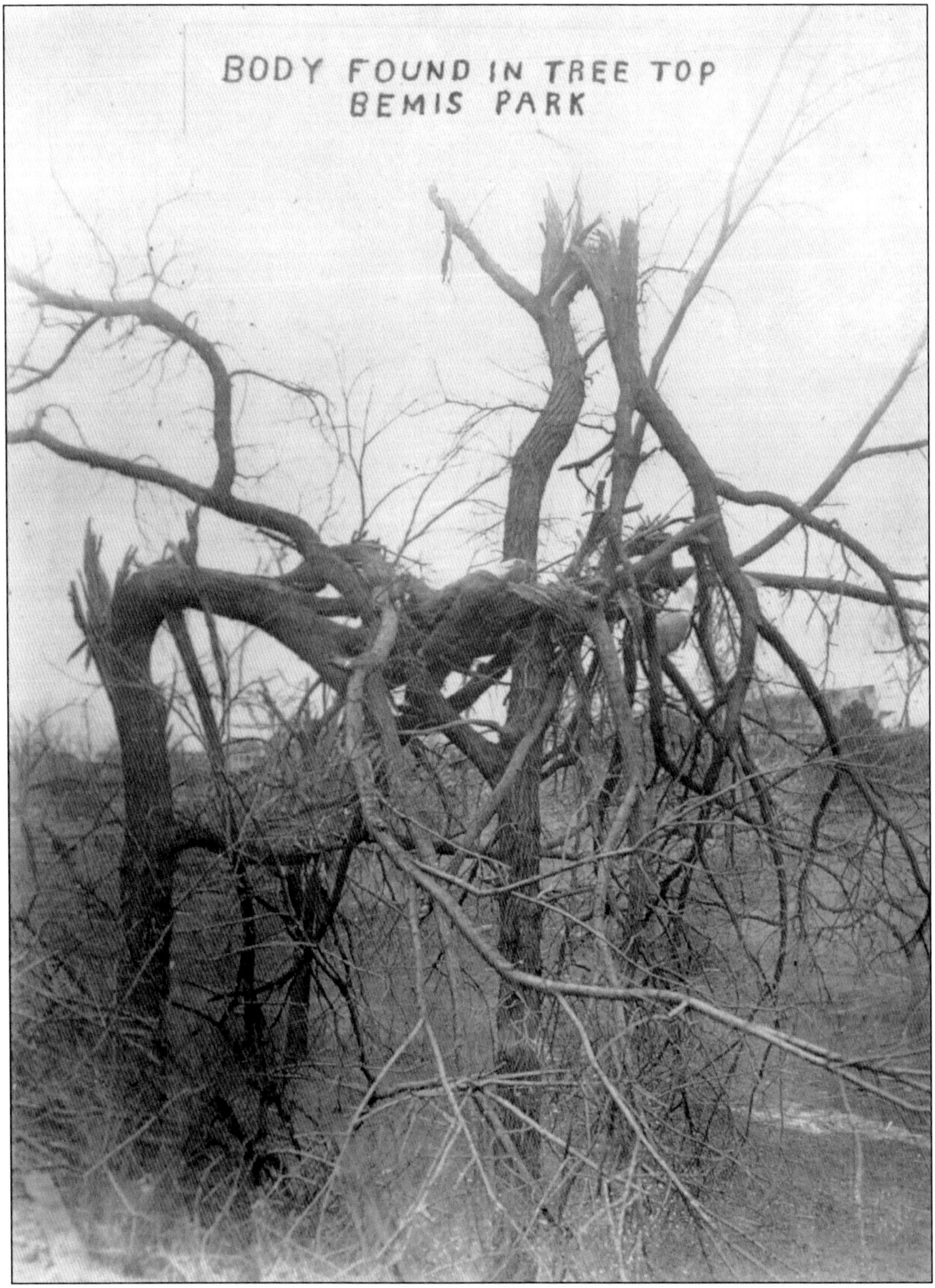

CORPSE IN TREE. There were only a few truly gruesome images captured in the storm's aftermath; however, the authenticity of this photograph is in doubt. Local newspapers abounded with fantastic tales of death and survival, yet there are no mentions of a corpse in a tree in Bemis Park.

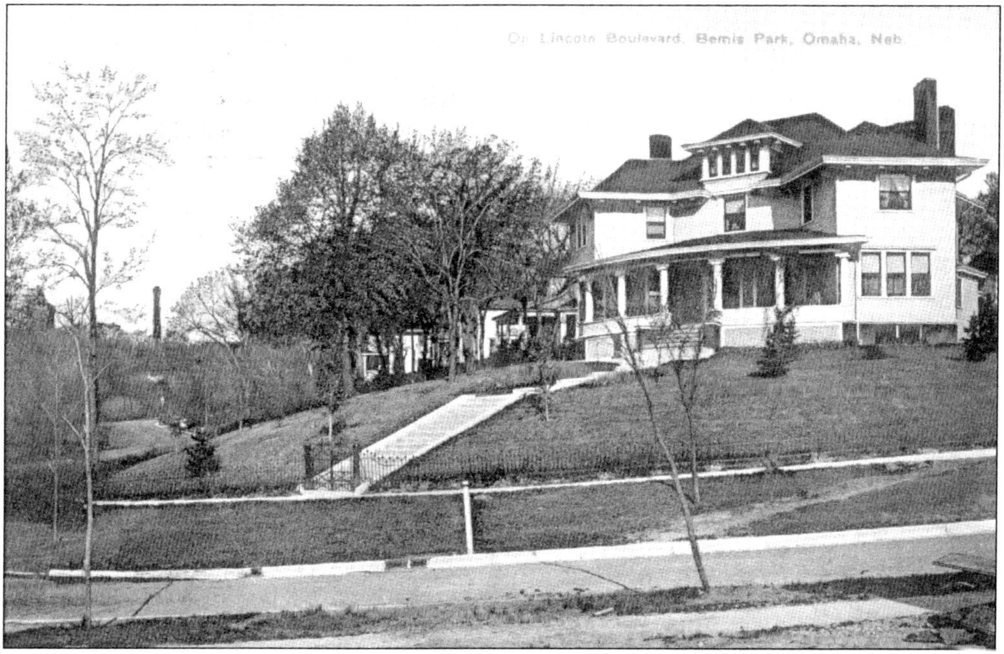

LINCOLN BOULEVARD, C. 1910. This is how Lincoln Boulevard looked running through the Bemis Park neighborhood c. 1910. In 1889, Bemis Park's land was donated to the city by future mayor George P. Bemis (1892–1896). The area was developed as a residential neighborhood from 1892–1908.

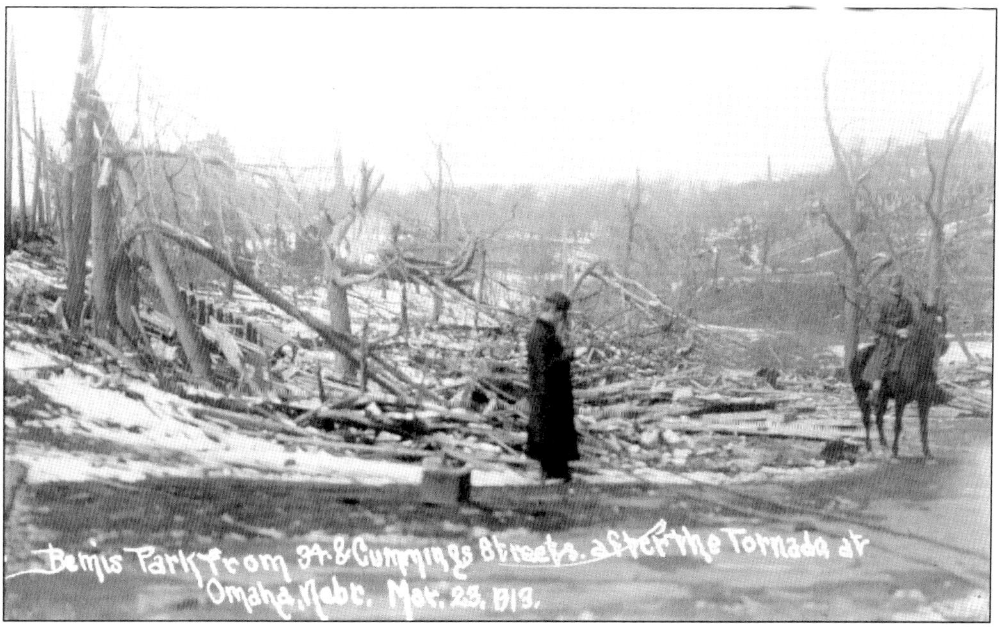

BEMIS PARK. Omaha was treated to several inches of snow after the tornado. Many of the trees in the district were blown over or greatly damaged. Some of the grand oaks in the park were over 100 years old.

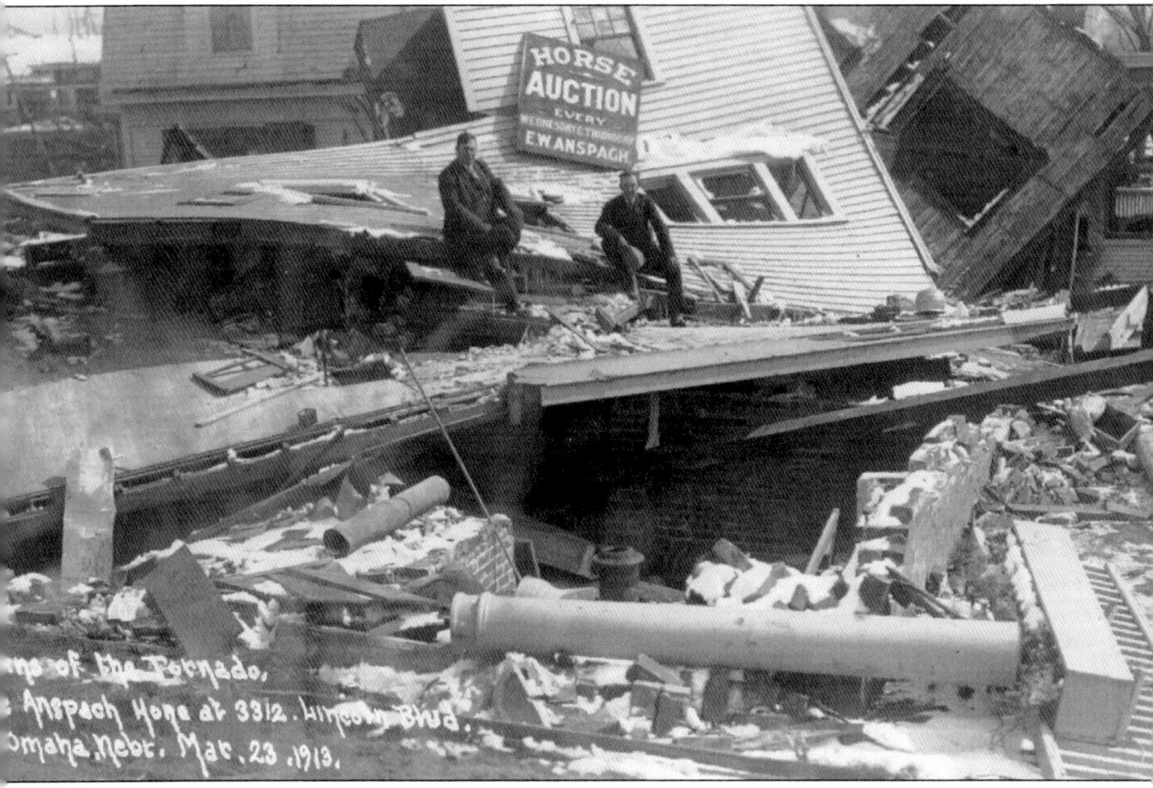

ANSPACH HOME. The walls of the Anspach home at 3312 Lincoln Boulevard are piled atop each other, exposing the basement. A sign for the family business is prominently featured.

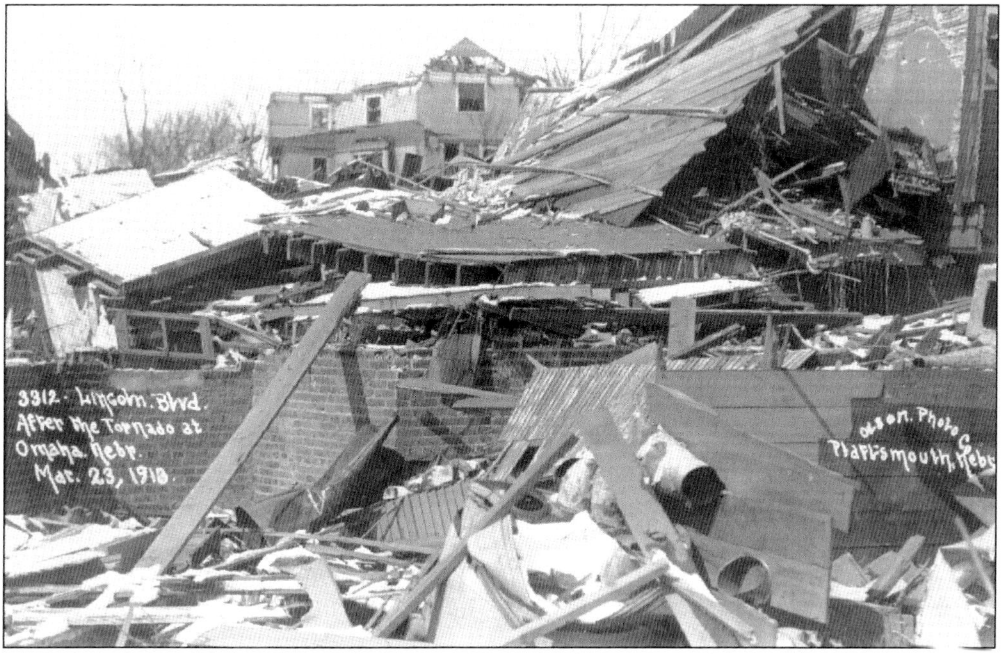

ALONG LINCOLN BOULEVARD. This photo shows another view of the Anspach home with the Hanson house in the background. Lincoln Boulevard is a major thoroughfare through the Bemis Park district, lined with fine homes.

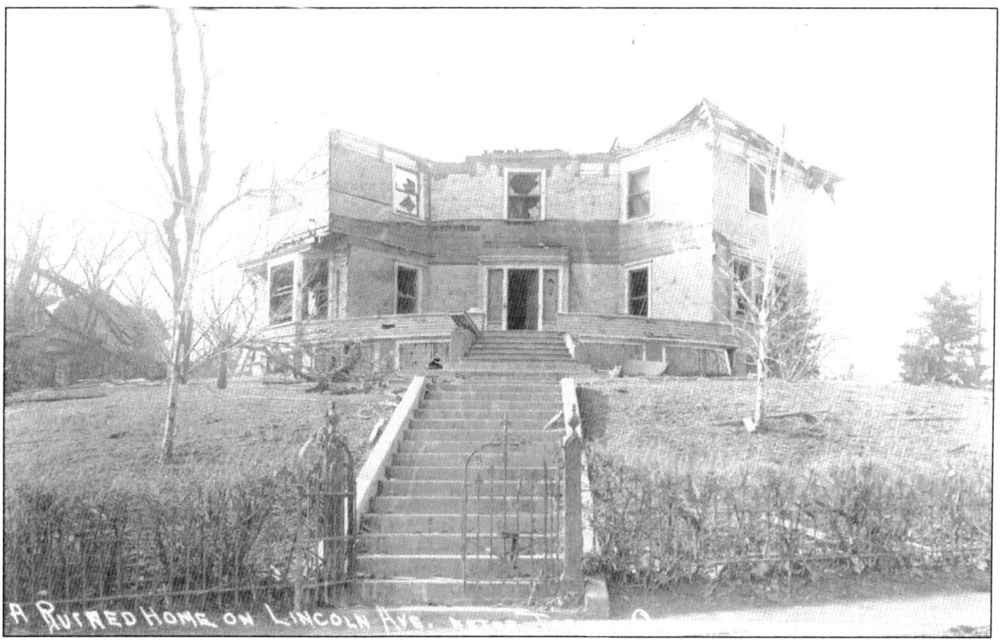

HANSON HOUSE. The late Christoff "Tolf" Hanson's residence at 3402 Lincoln Boulevard was one of the showplaces of Bemis Park. Hanson parlayed a career as a sandwich peddler into that of a restauranteur. This 14-room dwelling was built in 1904 for a grand sum of $7,500. In 1913 it was home to H.S. Clark Jr., whose wife was mistakenly placed on the list of the dead.

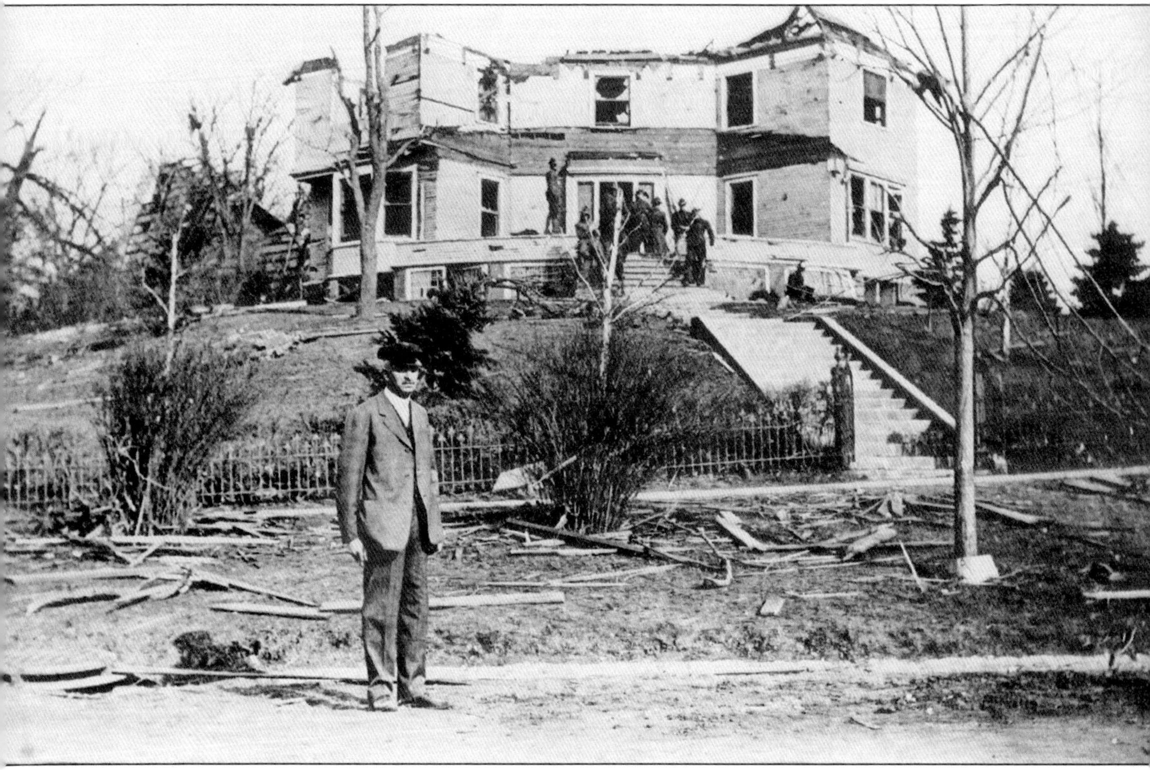

MILITIA ON THE PORCH. Members of the militia stationed in Bemis Park are pictured on the porch of the Hanson house. (Bostwick-Frohardt Collection, Durham Western Heritage Museum.)

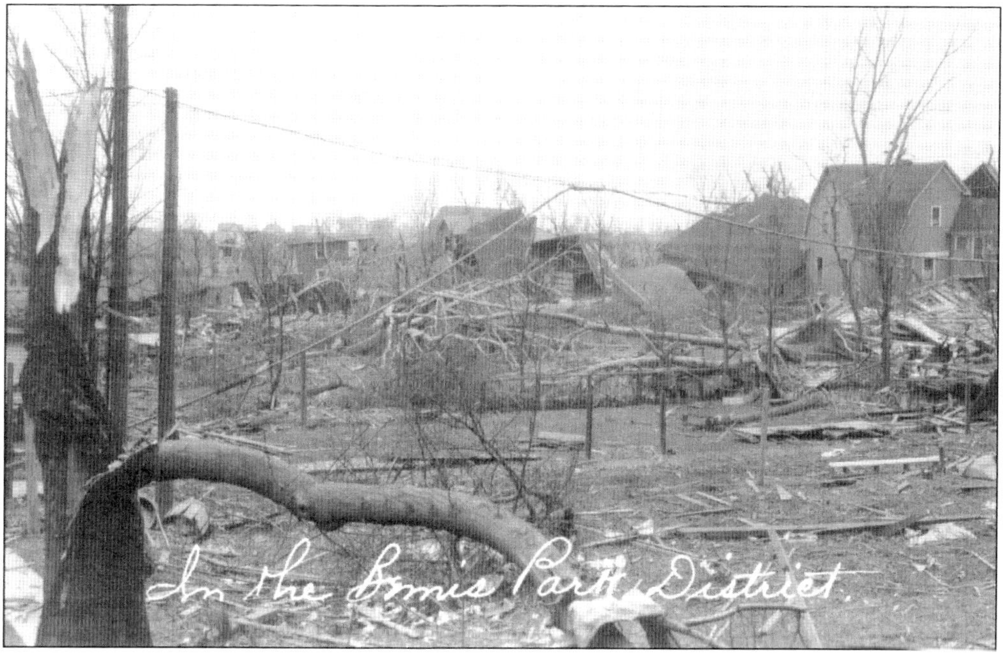

IN THE BEMIS PARK DISTRICT. Beautiful Bemis Park inspired a different form of awe after the storm, when it was rendered a wasteland of broken trees, downed power lines, and scattered debris.

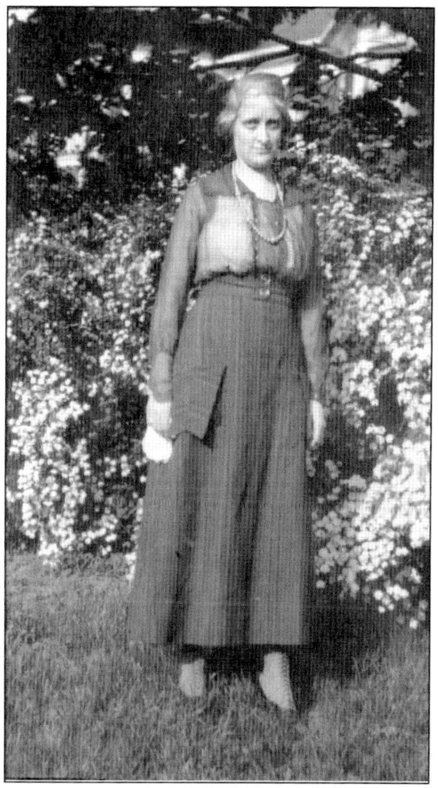

BEULAH ADAMS. Beulah Adams stepped off a streetcar at 33rd and Cuming Streets as the tornado bore down upon Bemis Park. She miraculously survived by lying in a ditch. Adams stated, "I put my umbrella down and lay flat, face downward… [w]ith my hand I held my face and my feelings were similar to those of a child who turns from an impending blow with helpless terror waits for what will come." (Douglas County Historical Society Library/Archives Center.)

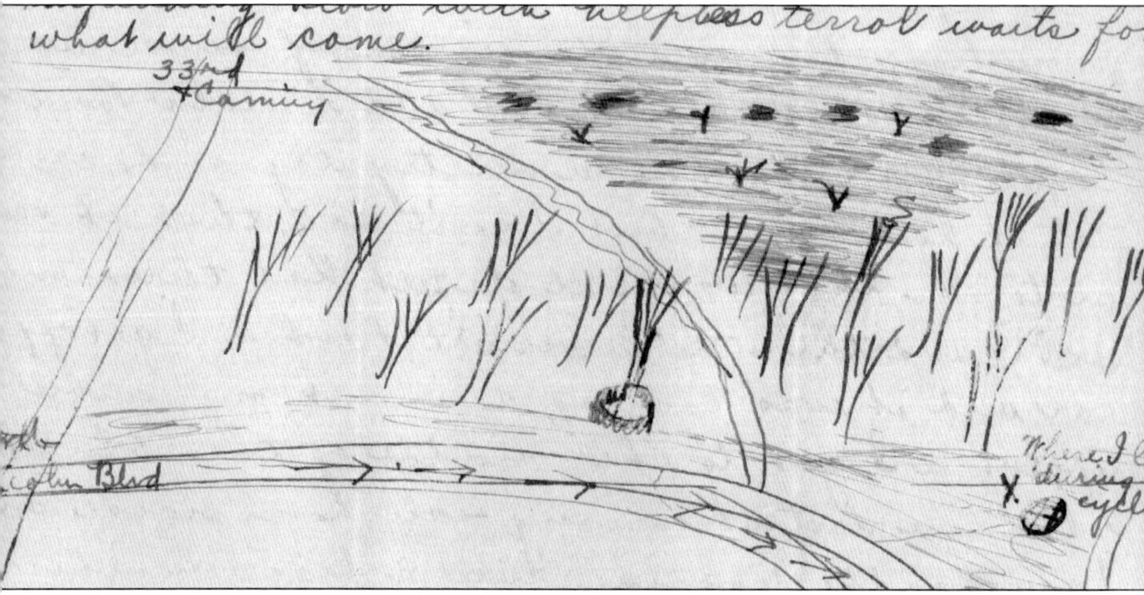

ADAMS SKETCH. This sketch is from a letter Beulah Adams wrote to her mother detailing her harrowing experience. (Douglas County Historical Society Library/Archives Center.)

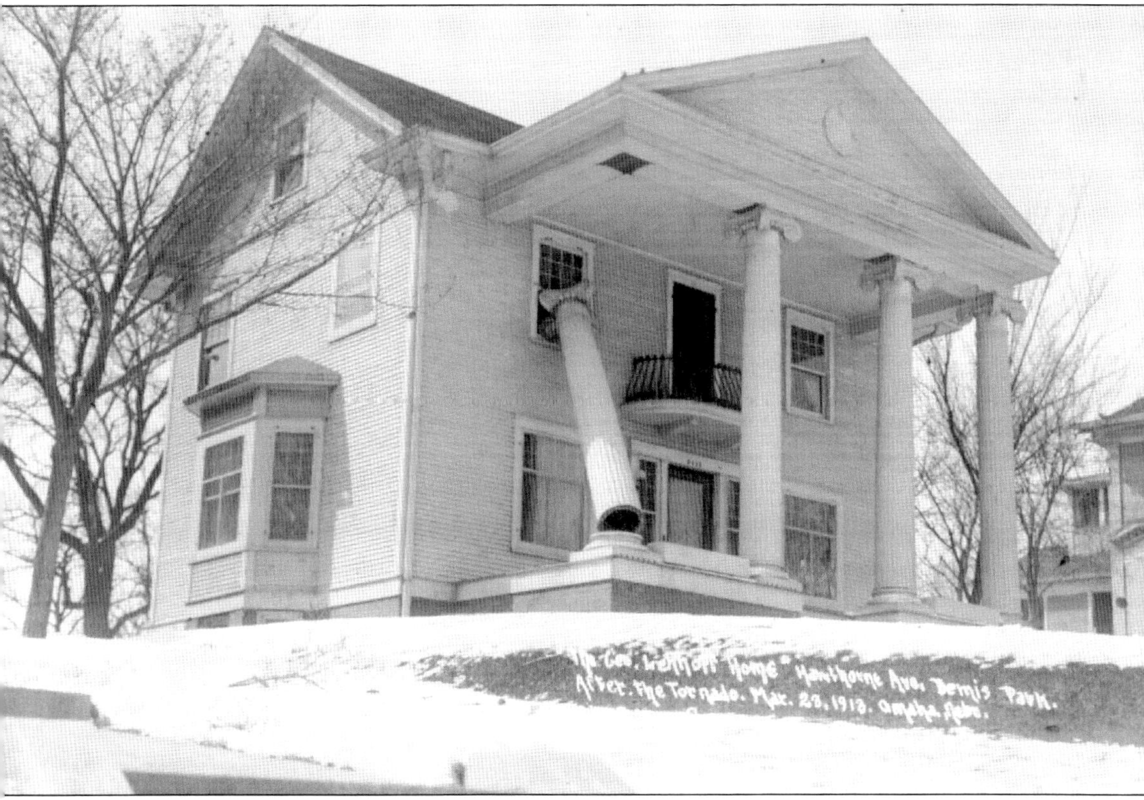

LEHNHOFF HOME. George and Minnie Lehnhoff's beautiful Neo-Classical Revival home at 3419 Hawthorne Avenue suffered slight damage, which included the fall of the easternmost column through a bedroom window.

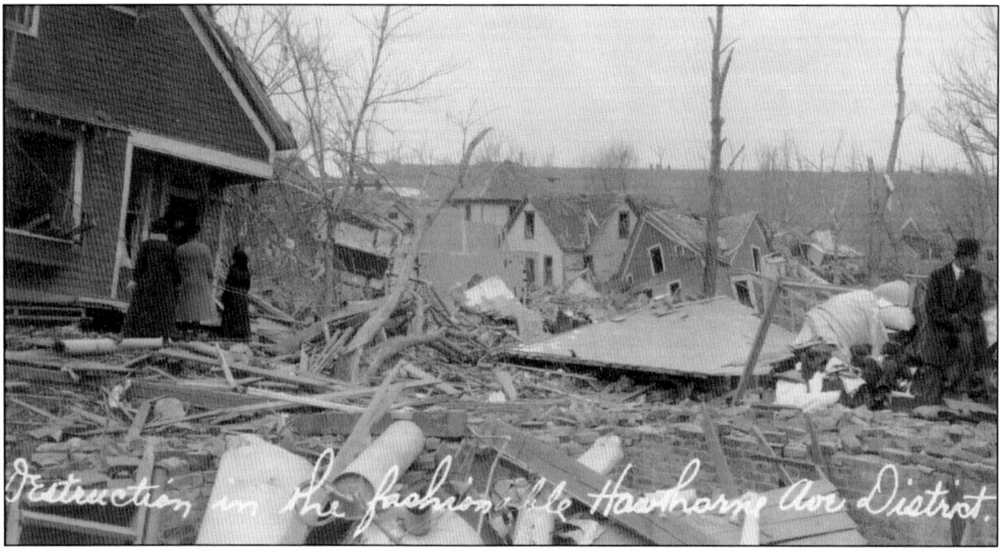

HAWTHORNE AVENUE. This view of Hawthorne Avenue illustrates the massive damage inflicted on the neighborhood. The *Omaha World-Herald* reported that "the ruin was so complete and the debris so heterogeneously mixed that it was actually impossible to determine in the darkness just where some of the structures had stood."

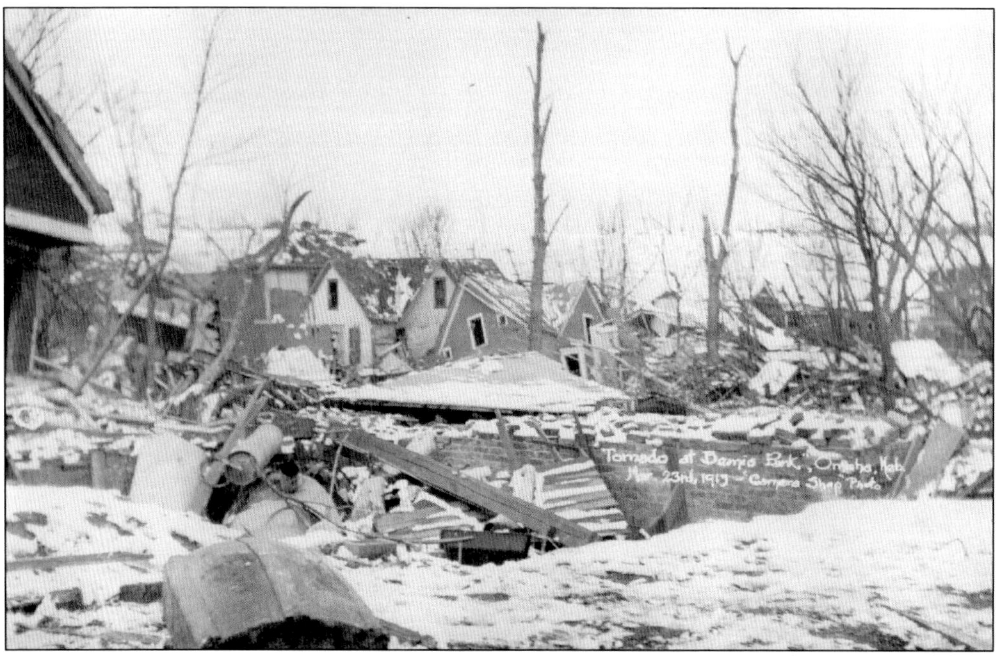

BEMIS PARK UNDER SNOW. A blanket of snow does little to soften the harsh scene in Bemis Park.

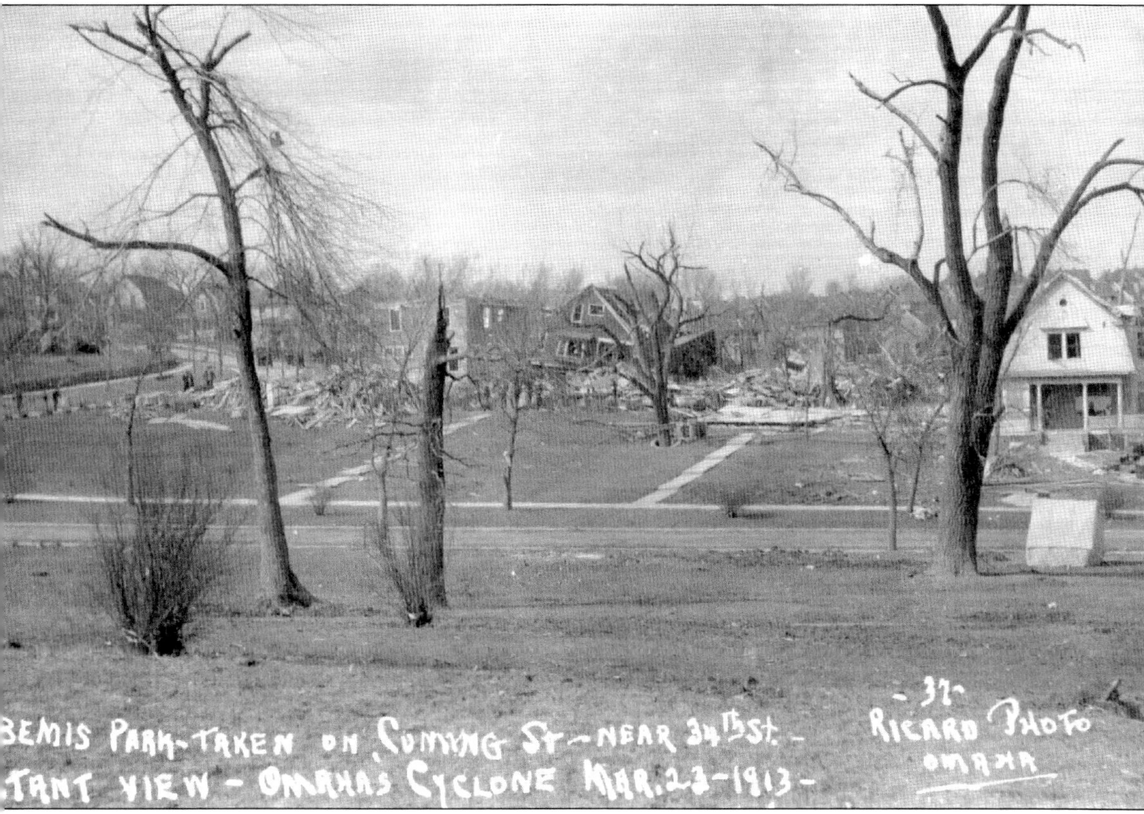

BEMIS PARK, FROM CUMING STREET. In this view of Bemis Park, the path of the tornado can be traced by demolished homes, or homes wiped clean of their foundations. A shipment of 400 military tents was sent to Omaha for temporary housing, and 25 were used in Bemis Park.

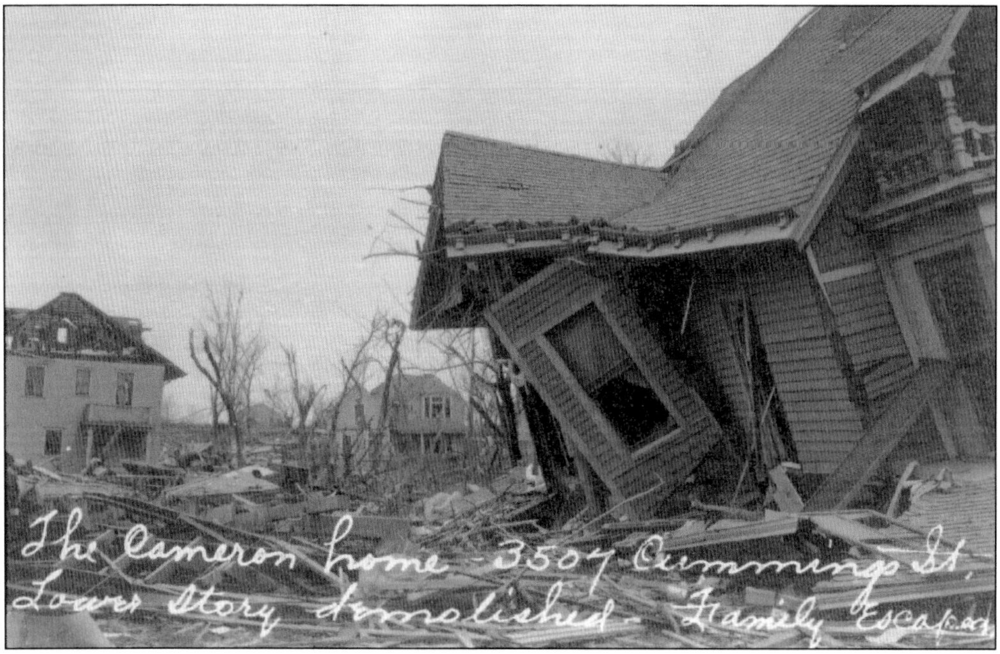

CAMERON HOME. The lower floor of the M.A. Cameron home at 3507 Cuming Street was demolished, and the upper floor came crashing down. All members of the family escaped.

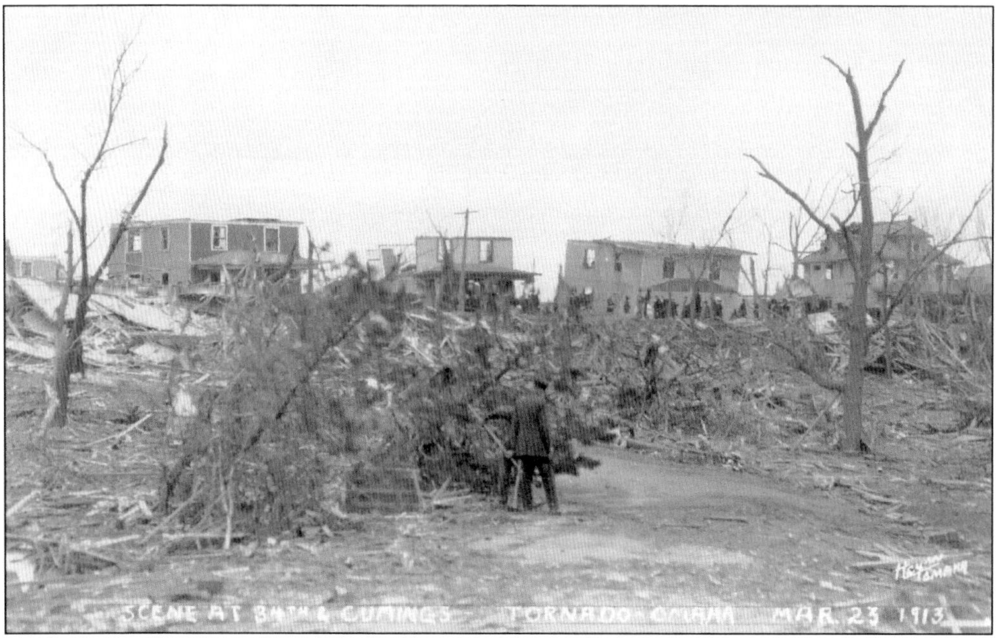

SCENE AT 34TH AND CUMING. A view of Cuming Street from Bemis Park shows mangled trees and roofless homes.

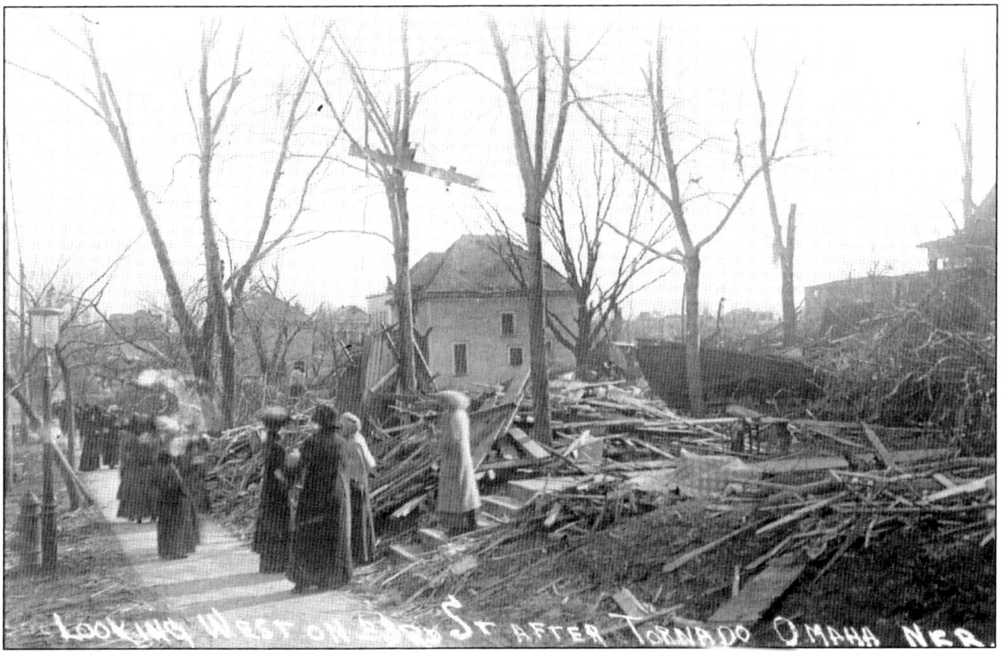

LOOKING WEST ON 33RD STREET. On Cuming Street, these women survey the damage and the debris in the treetops.

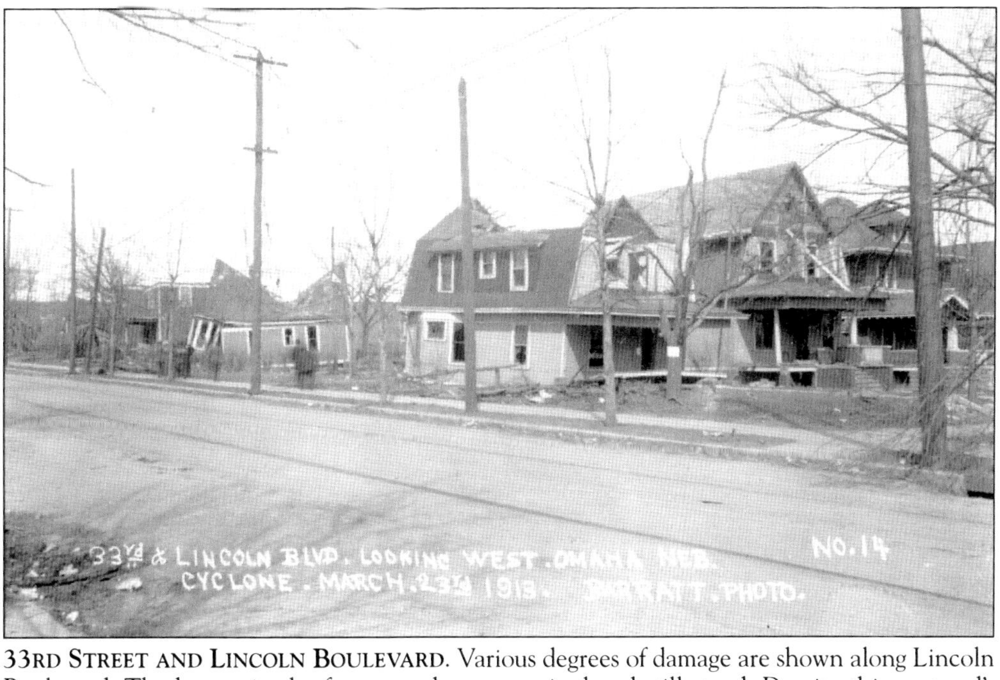

33RD STREET AND LINCOLN BOULEVARD. Various degrees of damage are shown along Lincoln Boulevard. The homes in the foreground were repaired and still stand. Despite this postcard's caption, the view does not look west, but northeast as the storm is tracked.

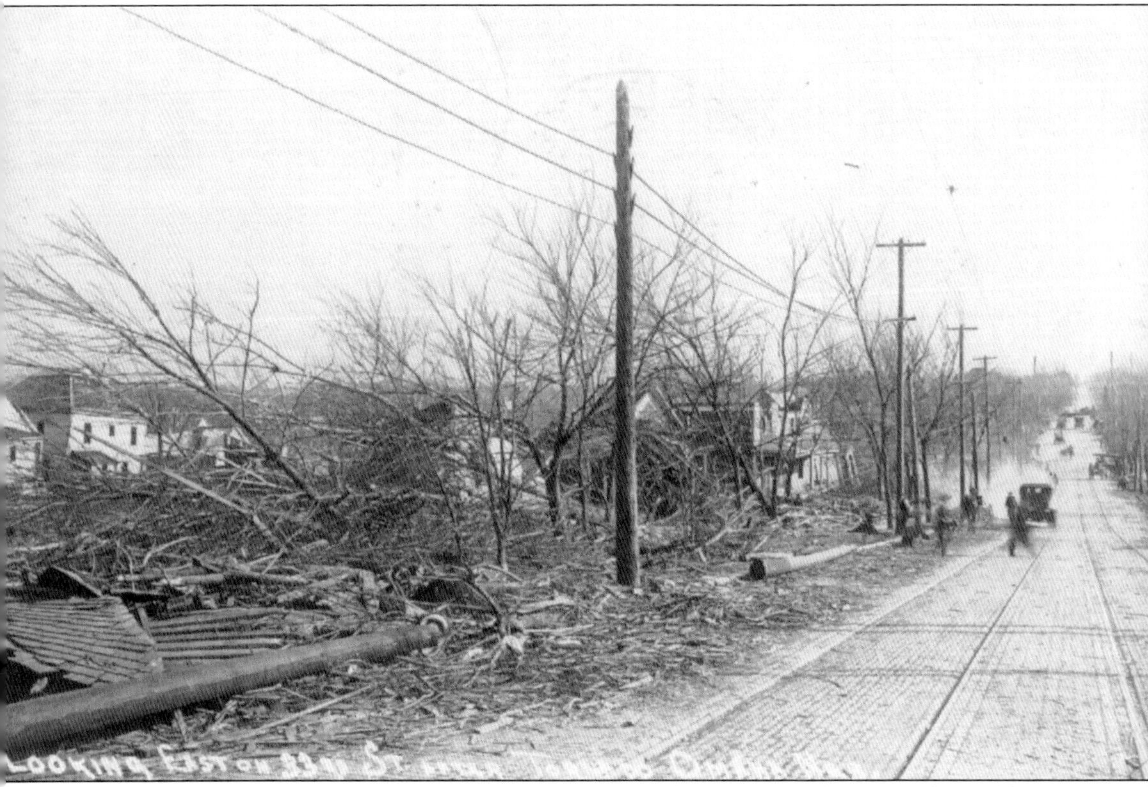

LOOKING EAST ON CUMING STREET. This photo was taken after the cleanup and rebuilding was initiated. Streetcars are running on the Cuming Street line, one of the last to open after the storm. New utility poles have been installed, and the old poles can be seen lying on the ground. The card's label is misleading, as it was taken from the intersection of 33rd and Cuming Streets.

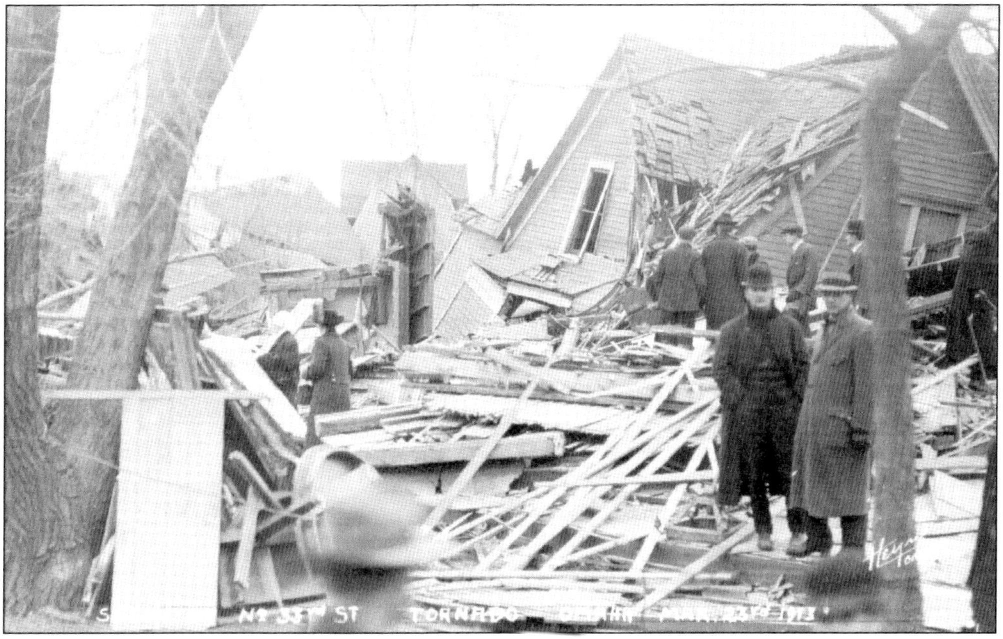

SCENE ON NORTH 33RD STREET. Some homes collapsed as if made of cards. Lower stories could literally be blown out from under the upper story or roof.

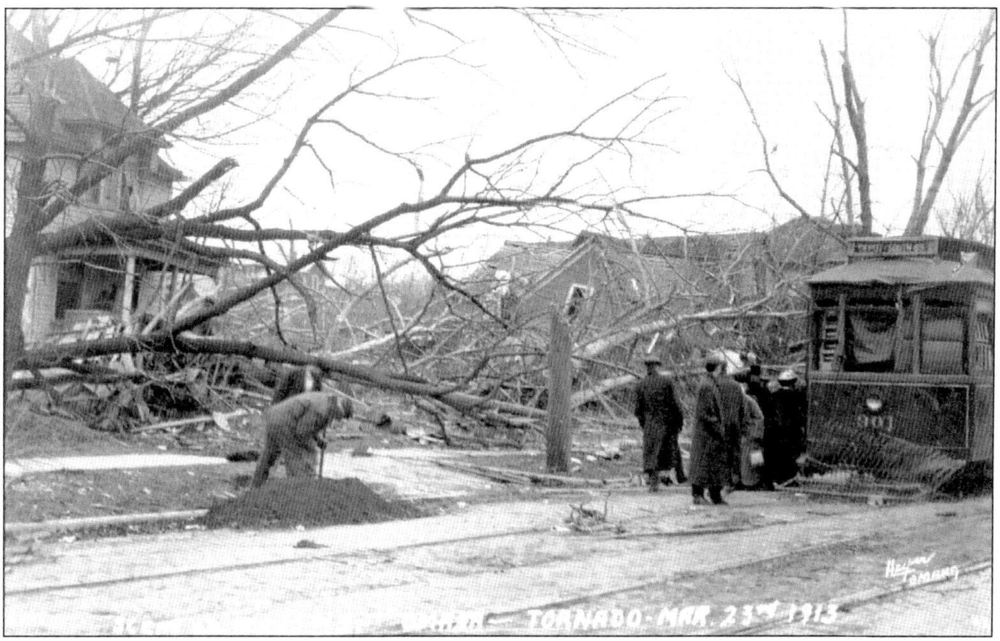

ANOTHER SCENE ON NORTH 33RD STREET. Felled trees, broken utility poles, and a halted streetcar mark a scene on 33rd Street. Visitors look around while men dig as part of the rebuilding effort.

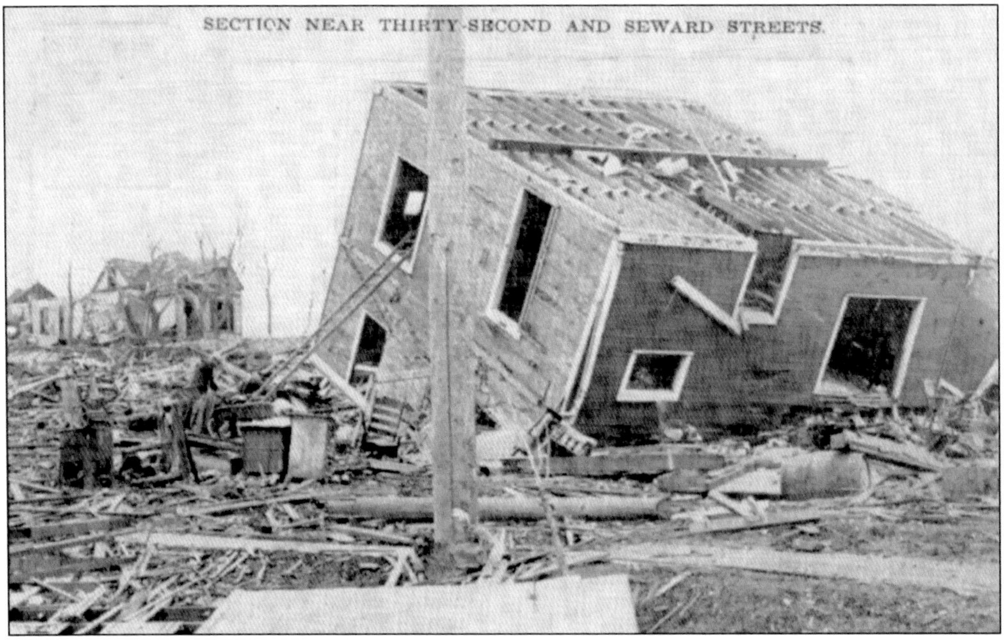

UPSIDE-DOWN HOUSE. Near 32nd and Seward Streets, the wrecked house in the foreground features a ladder leading up to what had been a first-floor window. Pipes can be seen through the "top" of the home. It was reported that the entire house was tossed 200 feet by the tornado.

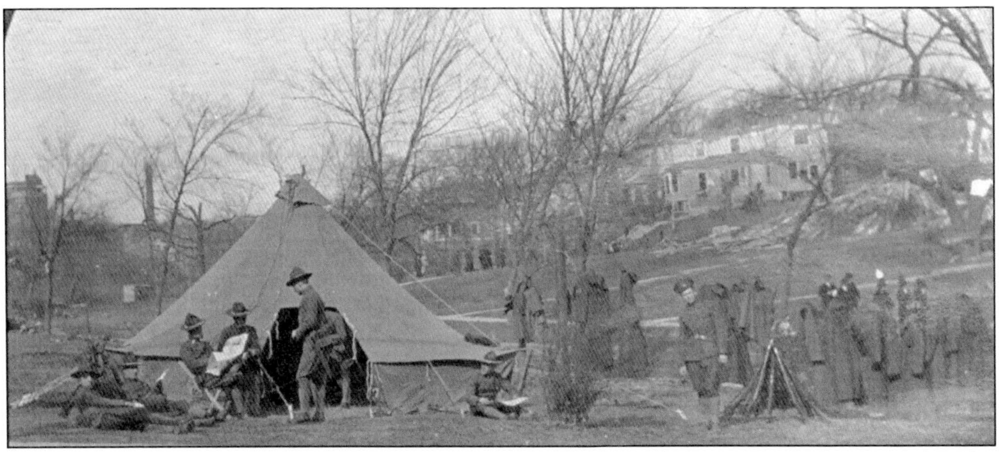

MILITIA IN BEMIS PARK. A group of militiamen are pictured at repose in Bemis Park. The militia's field headquarters for the entire tornado district was in the centrally-located Bemis Park. Somewhat more temperate weather is evidenced by the row of heavy coats hanging on a line between trees. (Douglas County Historical Society Library/Archives Center.)

Six

24TH AND LAKE

I was on the back platform, when I saw the cyclone coming. I gave the signal to stop, shouted to my passengers that a cyclone was coming, and ran for a basement of an unfinished building. I jumped into the basement, and three or four passengers were beside me. Wreckage flew over us, and a lot of boards were piled on top of us. It seemed to me that the horror lasted about two minutes. Then I crawled out and picked up two of my passengers, a man and a woman, who were lying unconscious in the street.

—*Charles Caldwell, conductor of streetcar #862*

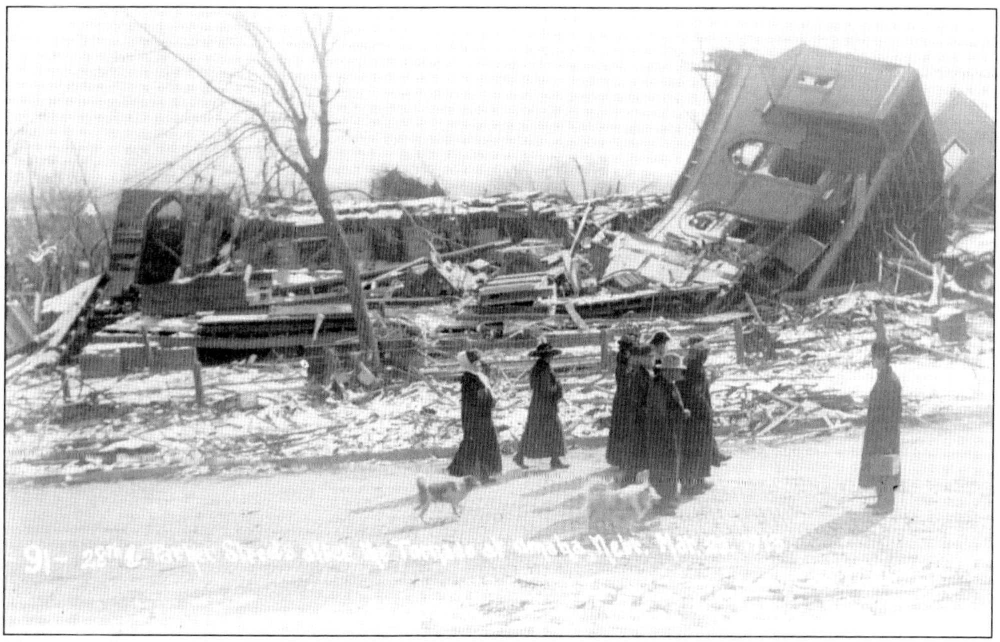

GERMAN LUTHERAN CHURCH. A group strolls past the remains of the German Lutheran Church at 28th and Parker Streets. A wedding ceremony was interrupted by the storm. After hasty vows, the newlyweds fled in an automobile, while the celebrants sought shelter in the church basement. The frame structure collapsed, but rescuers freed all guests.

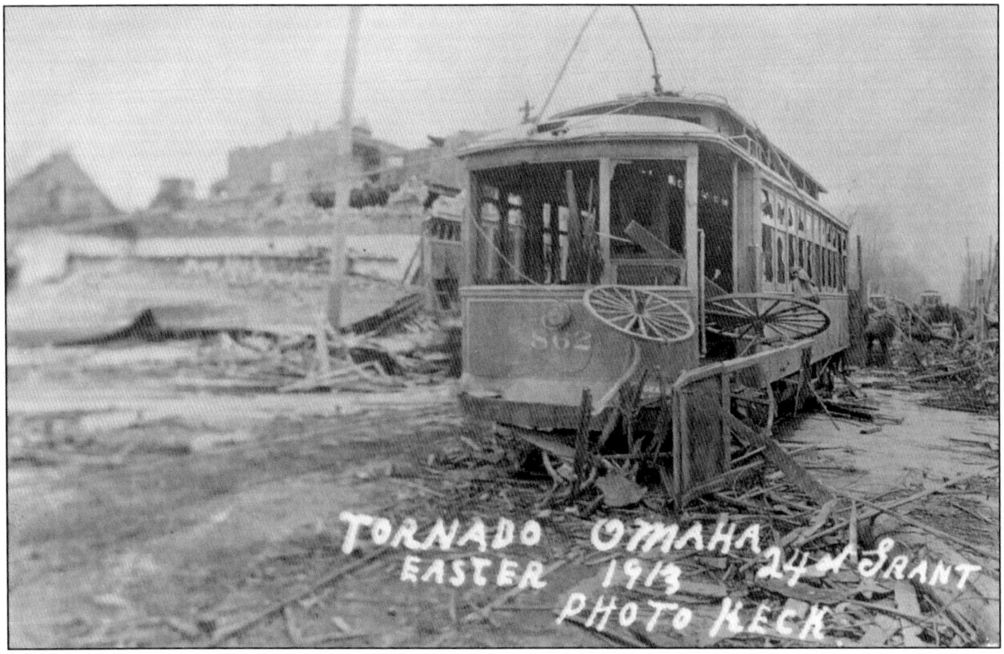

STREETCAR #862. Omaha & Council Bluffs Street Railway car #862 is halted on the 24th Street line. The carriage wedged underneath the car was blown there by the storm. Every window of the streetcar was broken. All those aboard sustained injuries, but no passengers perished due to the quick thinking of the conductor.

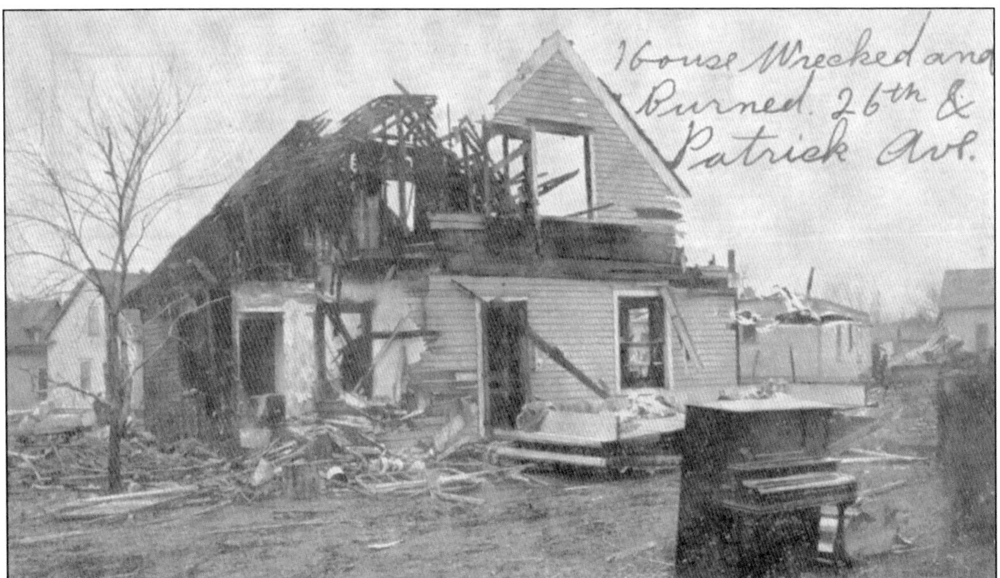

BURNED HOUSE. After the tornado, many fires were started due to ruptured gas lines. This home at 26th and Patrick Streets was only one of the victims of such fires.

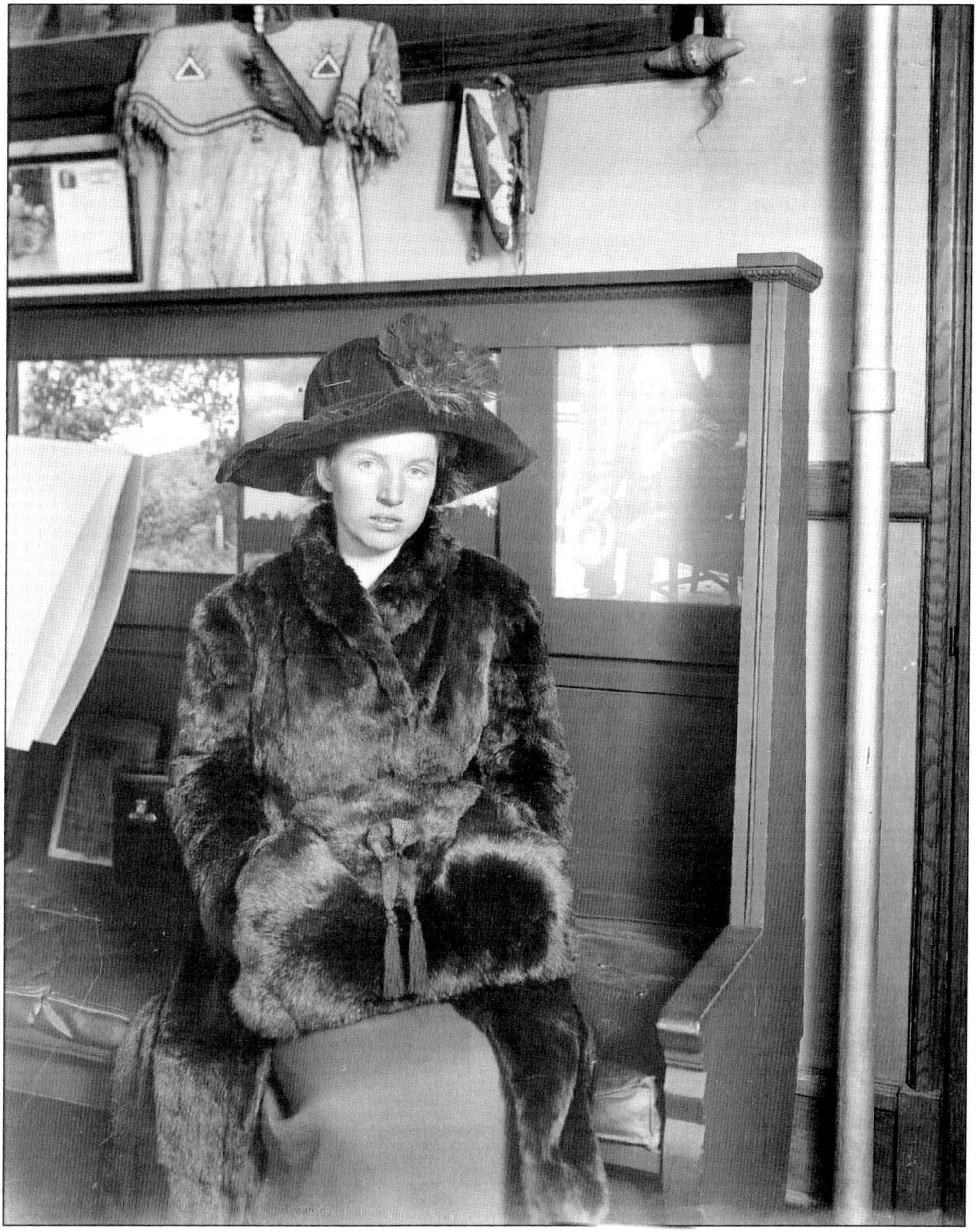

MARY GAMBLE, "HELLO GIRL." Although she had not worked at the Webster Telephone Exchange at 2213 Lake Street for three years, Mary Gamble left her baby with her mother and walked through the storm debris to aid the other operators for 20 hours. Heroines of the day, the "hello girls" kept their switchboard positions as the storm raged and chaos surrounded them. The telephone exchange building became a makeshift hospital and morgue. This photo was taken at Louis Bostwick's studio in the Brandeis Building. (Bostwick-Frohardt Collection, Durham Western Heritage Museum.)

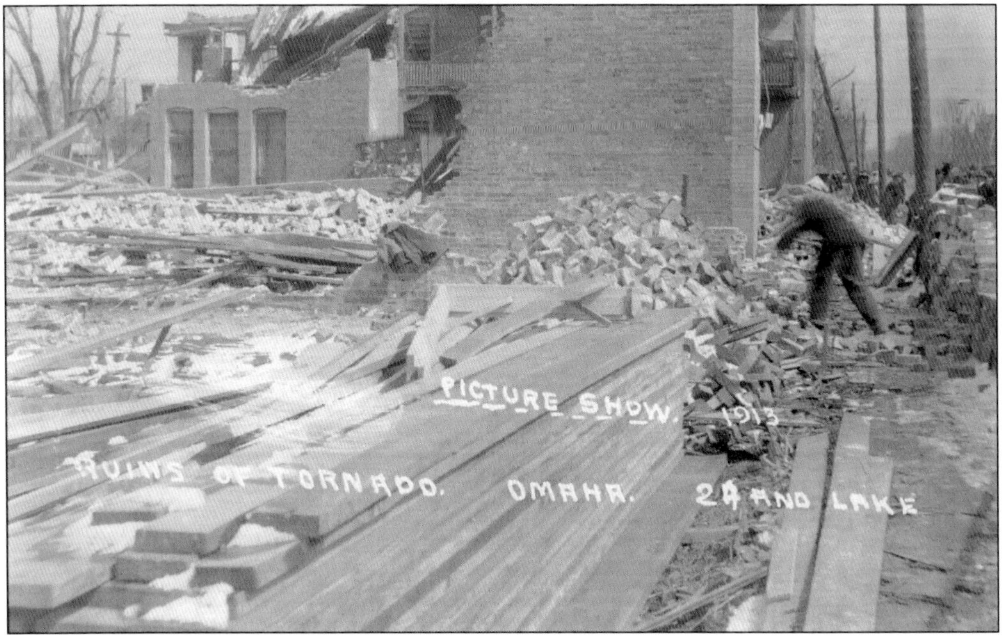

DIAMOND MOTION PICTURE THEATER. One of the fastest circulating rumors was that the movie house had collapsed, killing hundreds. The rumors proved untrue as all patrons, approximately 60, escaped alive.

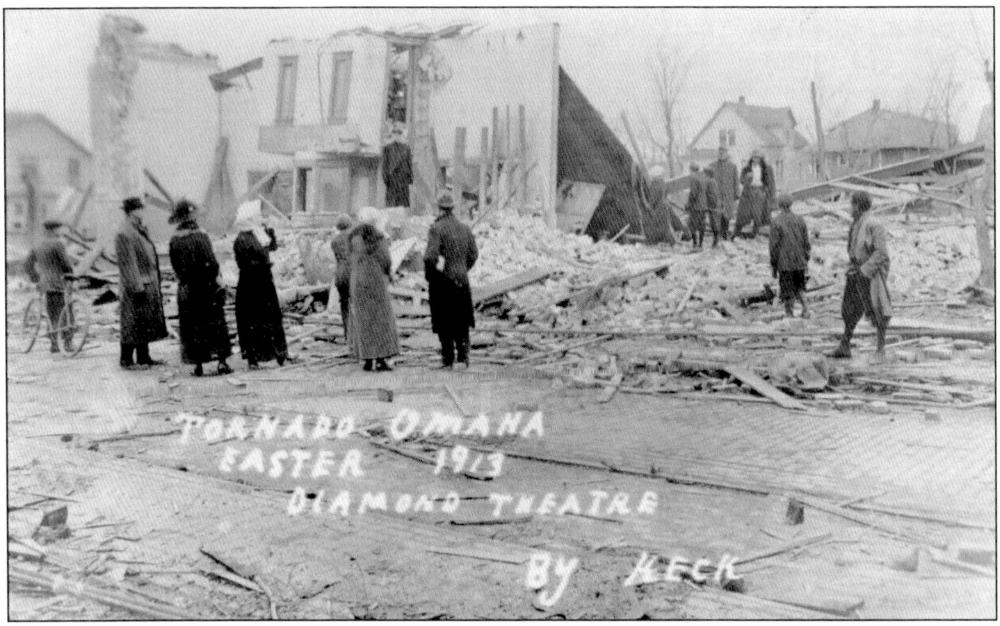

RUINS OF DIAMOND THEATER. According to R.C. Long, a newsreel showing President Wilson's inauguration had just finished when "the walls began to crumble and fall and the roof dropped. Most of the persons had time to drop to the floor. The roof fell flat upon the tops of the seats pinning the inmates." His wife and other patrons made their way through the aisles and out the front entrance, while Long himself and others had to wait 15 minutes for rescuers to remove debris.

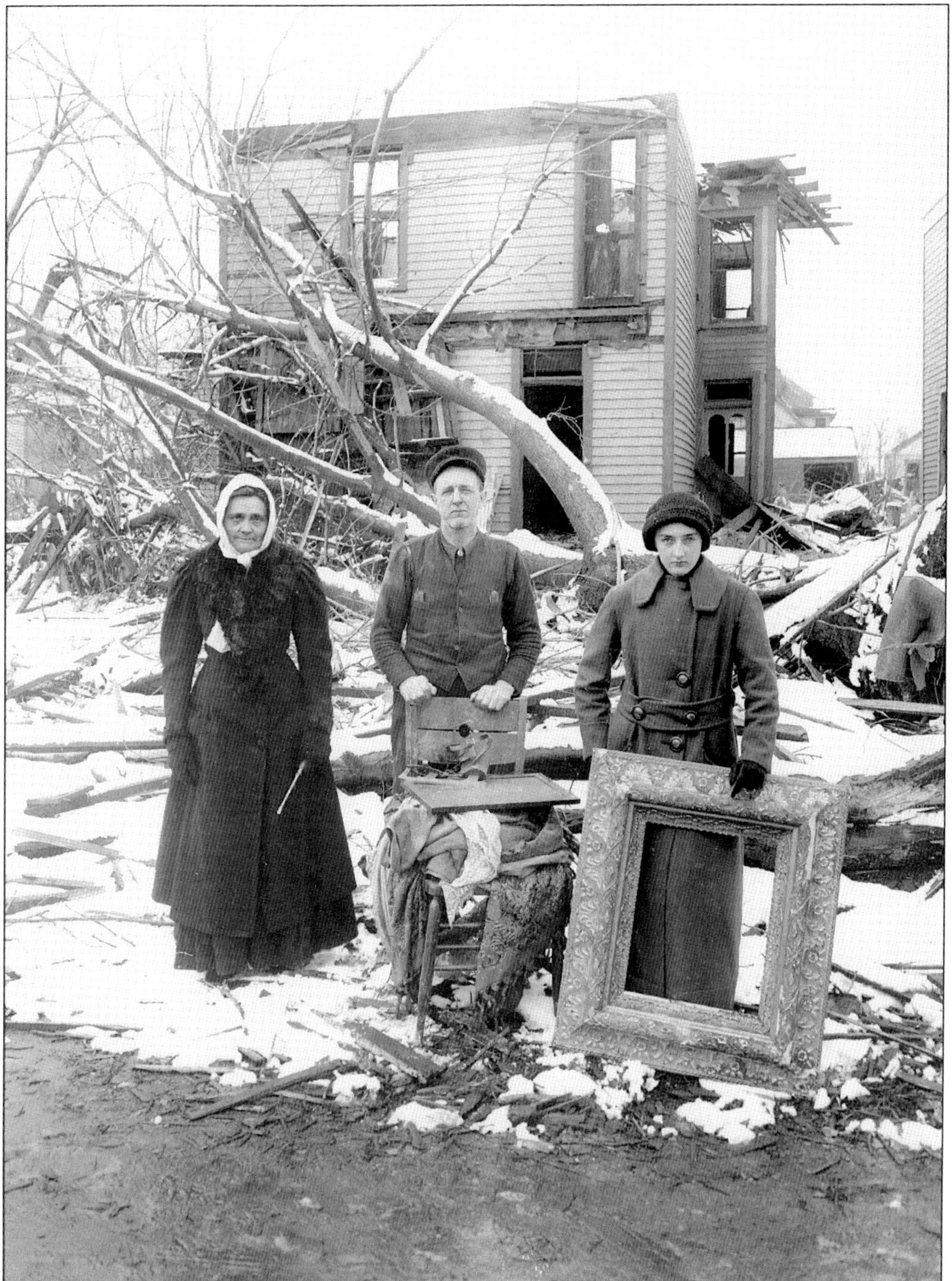

WILLIAMS FAMILY. The J.W. Williams family is pictured at their residence near 24th and Lake Streets with a few salvaged possessions. They clung to the piano until they were blown from the second story of the house, sustaining only minor injuries. (Bostwick-Frohardt Collection, Durham Western Heritage Museum.)

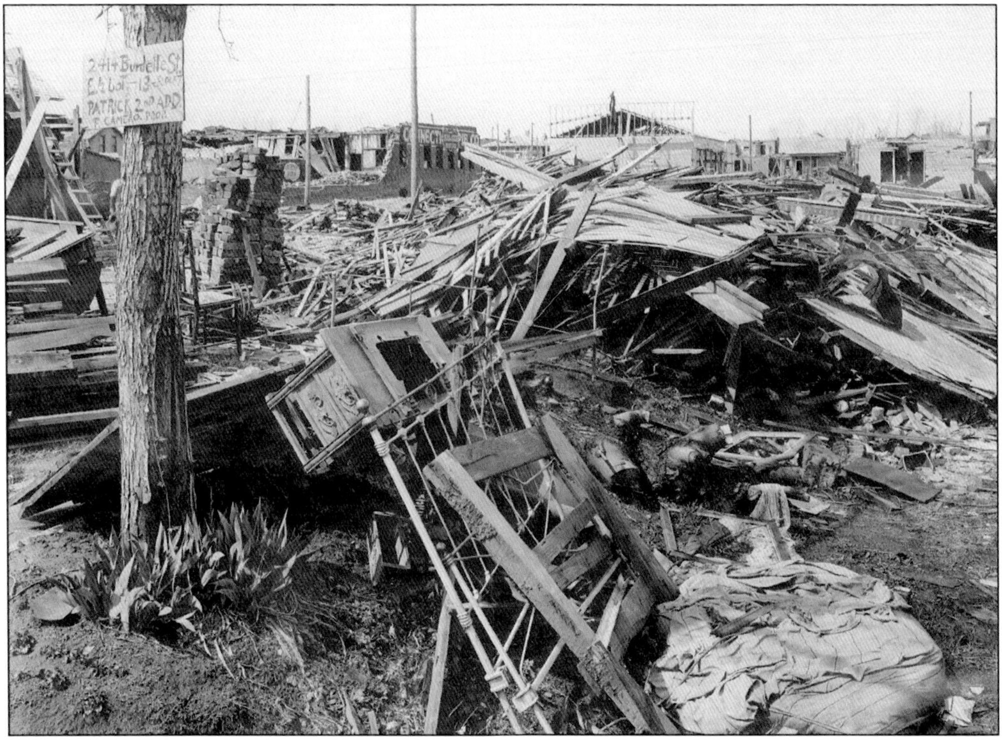

CAMERO HOME. Where the home of Angelo Joseph and Rachel Camero once stood, a sign nailed to a tree conveys vital information about the property. (Bostwick-Frohardt Collection, Durham Western Heritage Museum.)

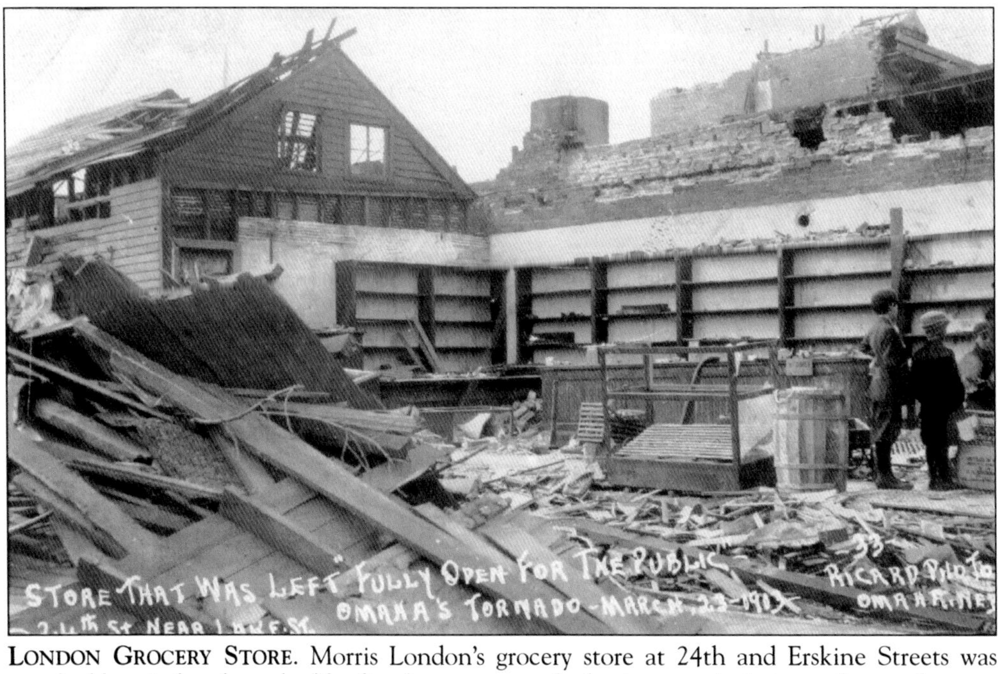

LONDON GROCERY STORE. Morris London's grocery store at 24th and Erskine Streets was wrecked by wind and touched by fire, but was open for business again in just a few weeks.

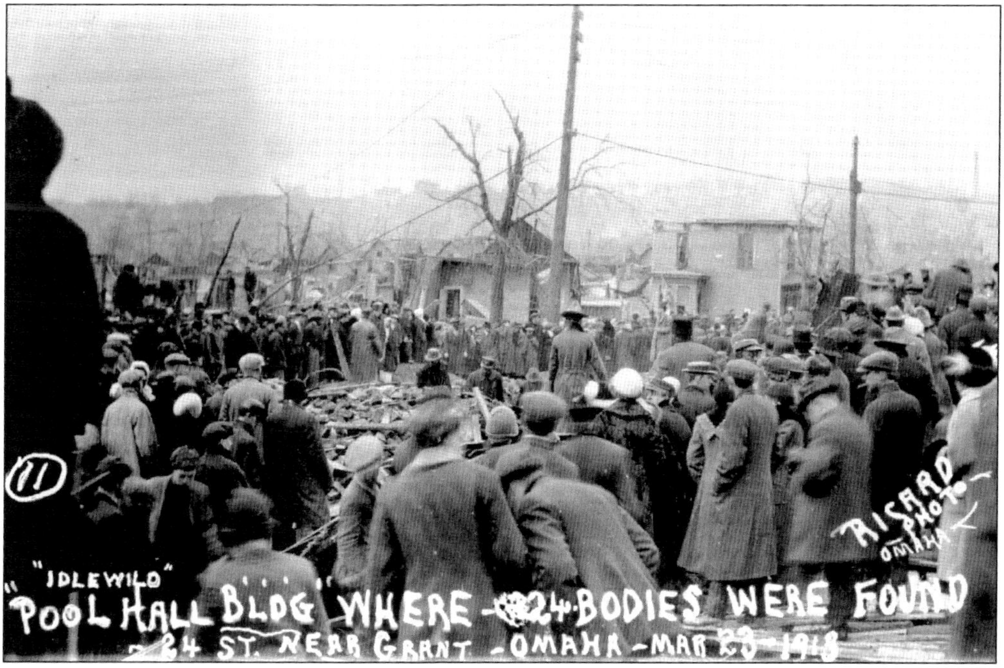

IDLEWILD POOL HALL. A crowd gathers at the all-black Idlewild Pool Hall at 24th and Lake Streets to survey the recovery of bodies. The tornado picked up the building, slammed it down, and then set it ablaze. While 25 men perished here, there were three survivors in the rubble.

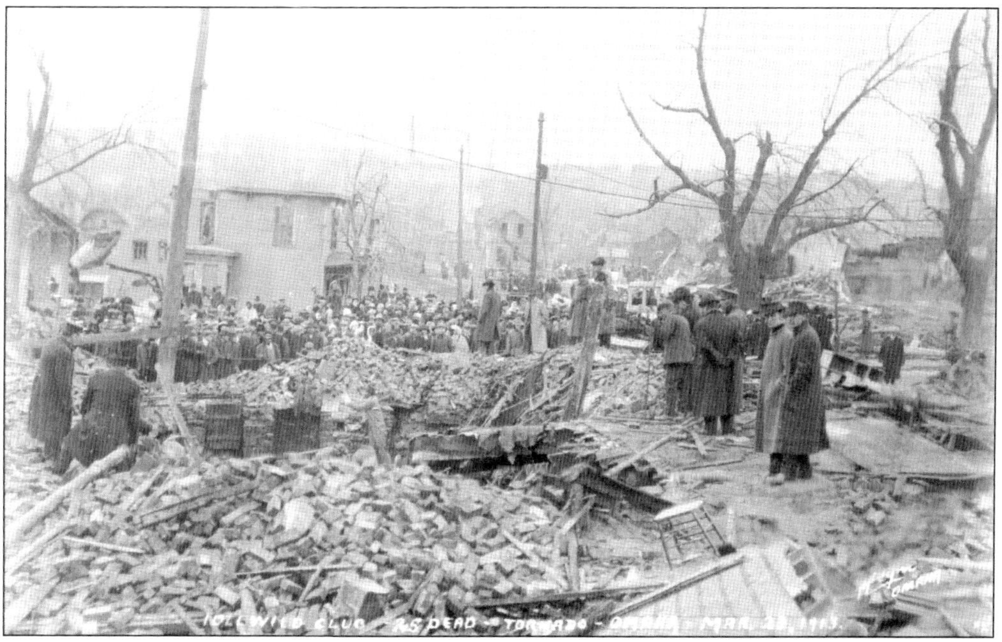

LARGE CROWD AT IDLEWILD. A large crowd gathered to view the terrible scene at Idlewild hall. An undertaker reported that while removing the coat of one of the victims—a well-liked gentleman who was a surprisingly good poker player—an ace of spades fell from the sleeve of the garment.

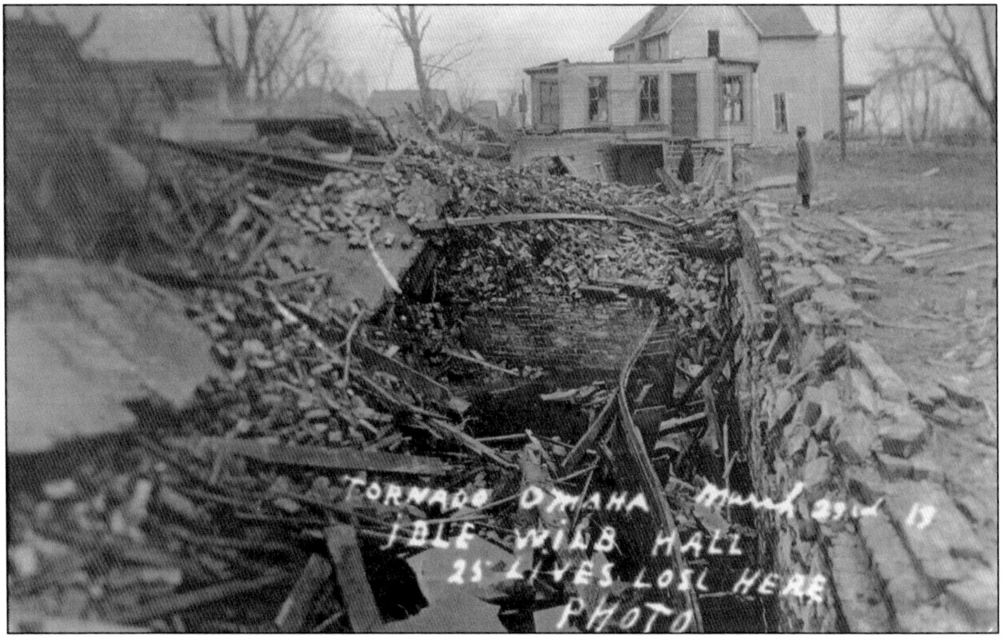

IDLEWILD ONLOOKER. The area around the Idlewild Pool Hall was usually crowded with a throng of curious onlookers, but this image finds it at a quieter moment.

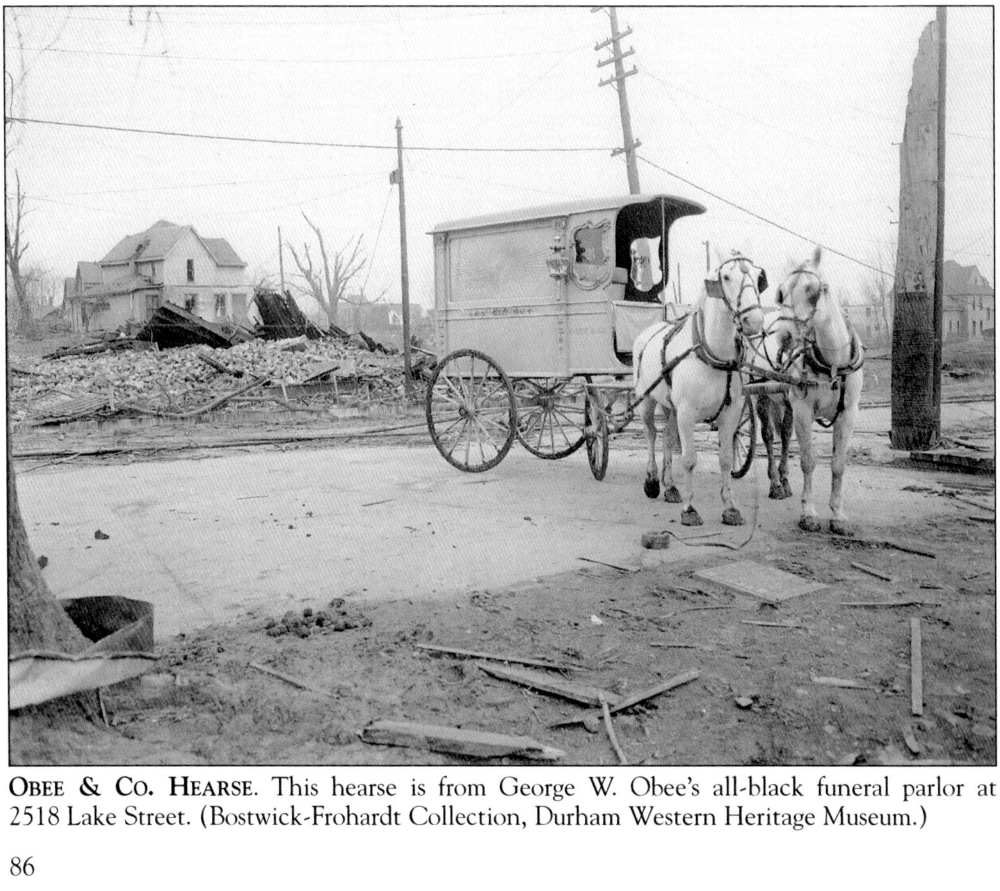

OBEE & CO. HEARSE. This hearse is from George W. Obee's all-black funeral parlor at 2518 Lake Street. (Bostwick-Frohardt Collection, Durham Western Heritage Museum.)

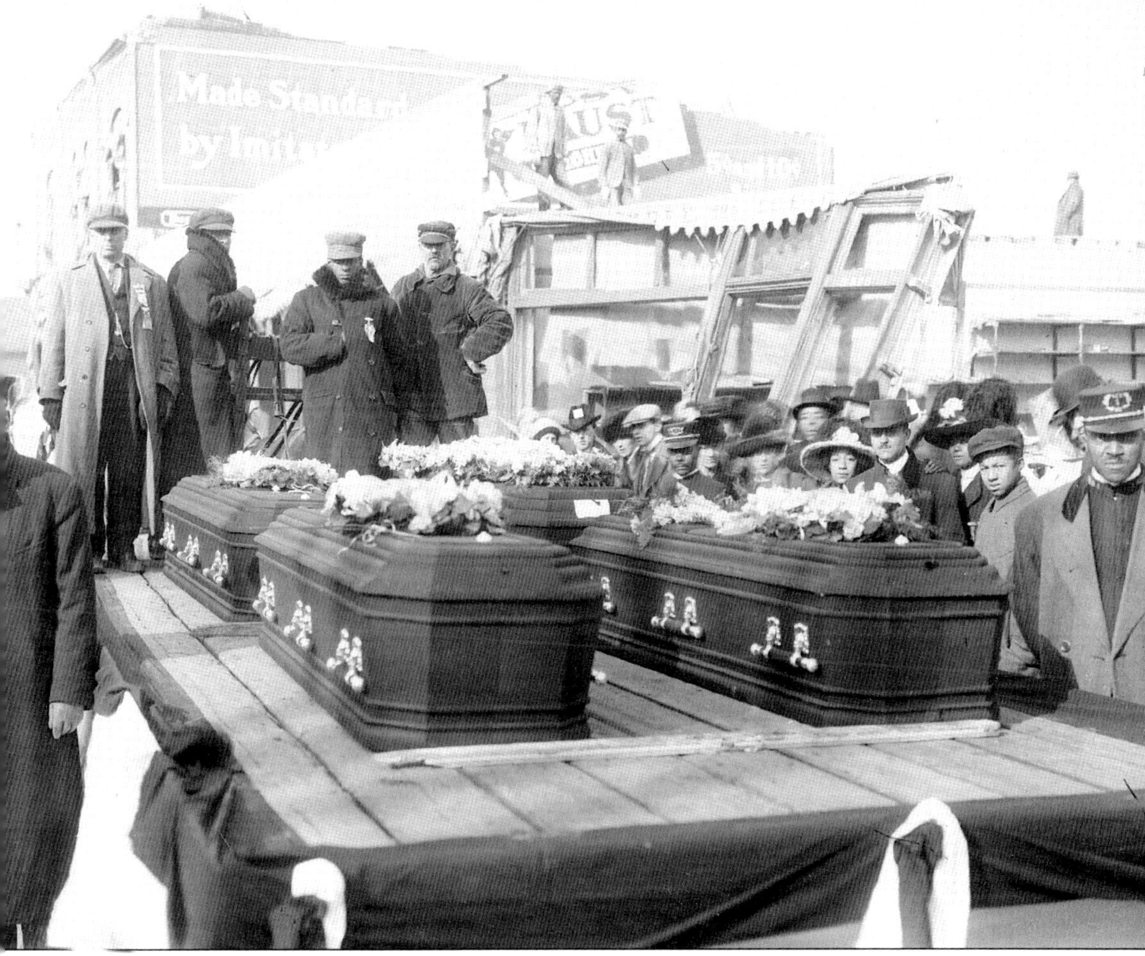

IDLEWILD PYTHIAN FUNERALS. The coffins of four Idlewild victims, all members of the Black Knights of Pythias, are pictured during the funeral parade. Pythian services were held at Obee's Chapel on Lake Street, under the auspices of the African Methodist Church. Due to the shortage of hearses, these men were conveyed to the cemetery on a specially-decorated "heavy truck," while two other lodge members killed at Idlewild were transported behind in individual hearses. (Bostwick-Frohardt Collection, Durham Western Heritage Museum.)

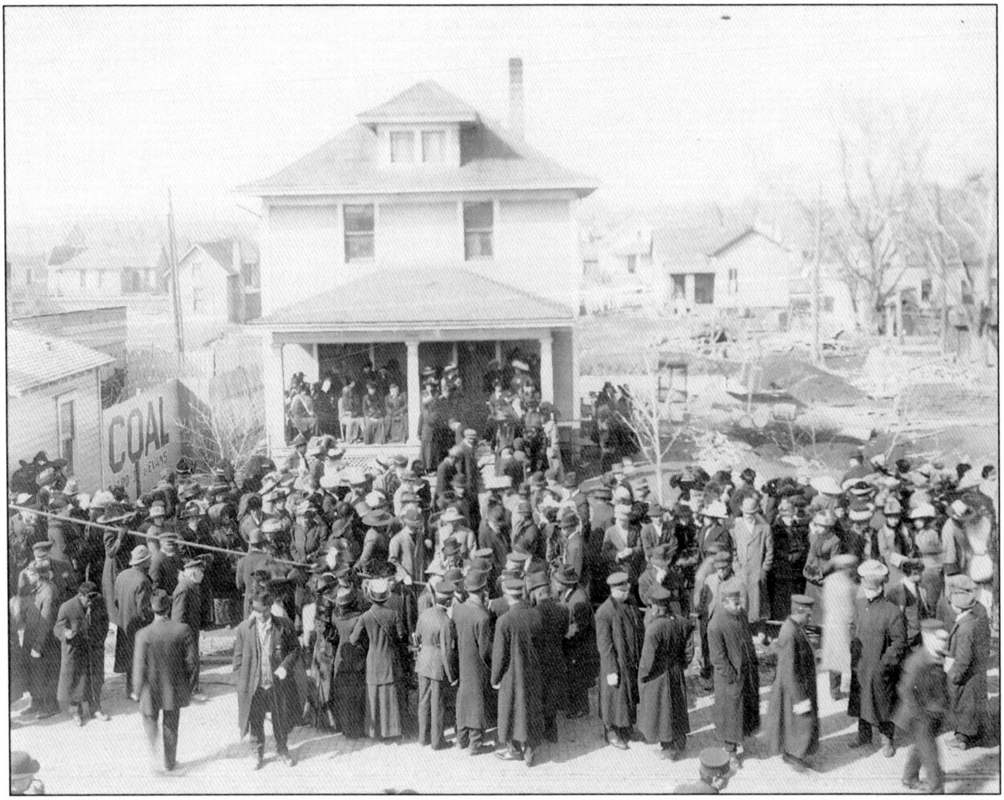

FUNERAL OF IDLEWILD VICTIM. Mourners teem around this house during one of the many funerals that occurred in the days following the tornado. (Bostwick-Frohardt Collection, Durham Western Heritage Museum.)

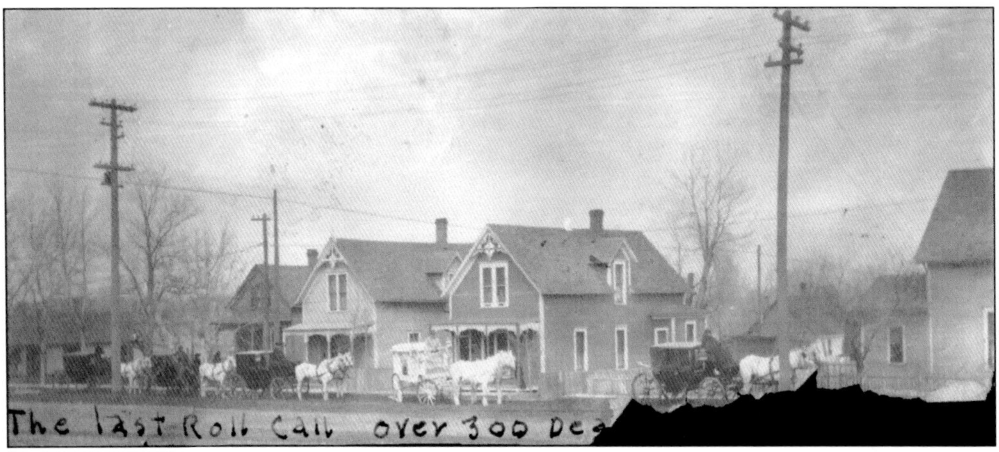

HEARSE PROCESSION. A large procession of hearses in north Omaha can be seen in this image. A hand-written claim conjecturing 300 fatalities is an exaggeration, as all estimates were less than half that number. (Douglas County Historical Society Library/Archives Center.)

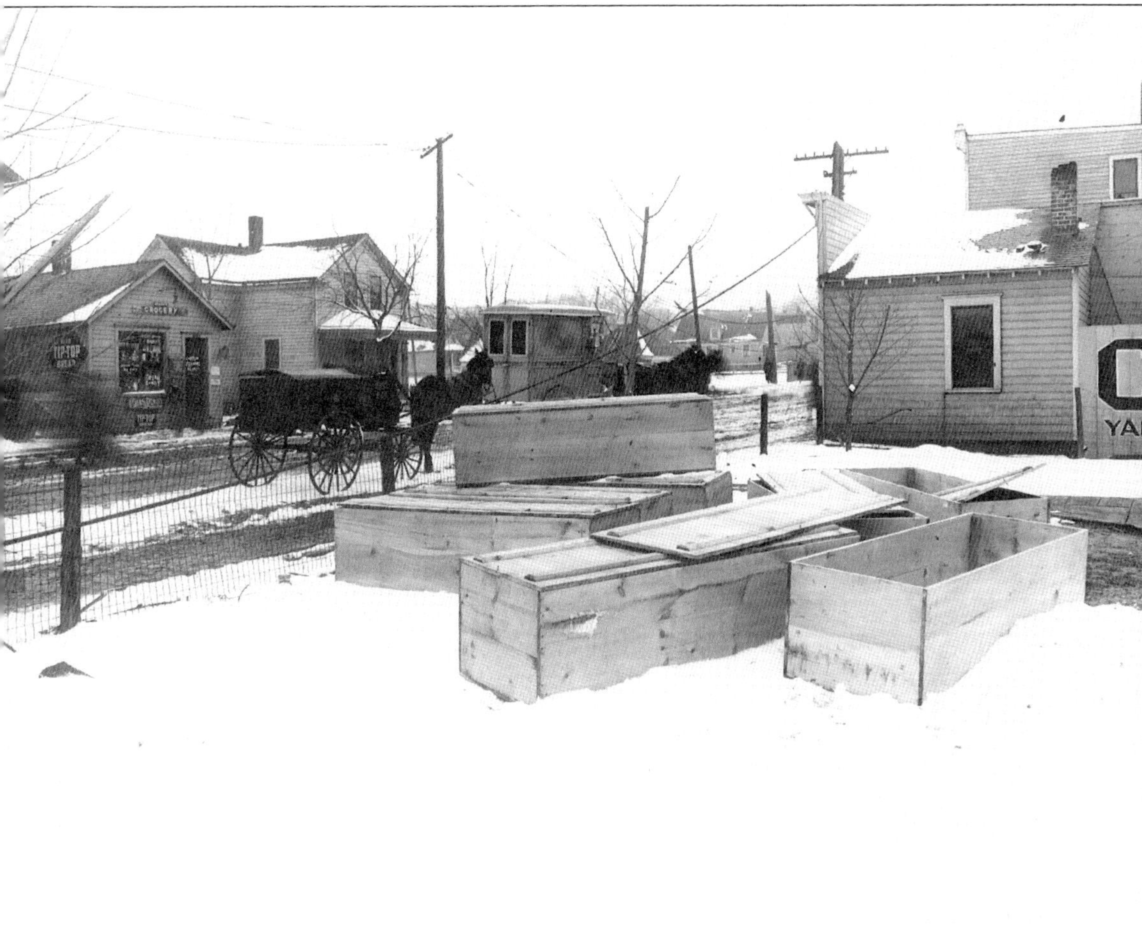

COFFINS IN SNOW. These rough-hewn coffins lie in the post-tornado snow. The horse-drawn vehicles in the background are hearses. (Bostwick-Frohardt Collection, Durham Western Heritage Museum.)

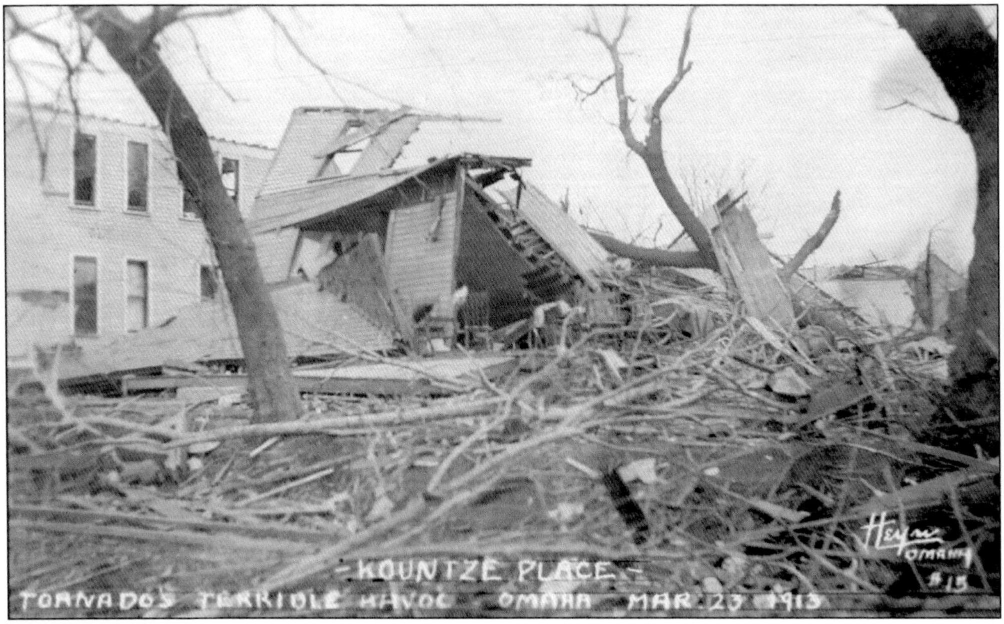

TORNADO'S TERRIBLE HAVOC AT KOUNTZE PLACE. Kountze Place was established in the late 1880s by banker and real estate developer Herman Kountze as a fashionable upper-middle-class neighborhood.

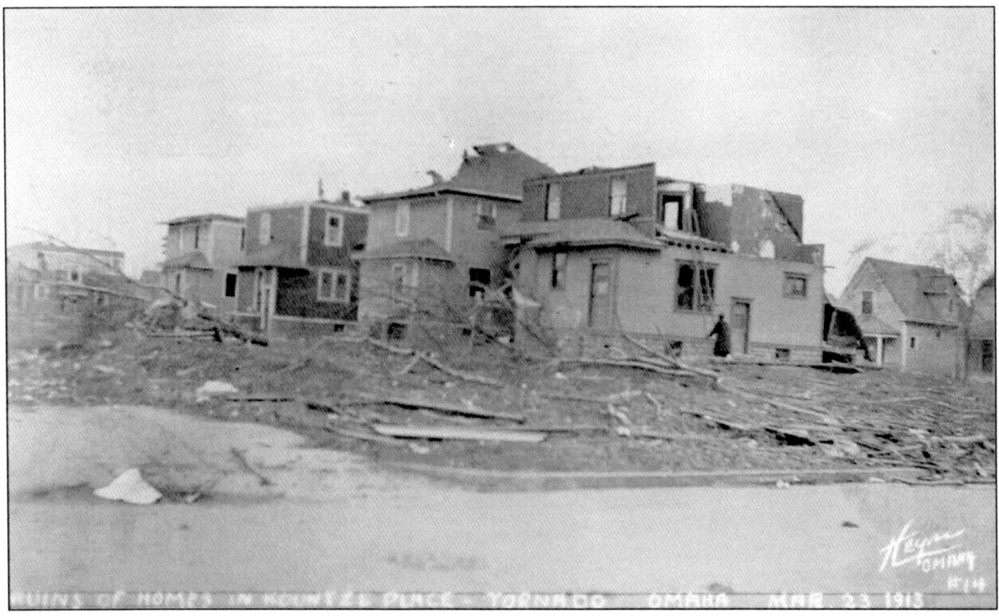

RUINS OF HOMES AT KOUNTZE PLACE. This line of homes in Kountze Place were partially or completely unroofed, and the trees blown down.

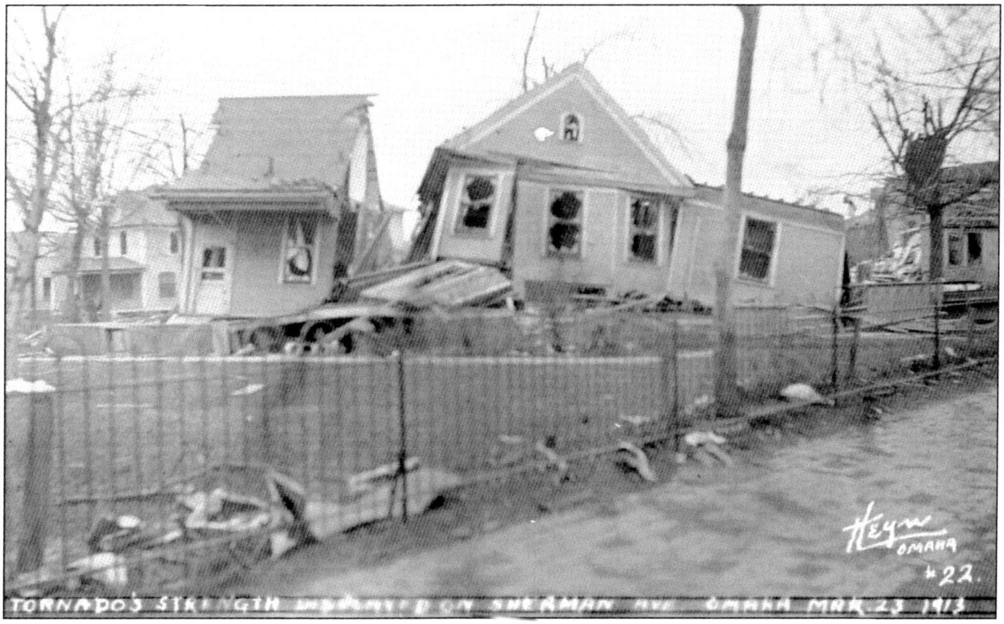

TORNADO'S STRENGTH DISPLAYED. This house that once sat on Sherman Avenue was split apart and moved out into the street.

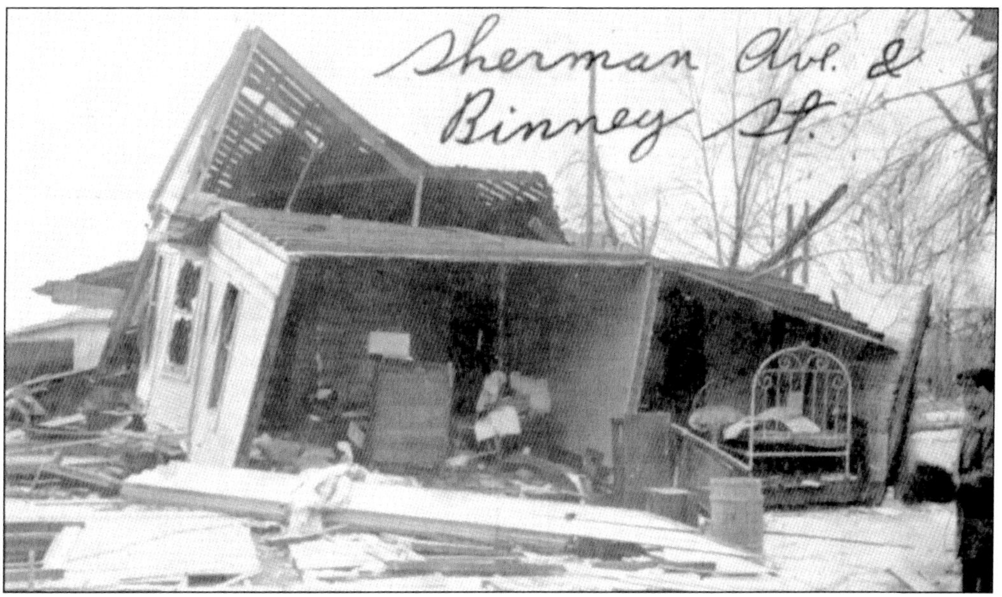

SHERMAN AVENUE AND BINNEY STREET. A boy views the remains of a home that had the wall sheared off, exposing the interior to the elements. The bed looks as if it was completely undisturbed.

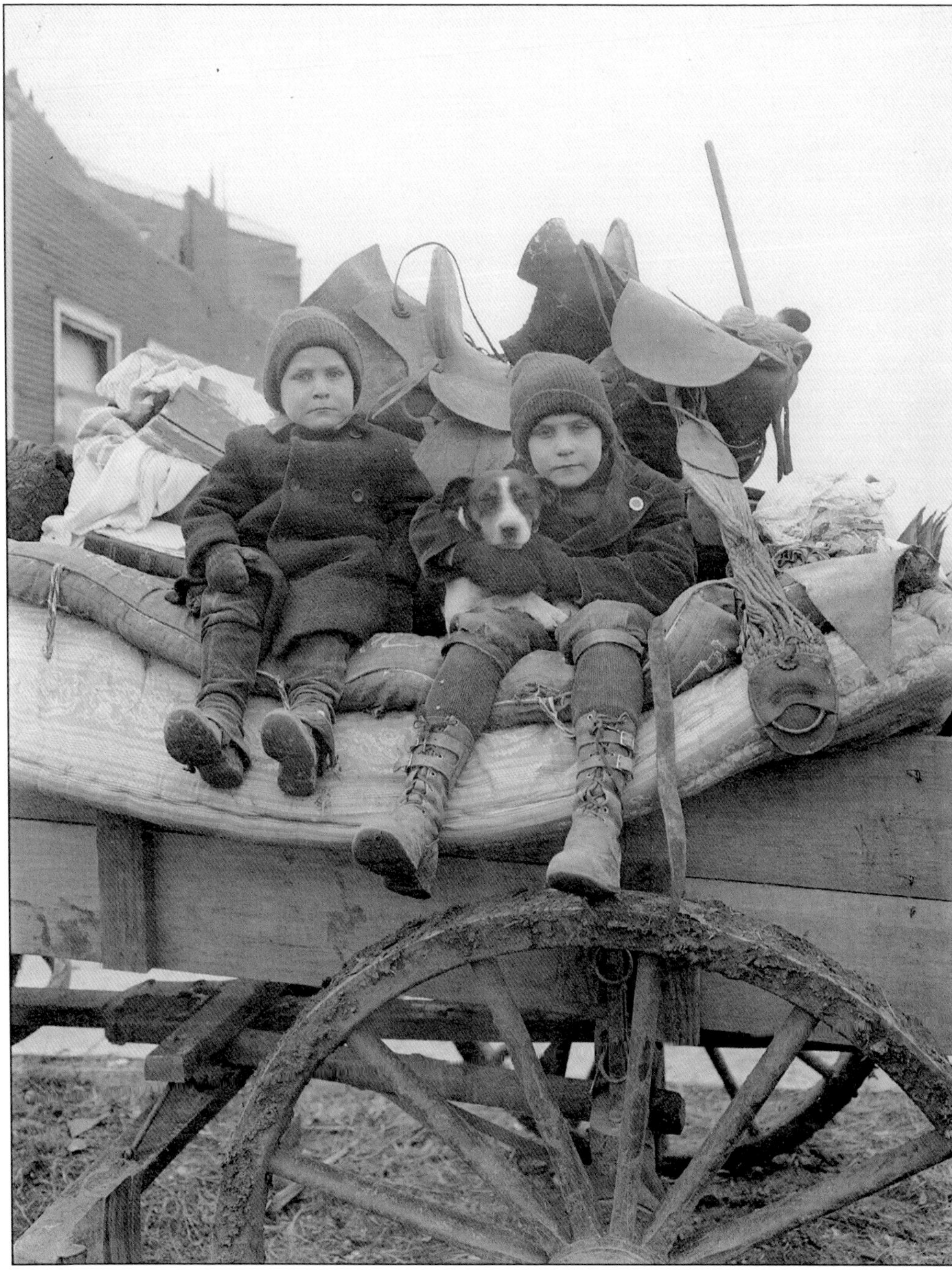

THE HILL CHILDREN. Four-year-old Lyn, on left, and eight-year-old Alvin Hill ride atop a wagon piled with the possessions of their aunt, Minnie Swan, who lived at 24th and Emmett Streets. The boys lived in the vicinity of 19th and Lake Streets, and their home suffered damage, as well. (Bostwick-Frohardt Collection, Durham Western Heritage Museum.)

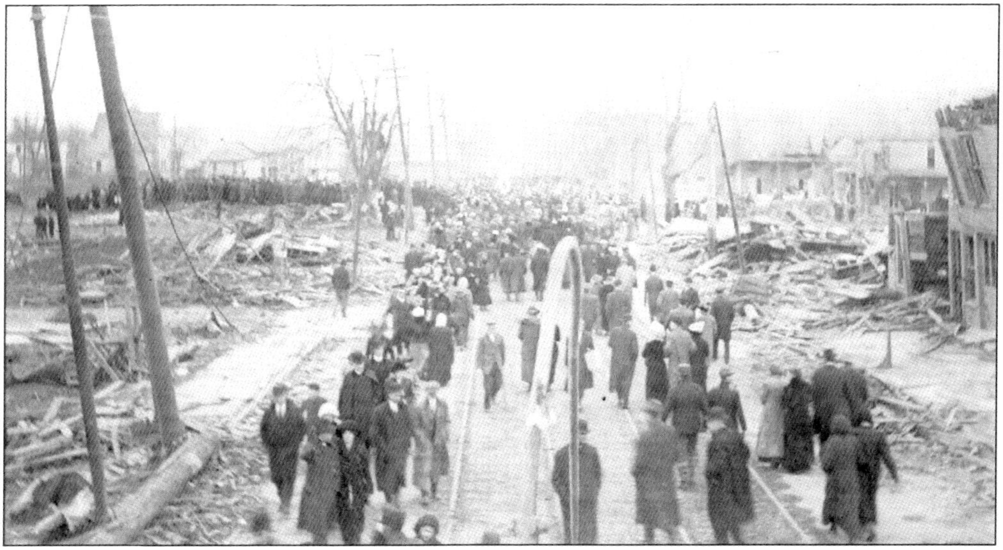

CROWD AT 24TH AND LAKE STREETS. Thousands of visitors traveled great distances to view the desolation at Omaha. On the Sunday following the storm, nearly 2,000 journeyed from Lincoln to witness the scene. Fifty collection boxes were placed about the tornado district for visitors to donate. This photograph was taken from atop a streetcar.

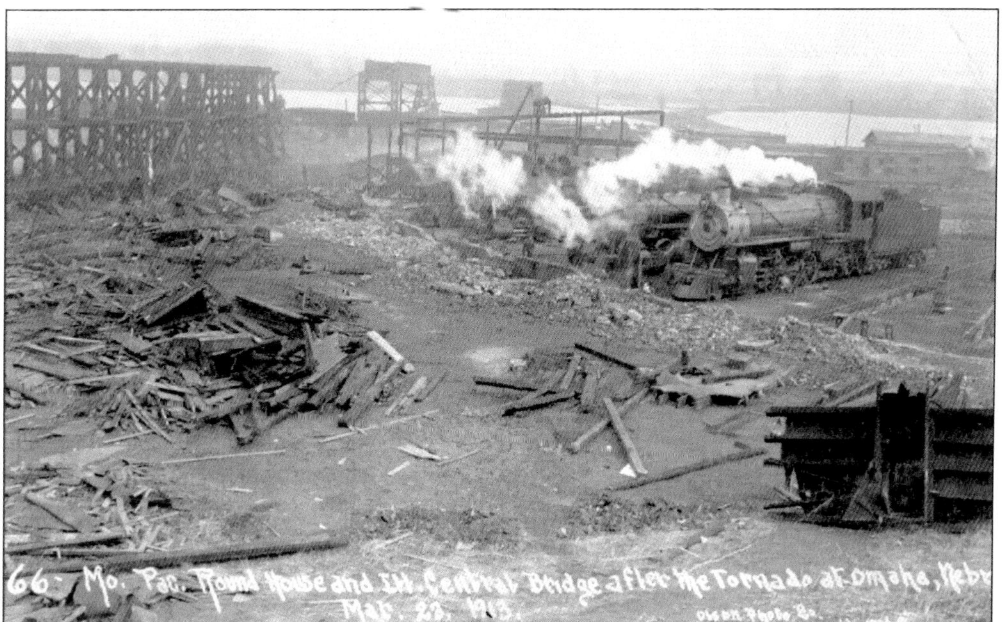

MISSOURI PACIFIC RAILROAD YARD. At least one man was killed here, and the Missouri Pacific sustained damages to four passenger cars, three Pullman sleepers, 30 freight cars, and seven engines.

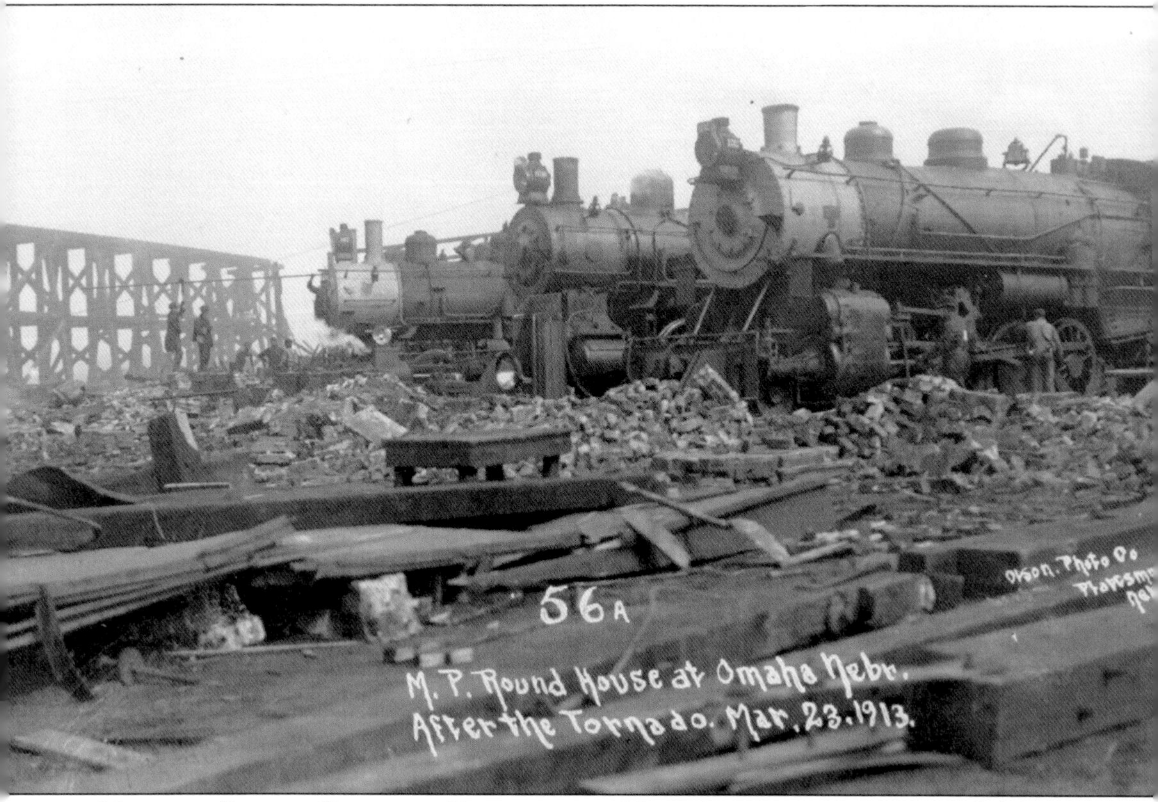

MISSOURI PACIFIC RAILROAD ROUNDHOUSE. These locomotives are surrounded by the remains of the roundhouse. MoPac General Superintendent DeBernardi vowed that a larger and better roundhouse composed of steel and concrete would go up immediately.

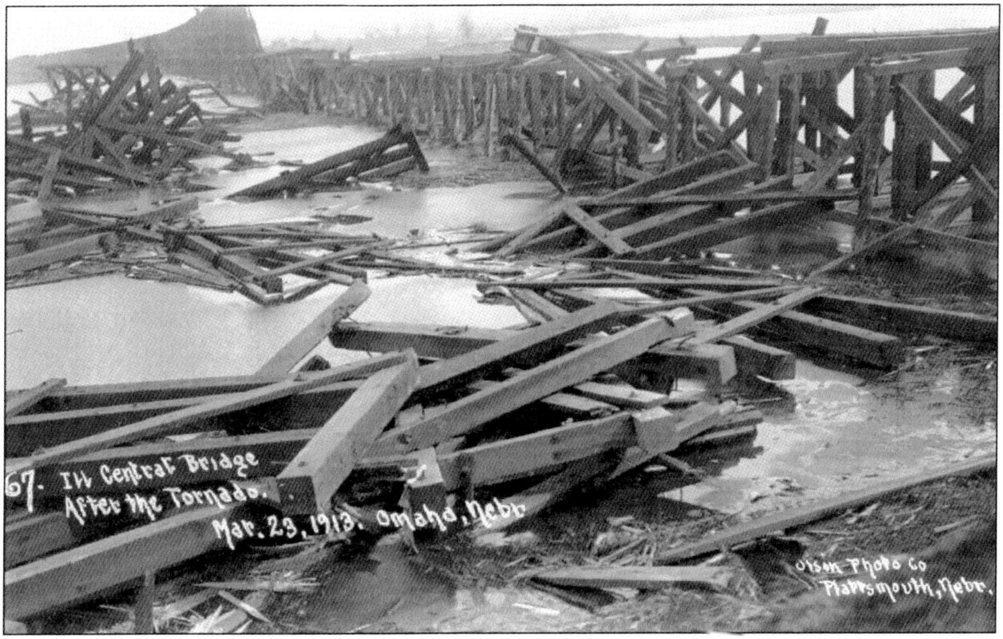

Illinois Central Railroad Bridge over Carter Lake. The Illinois Central Bridge was built over Carter Lake in 1899. It was one of the last Nebraska structures the tornado hit before traversing the Missouri River into Iowa.

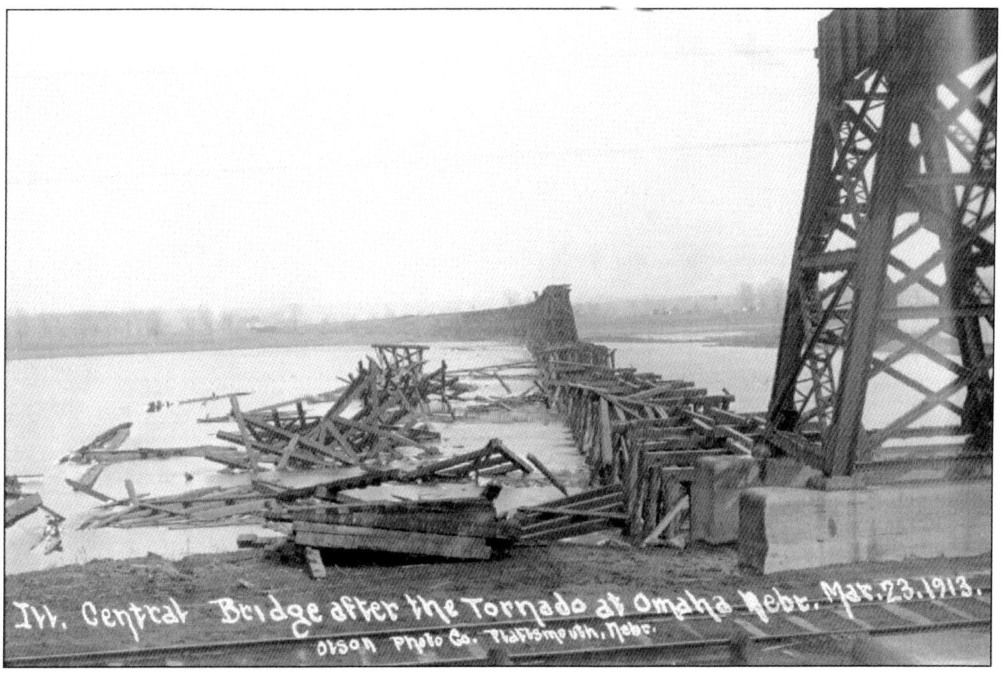

Illinois Central Railroad Bridge. This wide view of the Illinois Central Bridge shows larger devastation.

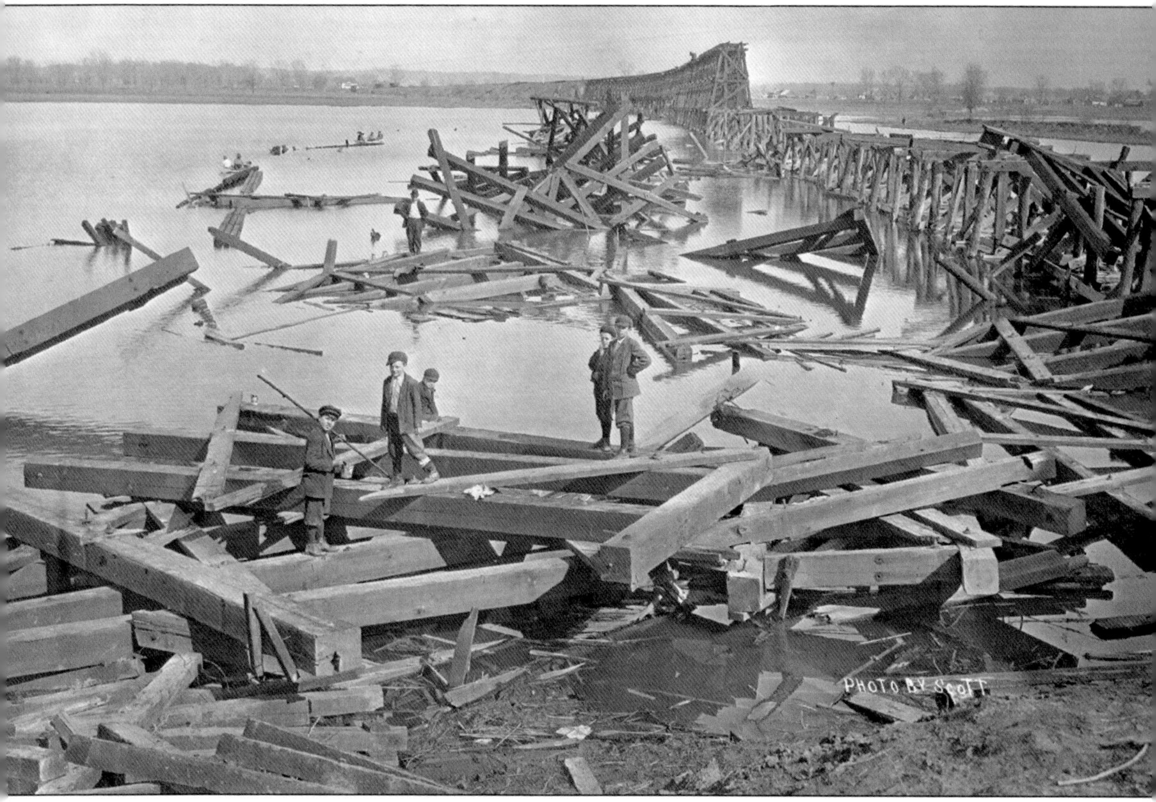

PLAYING ON THE BRIDGE. These boys are playing on the ruined Illinois Central bridge, while other sightseers are canoeing on Carter Lake. (Douglas County Historical Society Library/Archives Center.)

Seven

RELIEF

The city was placed up against its first real crucial test and it proved more than equal to the occasion. System solved the big problem in extending first aid to the injured and assistance to the hungry and unclothed. There are garments aplenty and food in abundance. Tender nurses are watching over the injured[;] on and in the fullness of time the relief committee will disburse the relief fund in a manner which it is believed will do the most good to the greatest number.

—Omaha Daily News, *April 30, 1913*

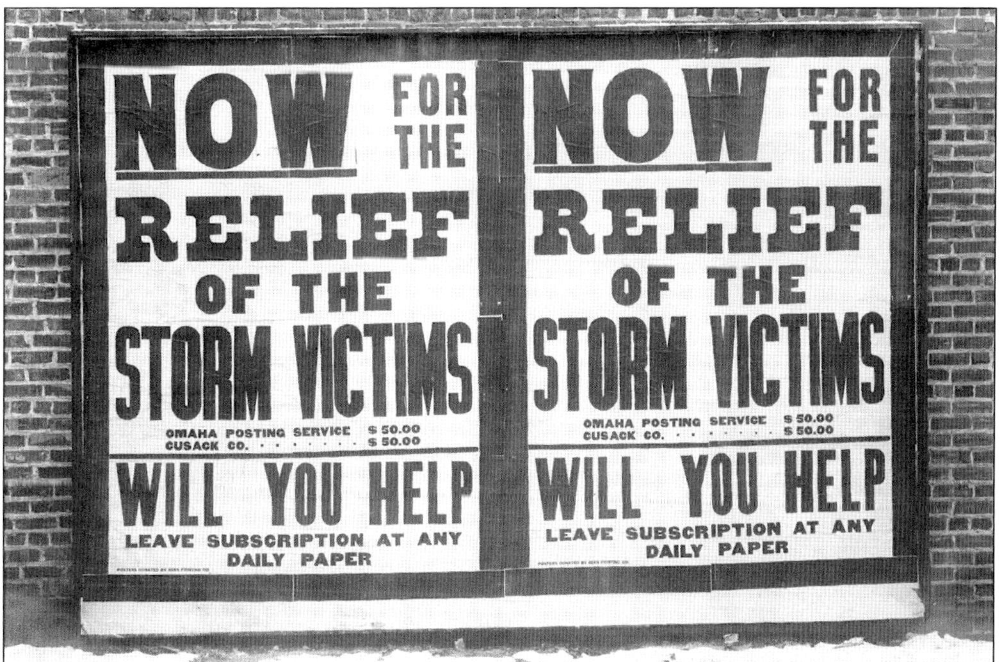

RELIEF POSTERS. Posters such as these were seen around the city, urging citizens to donate what they could, be it financially or materially. The relief slogan was: "Money Talks—Chip In." (Bostwick-Frohardt Collection, Durham Western Heritage Museum.)

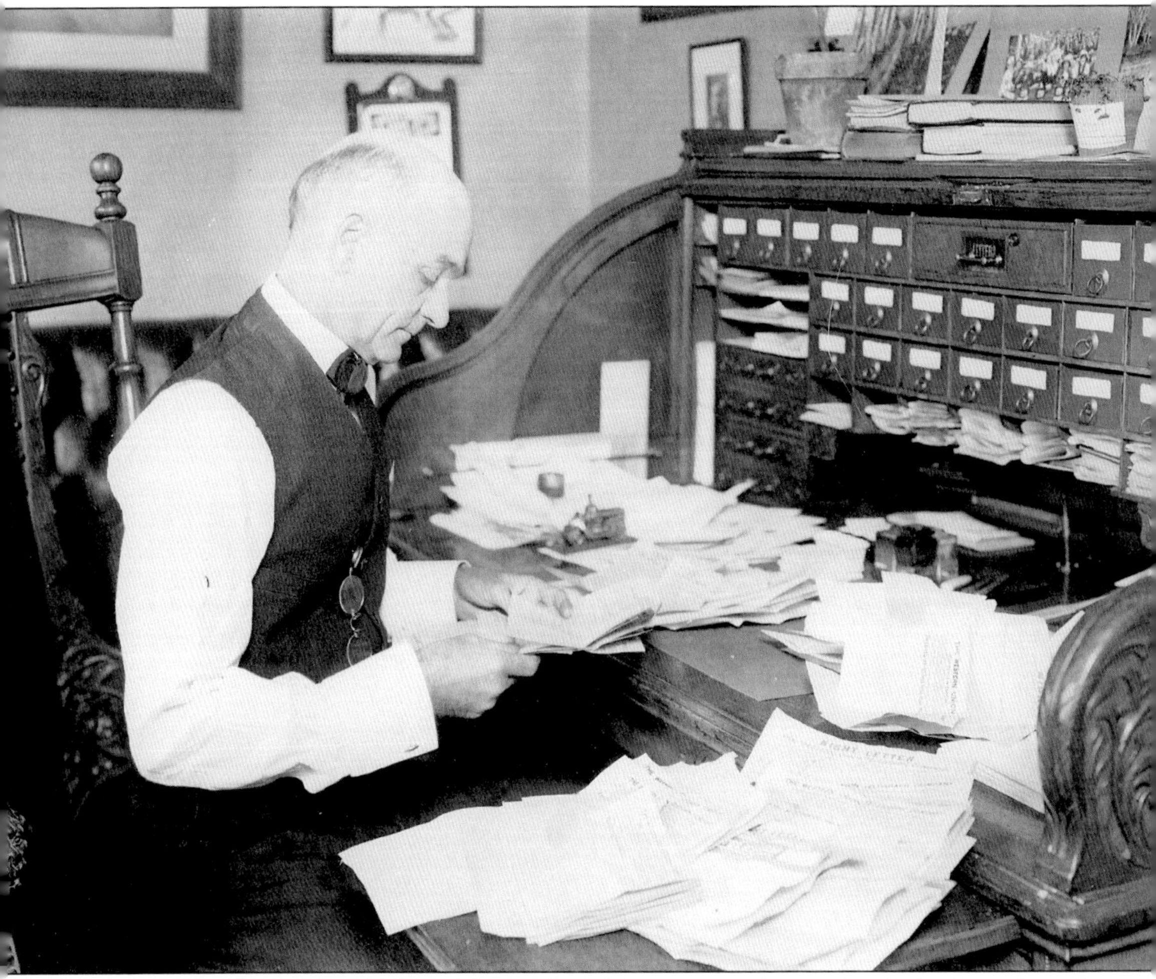

MAYOR DAHLMAN. Omaha Mayor James C. Dahlman is seen here at his desk sifting through the numerous letters and telegrams sent to him. His office was inundated with condolences and offers of monetary aid to the city. Dahlman and the Omaha Commercial Club initially refused all aid until the full spectrum of the havoc was recognized. Financial aid streamed into Omaha. Corporations like Studebaker Automobiles and American Harvester sent $1,000 each. Municipalities as far away as Regina, Saskatchewan, sent aid. Johnstown, Pennsylvania, sent money as a token of appreciation for Omahans sending $3,500 and supplies after its flood in 1889. (Bostwick-Frohardt Collection, Durham Western Heritage Museum.)

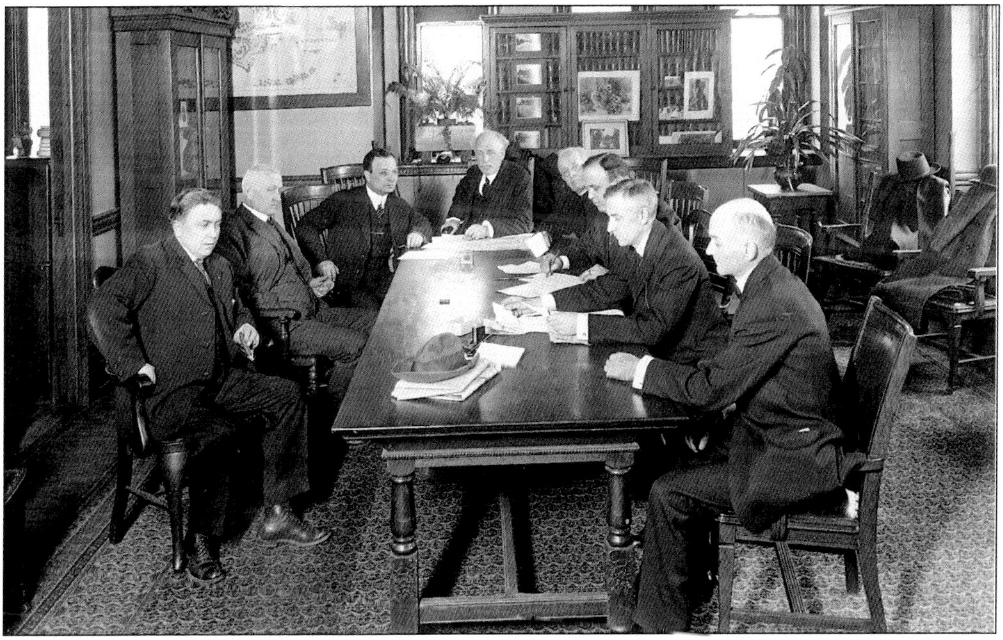

RELIEF COMMITTEE EXECUTIVE BOARD. The Omaha Relief Committee Executive Board was comprised of Superintendent of Police J.J. Ryder, T.C. Byrne, C.C. Rosewater, T.J. Mahoney, Rev. John Williams of St. Barnabas Church, Coucilman Dan B. Butler, J.M. Guild of the Omaha Commercial Club, and Mayor Dahlman. (Bostwick-Frohardt Collection, Durham Western Heritage Museum.)

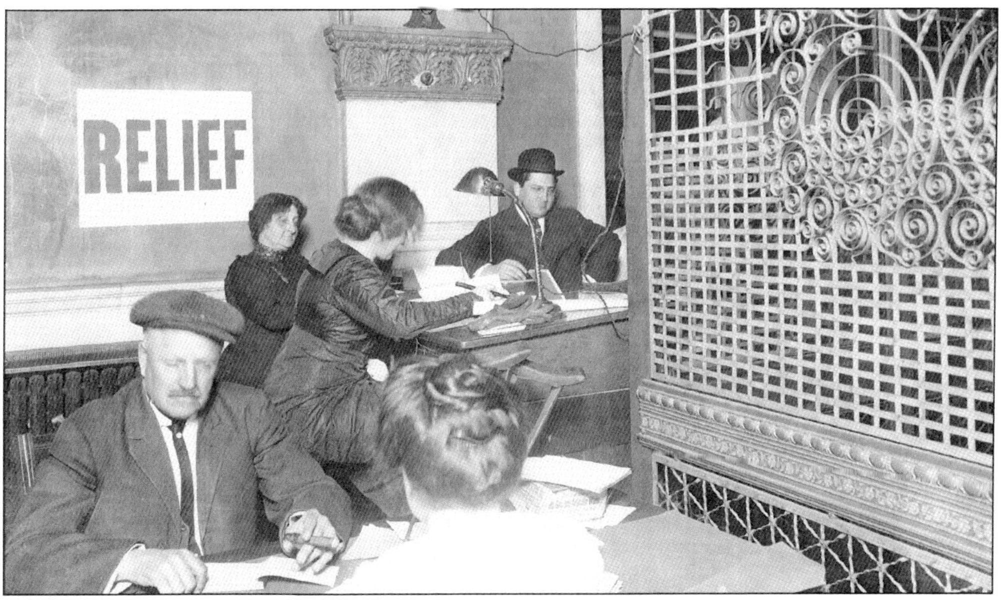

RELIEF AT CITY HALL. W.S. Jardine and Commercial Club stenographers assist relief applicants at City Hall. Within a week of the storm, nearly 2,100 families had sought relief. Although most applicants had legitimate needs, it was reported that "bums and hoboes were flocking" to Omaha, and "drug fiends" sold donated clothes for money to obtain more drugs. (Bostwick-Frohardt Collection, Durham Western Heritage Museum.)

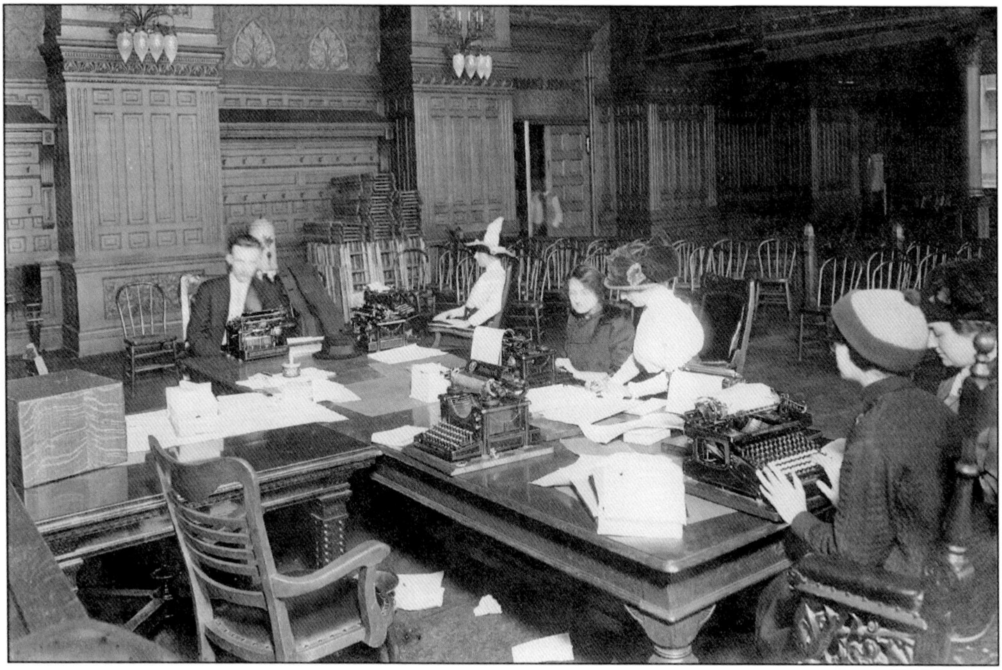

Commercial Club Stenographers. Commercial Club stenographers are pictured here at City Hall in the City Council chambers. They were responsible for much of the paperwork generated as relief claims were checked for validity. (Bostwick-Frohardt Collection, Durham Western Heritage Museum.)

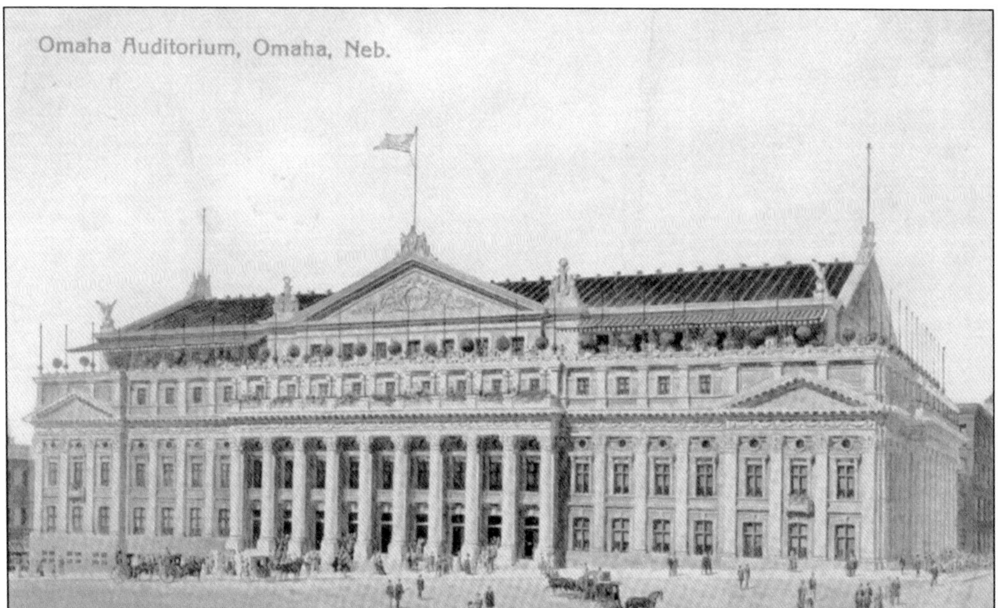

Omaha Auditorium. The Omaha Auditorium at 15th and Howard Streets was the central relief station where victims were fed, clothed, and housed.

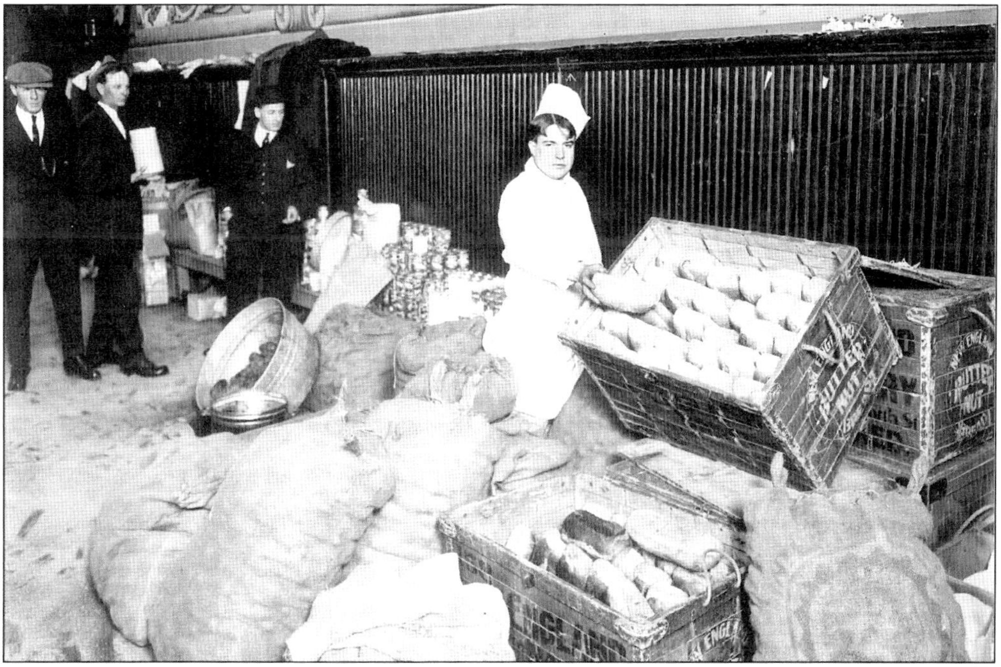

DONATED FOOD. Bread and other donated foodstuffs are being shown off at the city auditorium. Although workers planned to feed 2,000 people every 12 hours, much of the food was distributed to neighborhood relief stations. (Bostwick-Frohardt Collection, Durham Western Heritage Museum.)

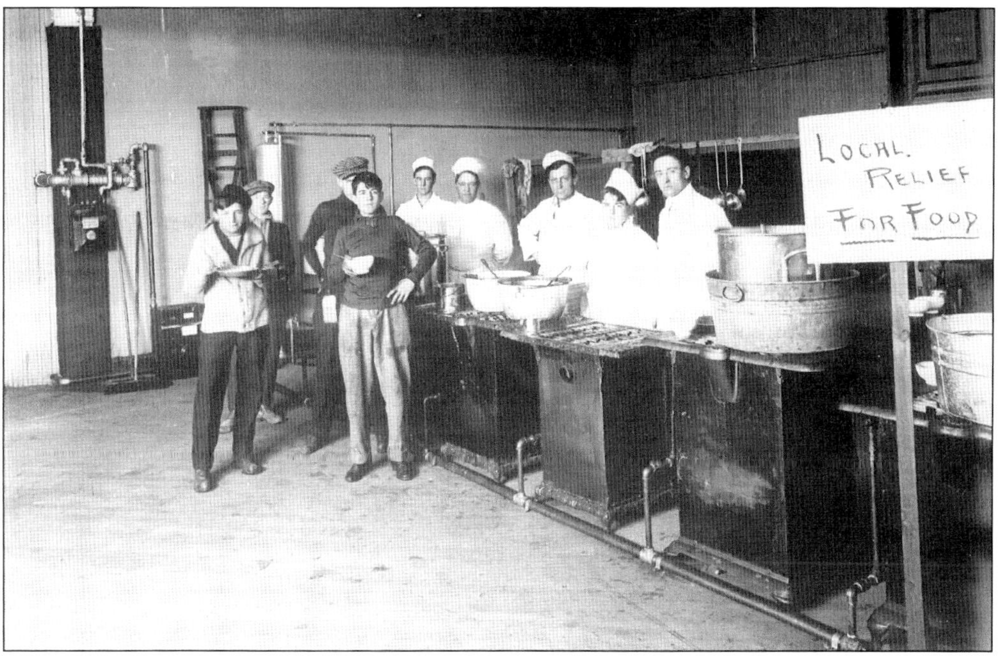

SOUP KITCHEN. This kitchen was established at the Omaha Auditorium, where soups, stews, bread, and coffee were offered to the victims. (Bostwick-Frohardt Collection, Durham Western Heritage Museum.)

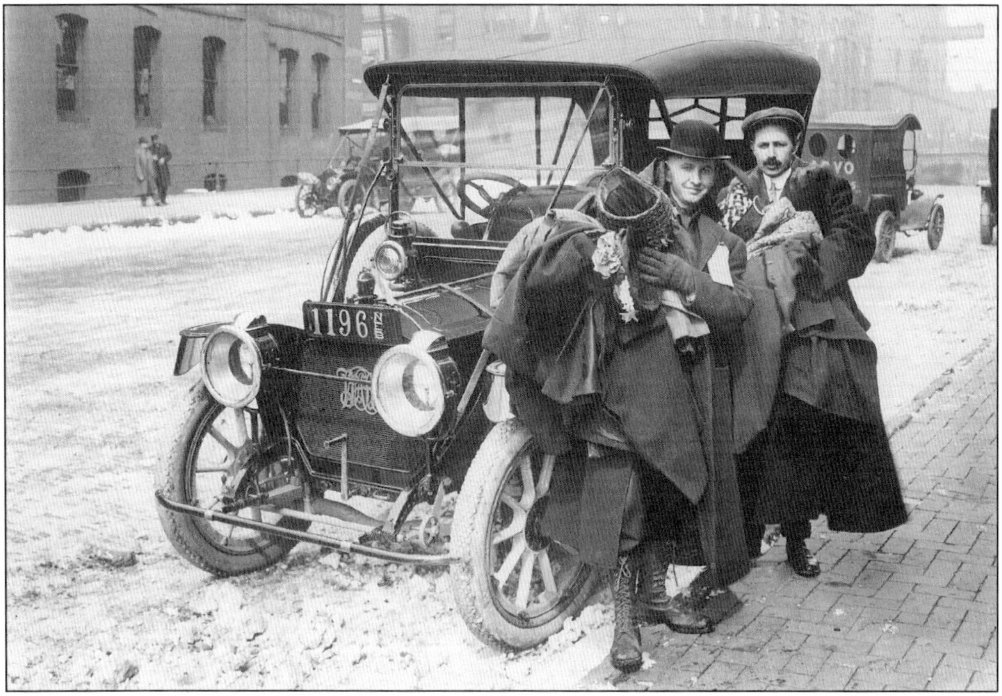

UNLOADING DONATIONS. Carloads of donations arrived at the auditorium. The man in the cap is John Redick, and it was reported that he was "on the job all day" making deliveries. (Bostwick-Frohardt Collection, Durham Western Heritage Museum.)

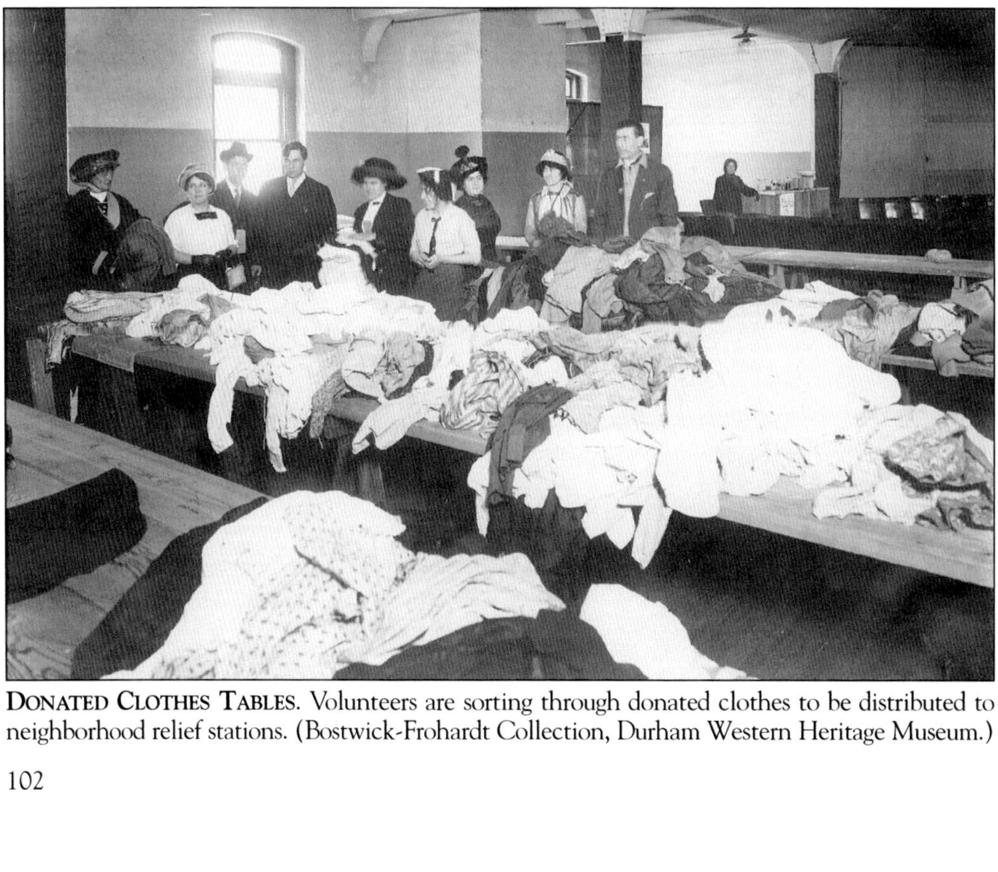

DONATED CLOTHES TABLES. Volunteers are sorting through donated clothes to be distributed to neighborhood relief stations. (Bostwick-Frohardt Collection, Durham Western Heritage Museum.)

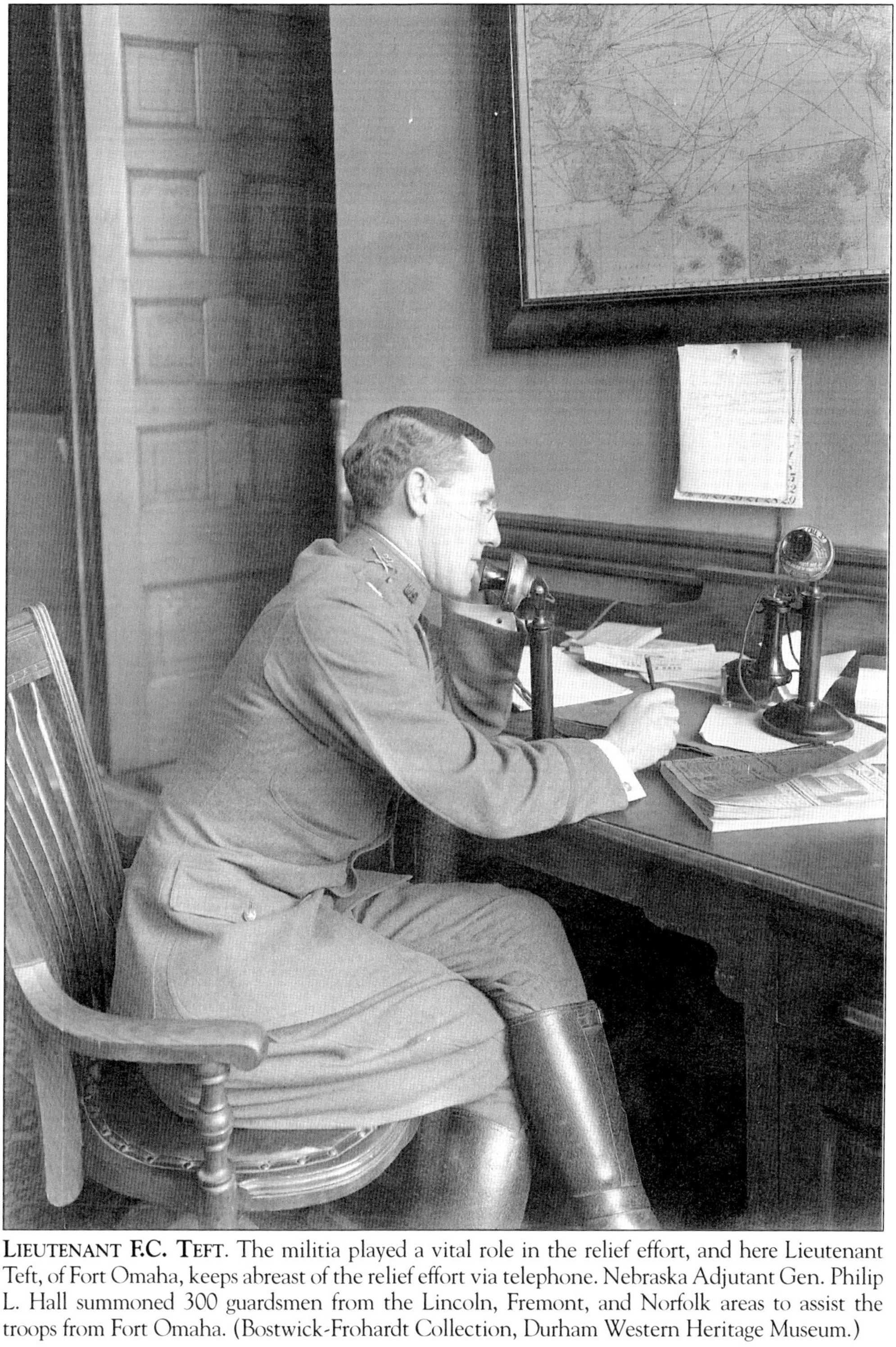

LIEUTENANT F.C. TEFT. The militia played a vital role in the relief effort, and here Lieutenant Teft, of Fort Omaha, keeps abreast of the relief effort via telephone. Nebraska Adjutant Gen. Philip L. Hall summoned 300 guardsmen from the Lincoln, Fremont, and Norfolk areas to assist the troops from Fort Omaha. (Bostwick-Frohardt Collection, Durham Western Heritage Museum.)

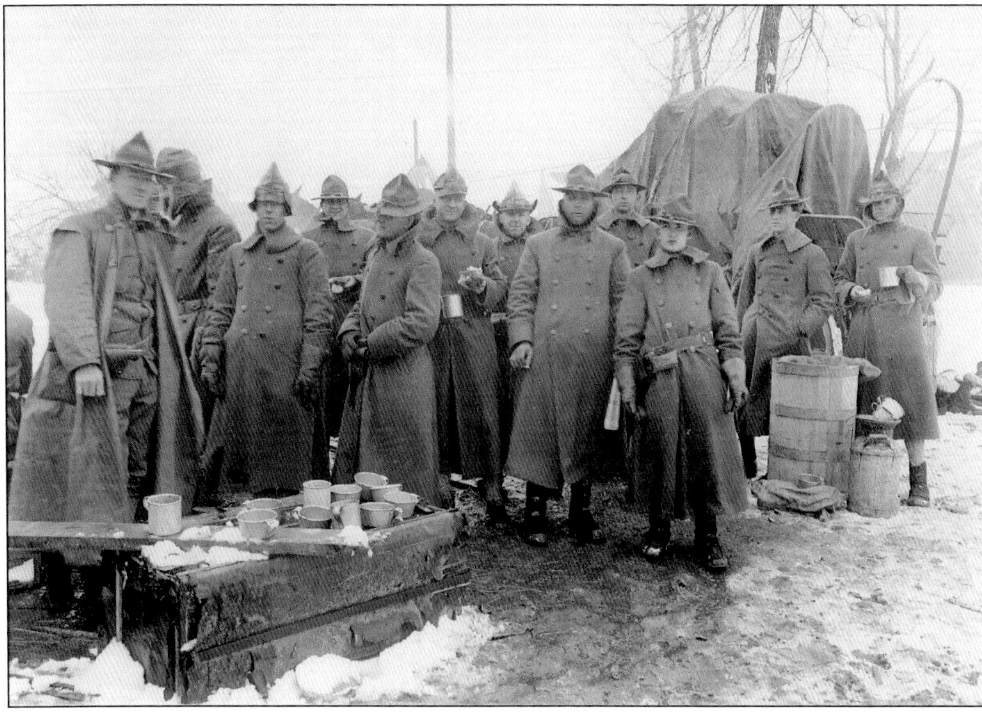

CHOW TIME. These militiamen are gathered for a hardy breakfast before they patrol the stricken area on a frigid day. A typical breakfast consisted of a fried-egg sandwich, a hard-boiled egg, and coffee. (Bostwick-Frohardt Collection, Durham Western Heritage Museum.)

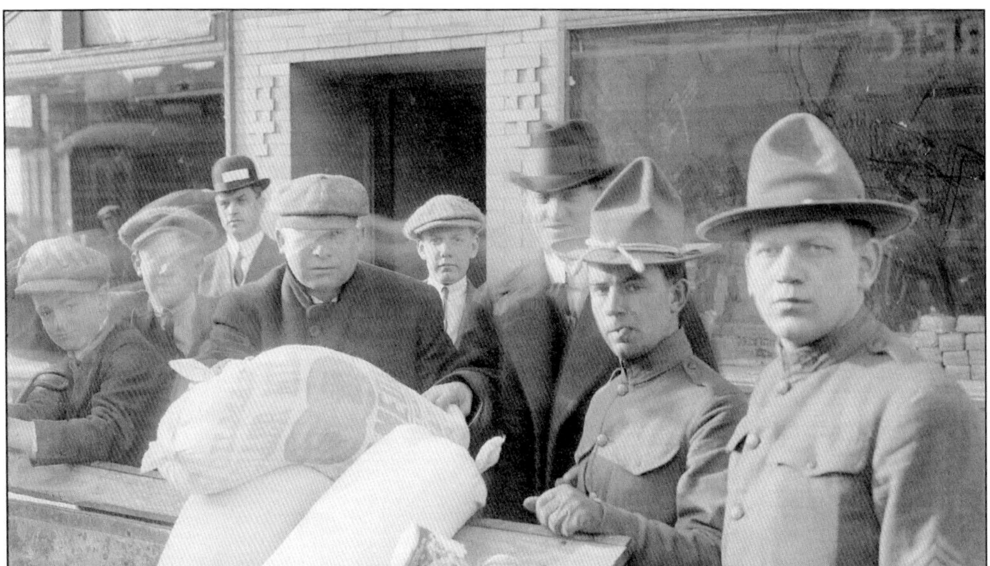

RELIEF STATION NUMBER 5. A scene at Relief Station No. 5 at 40th and Farnam Streets. The man with a bandage over his eye is Gus Renze, who, despite injury, was busy aiding the relief effort. Renze was well-known as the mastermind and designer for the Electric Night Parades in conjunction with AkSarBen pageants starting in 1895. (Bostwick-Frohardt Collection, Durham Western Heritage Museum.)

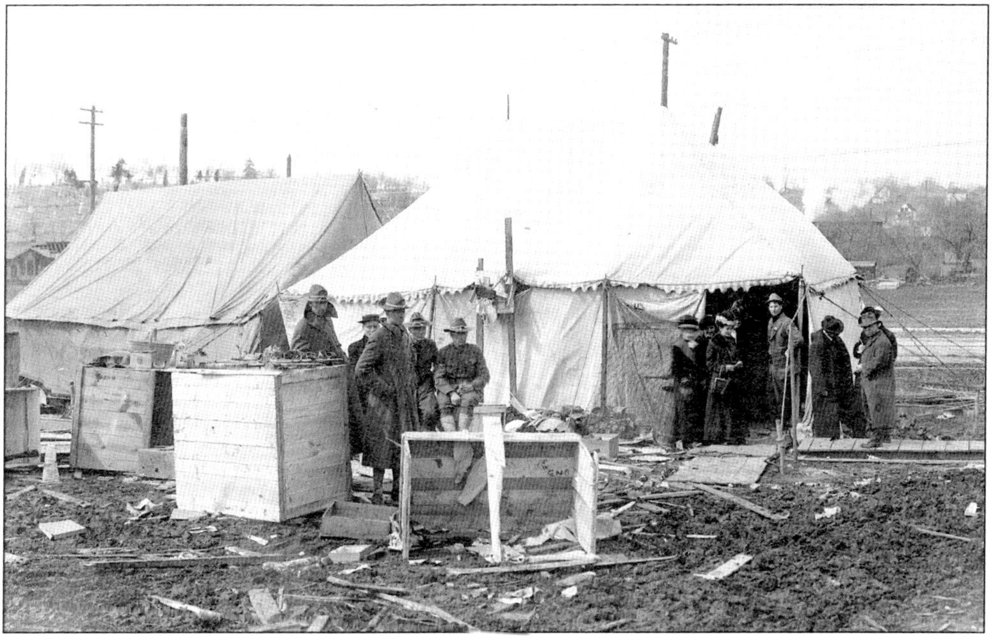

LEAVENWORTH RELIEF STATION. The No. 6 relief station at 46th and Leavenworth Streets was housed in a large tent. (Bostwick-Frohardt Collection, Durham Western Heritage Museum.)

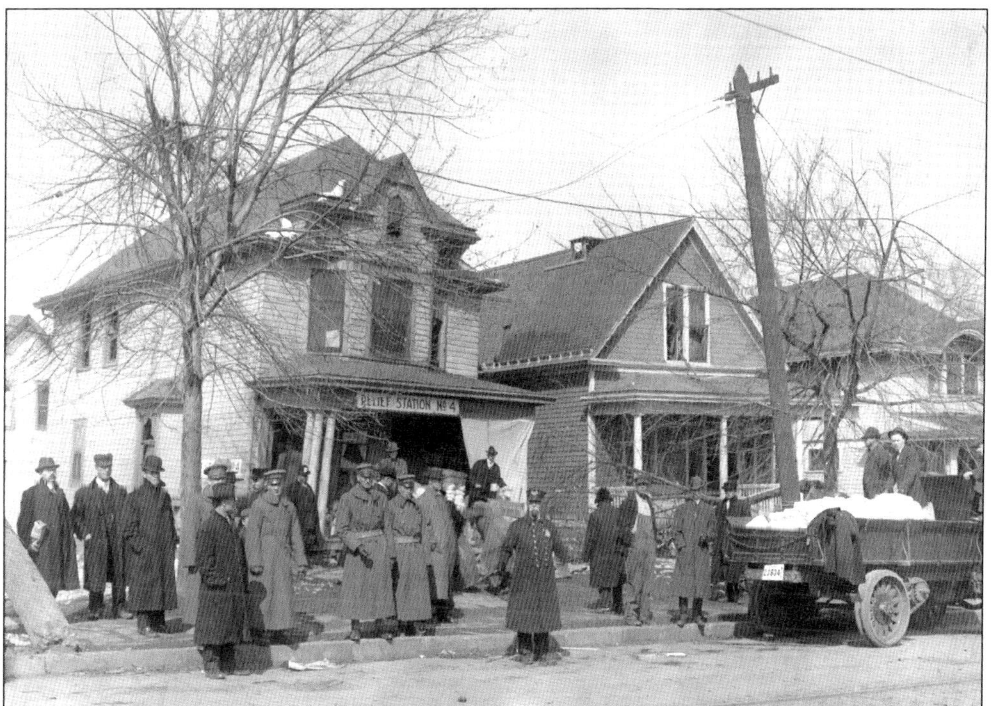

RELIEF STATION NUMBER 4. Relief Station No. 4 at 33rd and Cuming Streets was one of the busiest. (Douglas County Historical Society Library/Archives Center.)

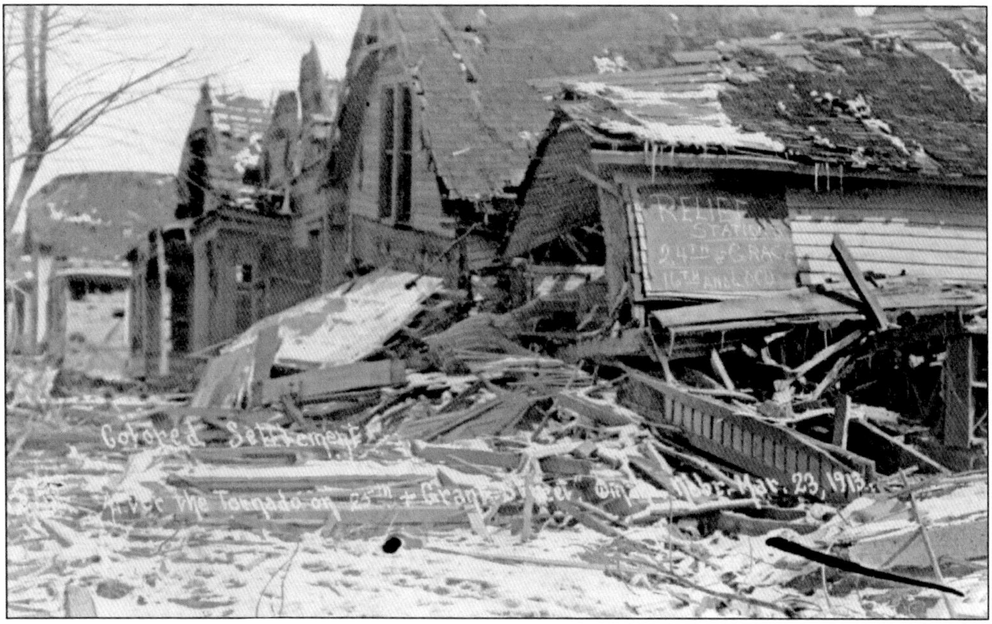

RELIEF STATION SIGN IN NORTH OMAHA. In the wreckage at 25th and Grant Streets, this sign informs victims of two nearby relief stations: one at 24th and Grace Streets and another at 16th and Locust Streets.

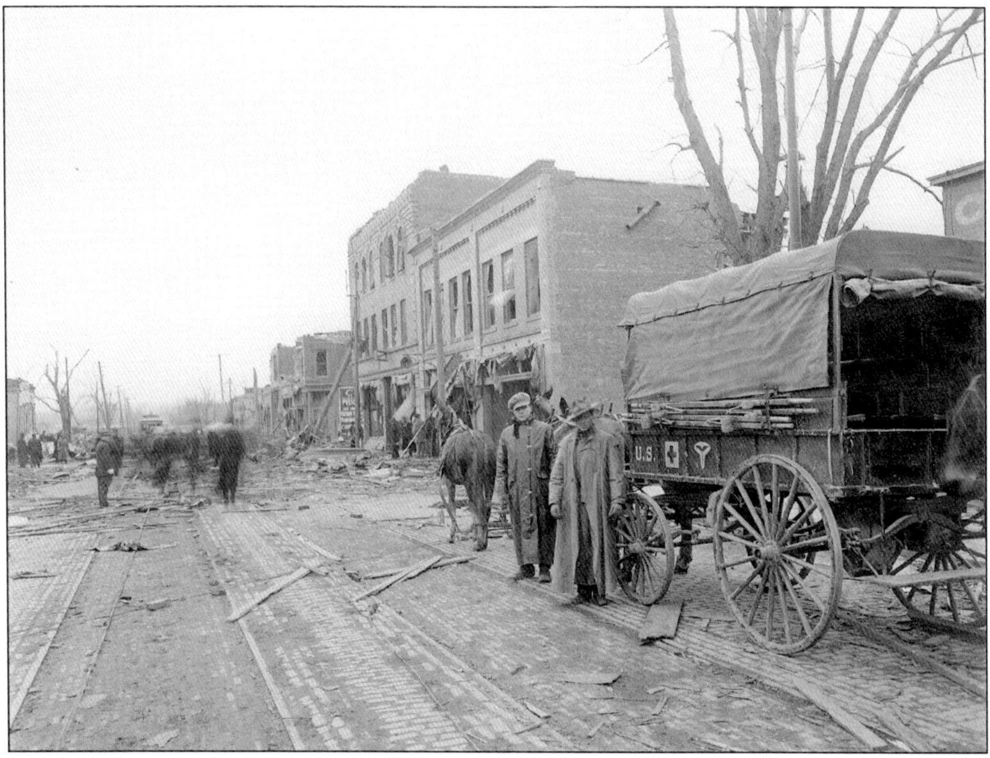

ARMY AMBULANCE WAGON. A Fort Omaha Army Signal Corps ambulance wagon is pictured near the vicinity of 24th and Lake Streets.

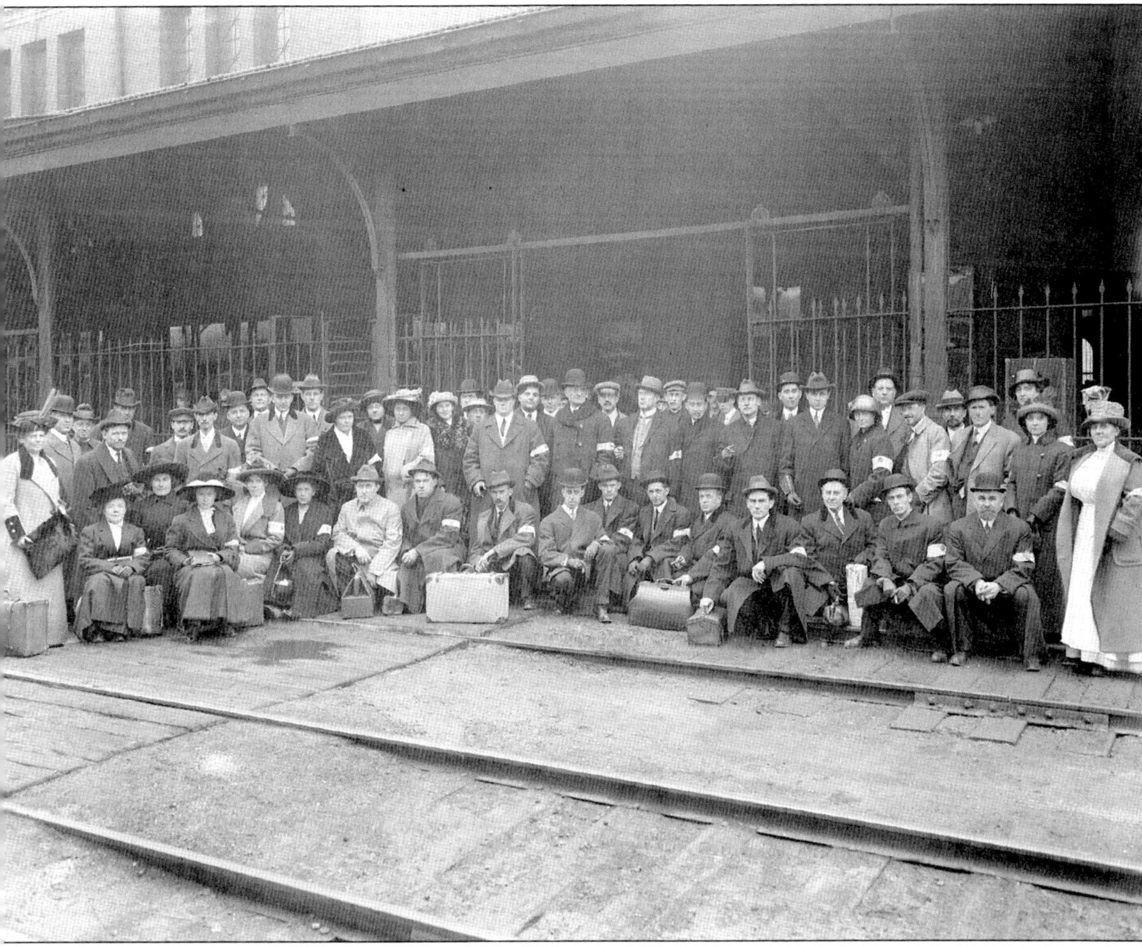

DES MOINES MEDICAL TEAM. This group of doctors and nurses from Des Moines, Iowa, arrived the morning after the storm. They are pictured at the old Union Station. (Bostwick-Frohardt Collection, Durham Western Heritage Museum.)

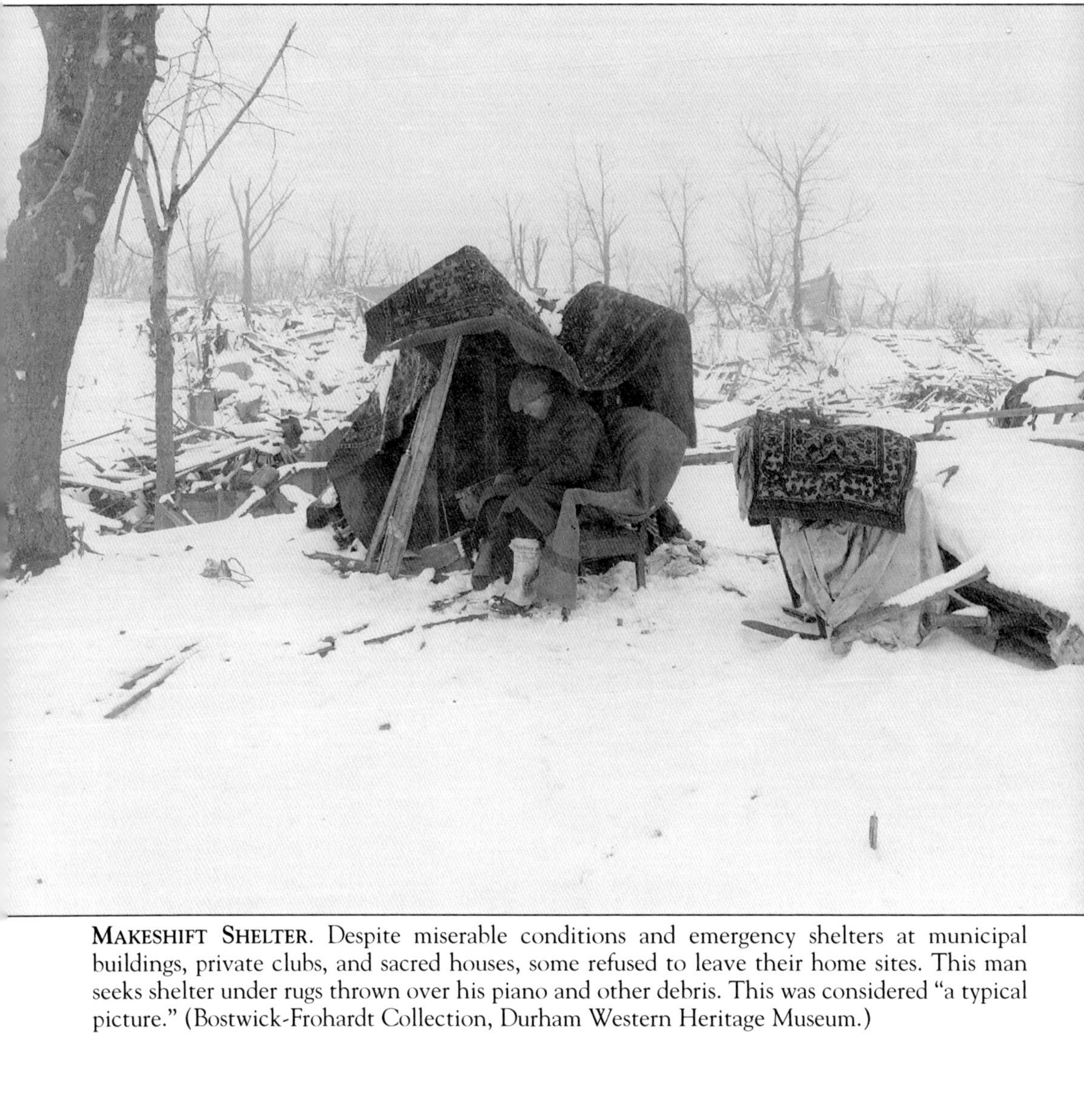

MAKESHIFT SHELTER. Despite miserable conditions and emergency shelters at municipal buildings, private clubs, and sacred houses, some refused to leave their home sites. This man seeks shelter under rugs thrown over his piano and other debris. This was considered "a typical picture." (Bostwick-Frohardt Collection, Durham Western Heritage Museum.)

Eight

Recovery

Omaha presents an unsightly condition, the result of the destructive tornado which passed through the residence district on March 23. The condition is but a natural result of this terrific tornado. Every citizen of Omaha desires to see all evidences of that terrible catastrophe removed as soon as possible. . . . We do not want Omaha to be known as the tornado[-] wrecked city, but as Omaha the wonder of the west, destroyed in a night, rebuilt in a day—the city that turned a calamity into an era of prosperity.

—*Mayor James C. Dahlman in a proclamation, April 2, 1913*

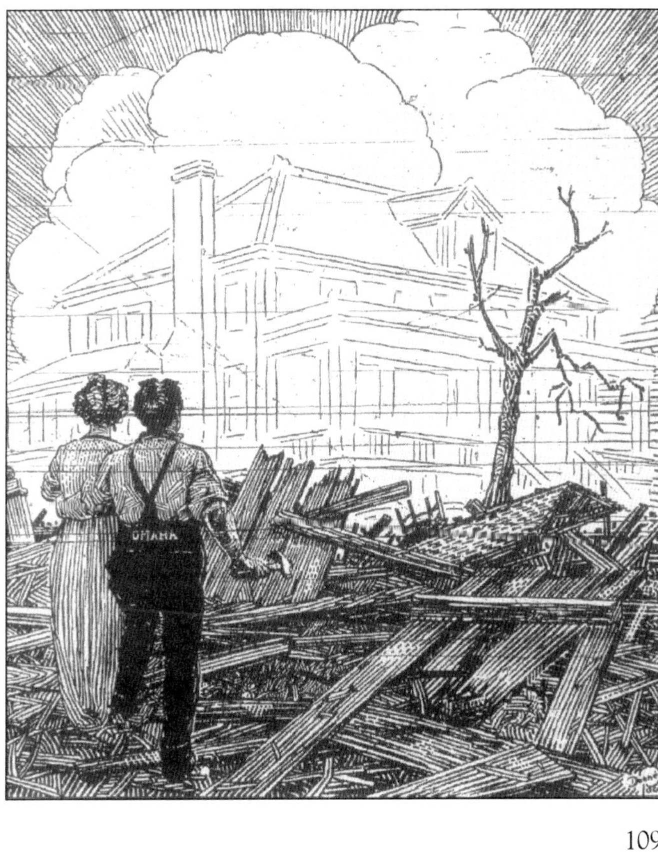

LOOKING AHEAD. This illustration appeared in the *Omaha Bee*, and once again Doane Powell captured the mood of the city.

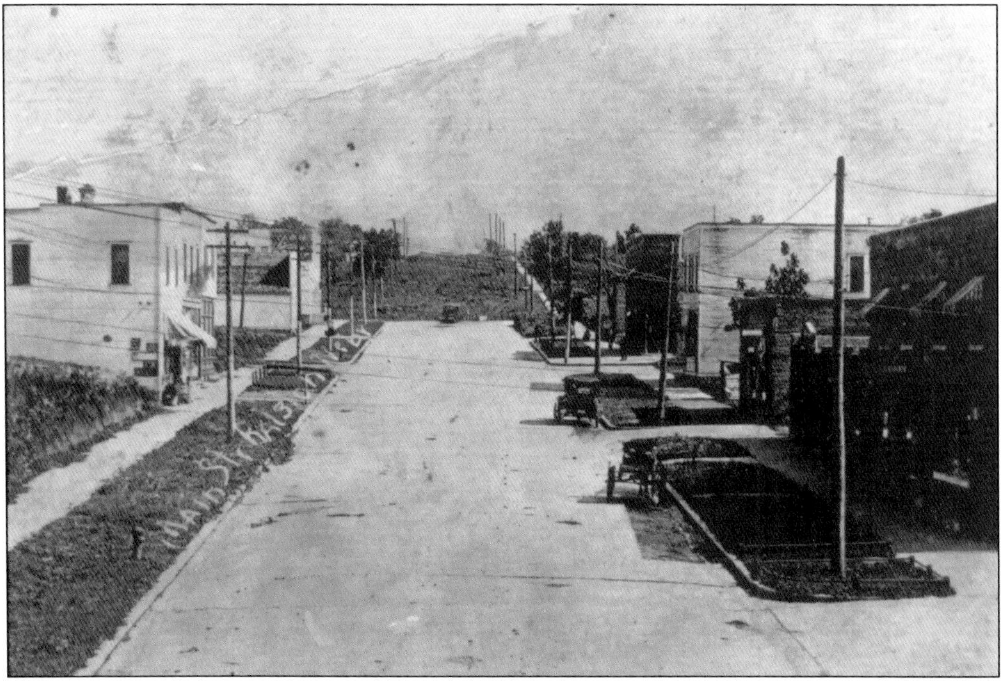

DOWNTOWN RALSTON. Downtown Ralston was quickly rebuilt and revitalized. This view looks north on 77th Street in 1913. (The Frank & Velma Johnson Ralston Archives Museum.)

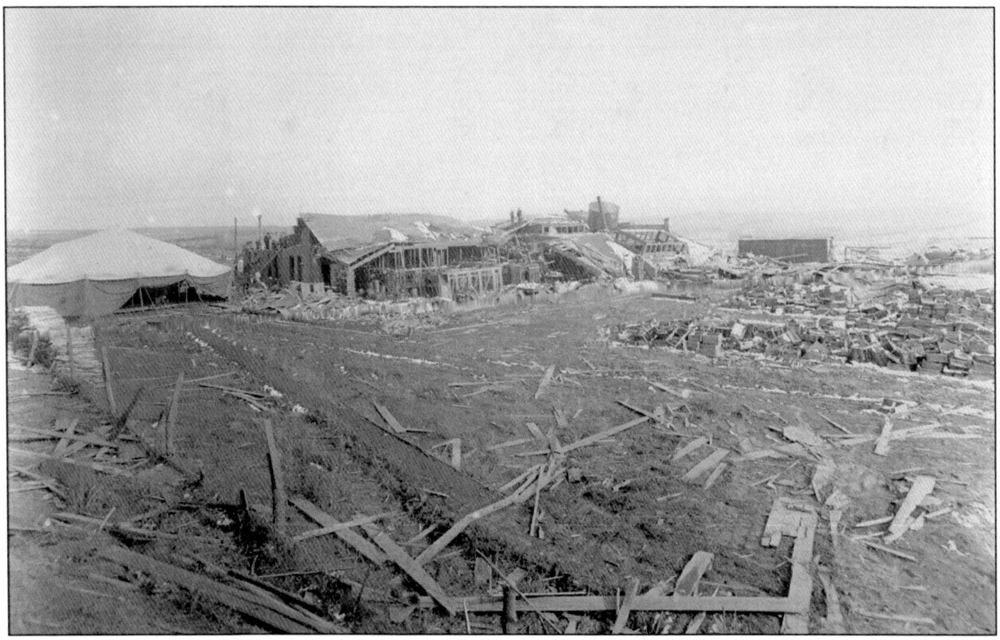

HOWARD STOVE WORKS REPAIR TENT. Rebuilding quickly began at the Howard Stove Works. Near the repair tent is a neat pile of new lumber, while the yard at right is still scattered with packing crates for stoves. (The Frank & Velma Johnson Ralston Archives Museum.)

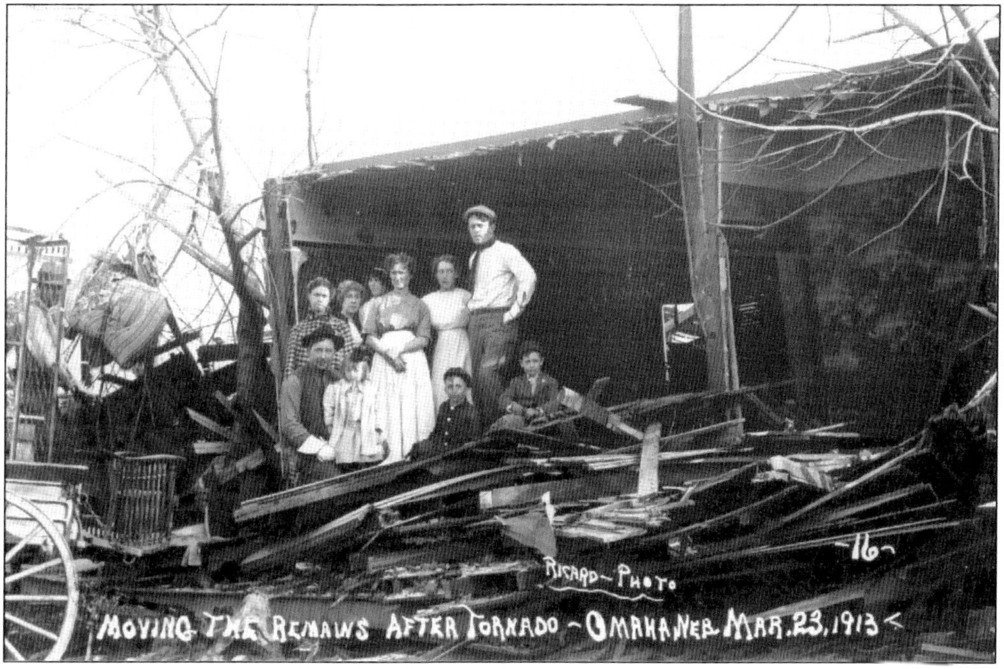

MOVING THE REMAINS. This family is gathered to move their remaining possessions to another location.

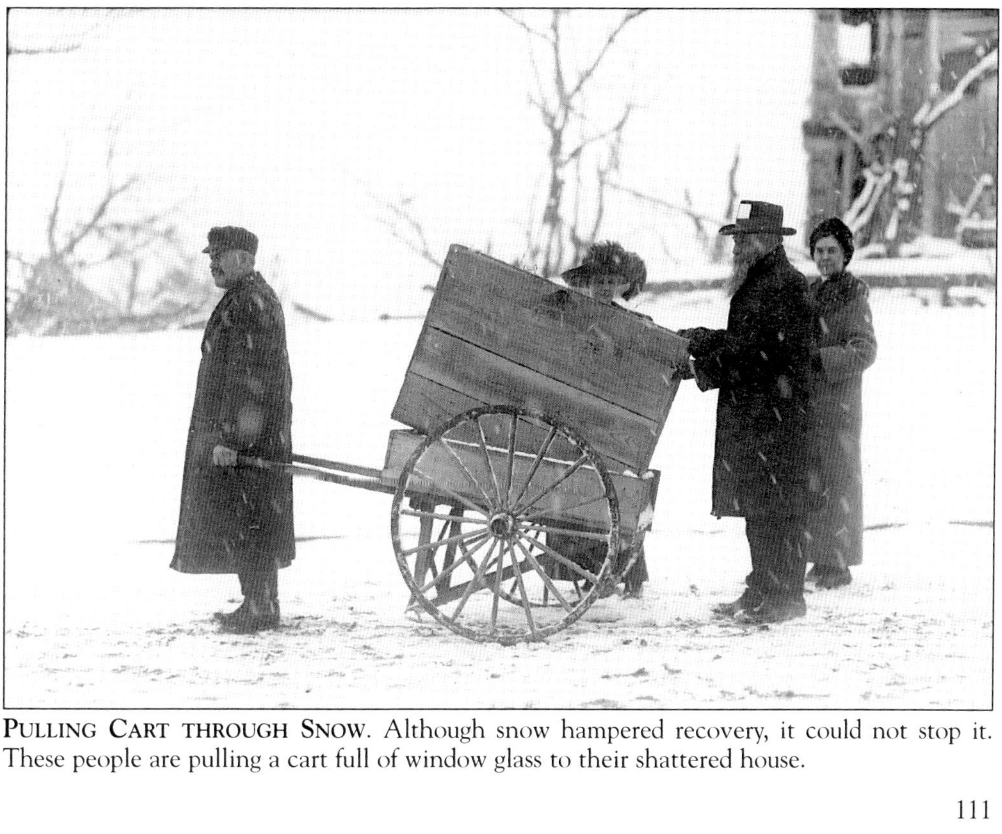

PULLING CART THROUGH SNOW. Although snow hampered recovery, it could not stop it. These people are pulling a cart full of window glass to their shattered house.

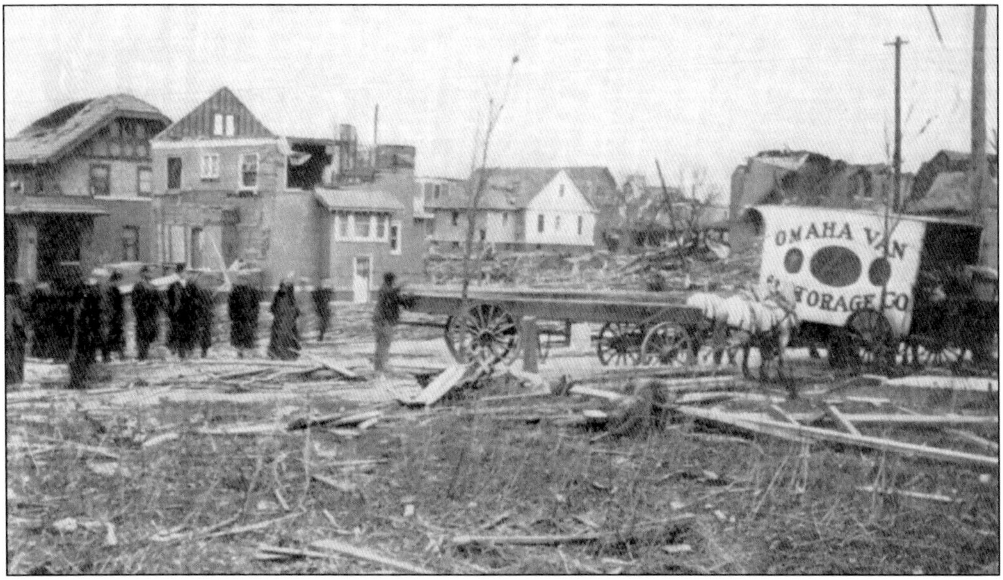

Omaha Van & Storage Company. Horse-drawn wagons were used for numerous purposes, including moving items, carting away debris, hauling relief supplies, and serving as ambulances and hearses. The Bekins Brothers founded the Bekins Van Line in Sioux City, Iowa. In 1893, Martin and John Bekins came to Omaha and established the Omaha Van & Storage Company.

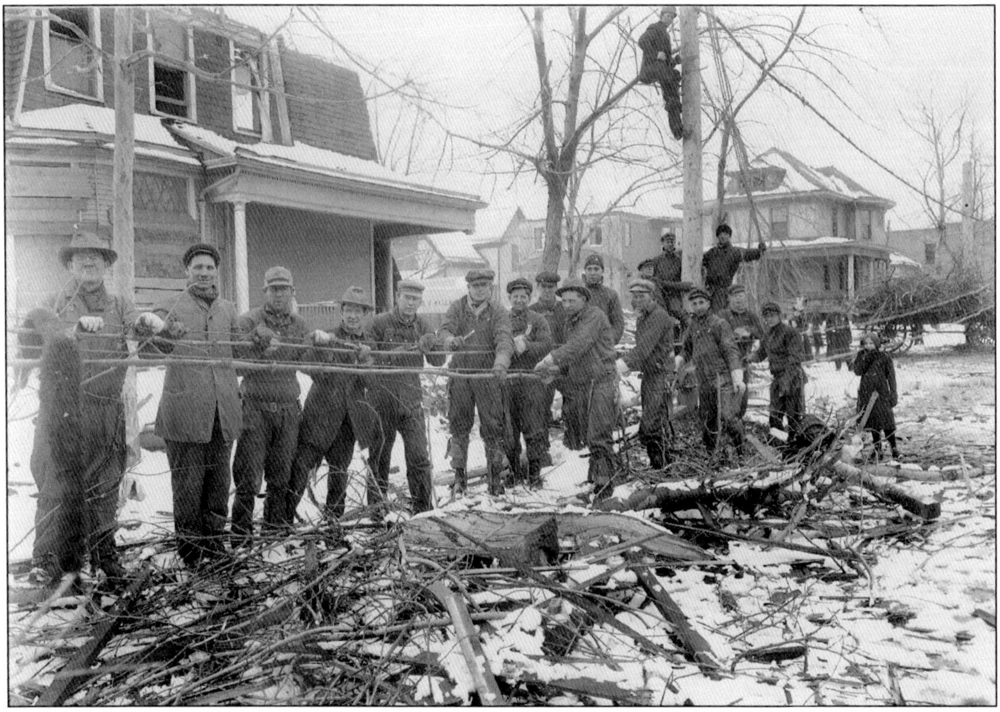

Utility Crew. The Omaha Electric Light Company dispatched 150 men with trucks and wagons to repair the lines. Light company losses for meters, poles, wire, other materials, and labor was estimated between $50,000 and $100,000. (Bostwick-Frohardt Collection, Durham Western Heritage Museum.)

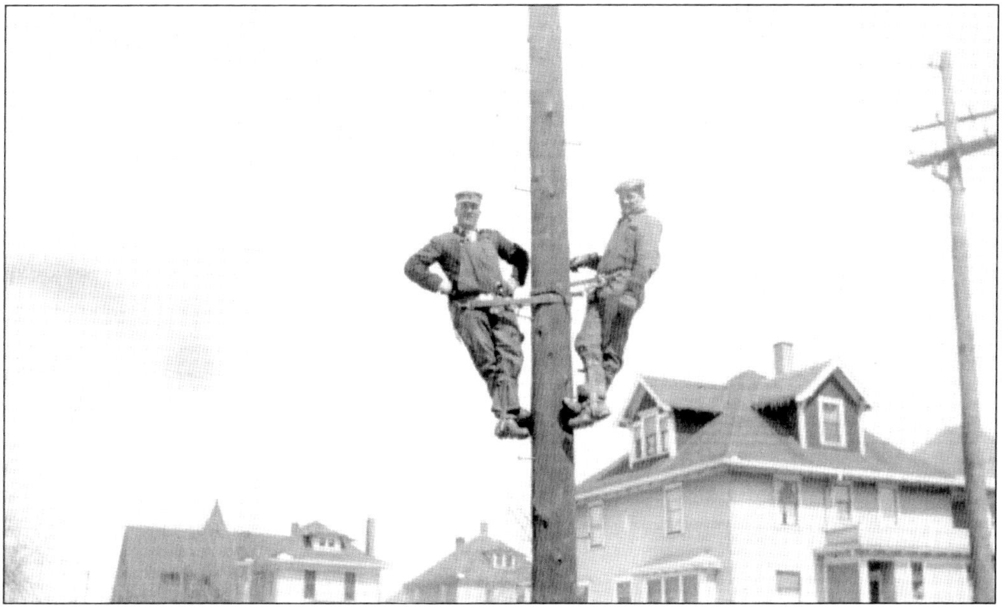

TWO LINEMEN. This tandem seems to enjoy posing for the camera as they perform repairs. Nebraska Telephone Company lost service to 2,500 phones and estimated losses at an enormous $200,000.

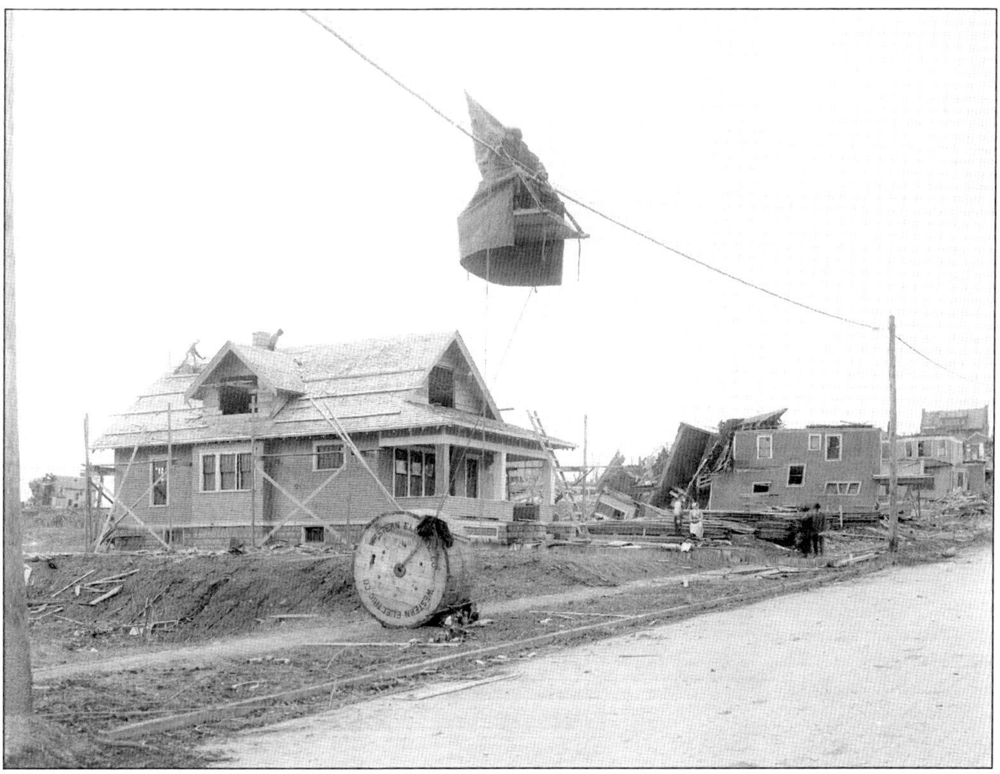

REPAIR GONDOLA. A repairman is seen here suspended in a gondola near 33rd and California Streets.

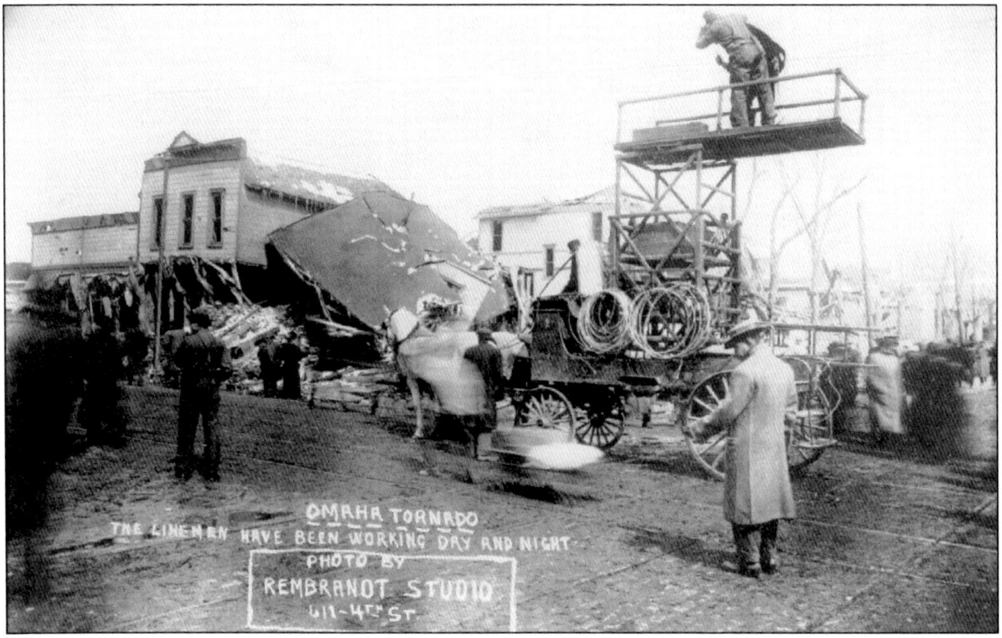

LINE TRUCK. This image depicts a horse-drawn truck with wire and scaffolding for restoring utilities.

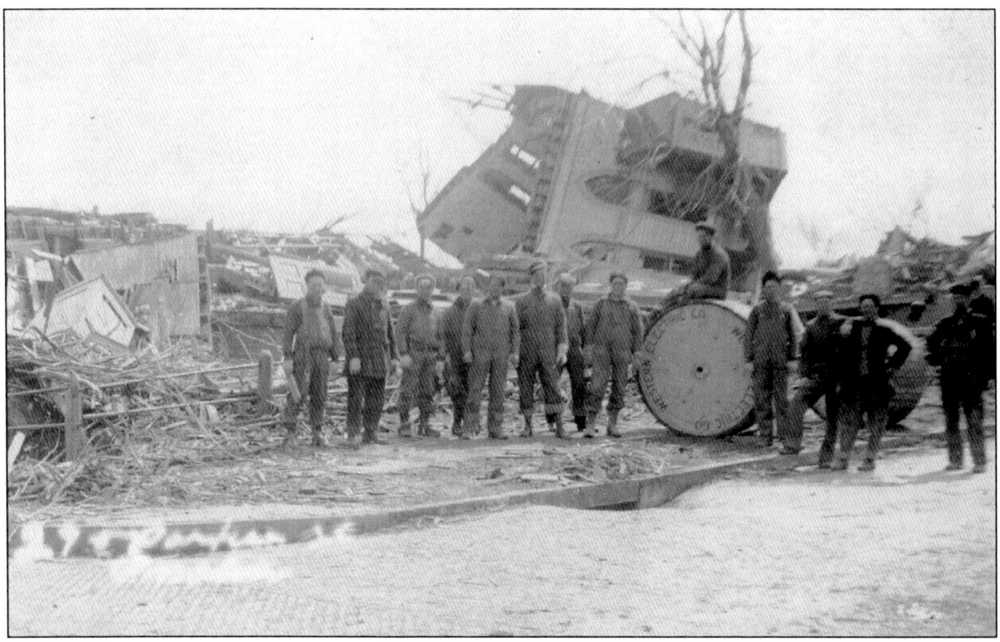

UTILITY REPAIR NEAR 28TH AND PARKER STREETS. A repair crew takes pause from its work near the twisted remains of the German Lutheran Church at 28th and Parker Streets.

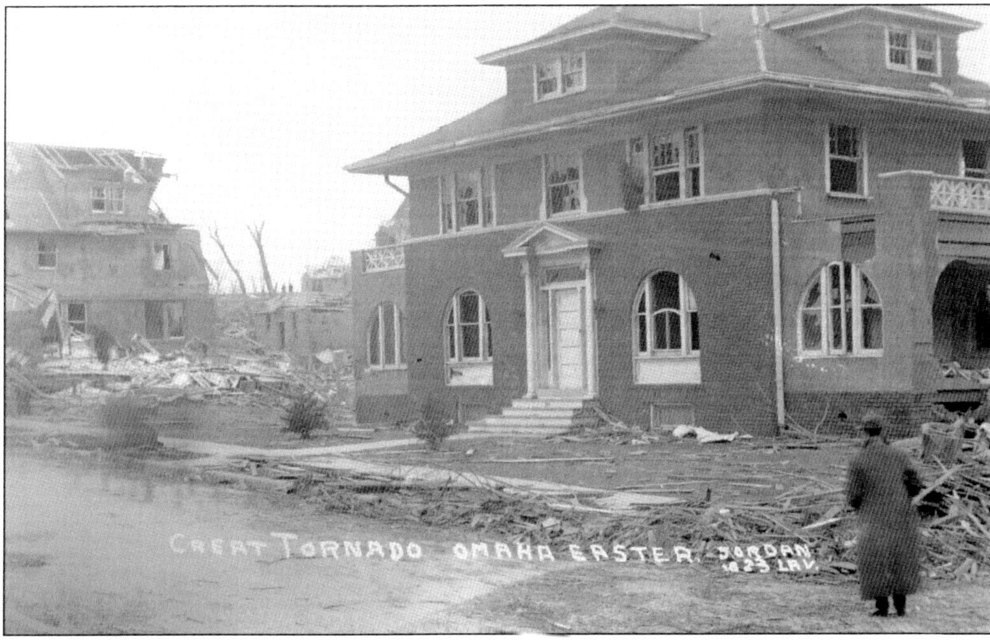

D.C. Patterson Home. Patterson's brick home on 38th Avenue was damaged, but remained inhabitable. Repairs began quickly, as evidenced by the glazier in an upper-story window.

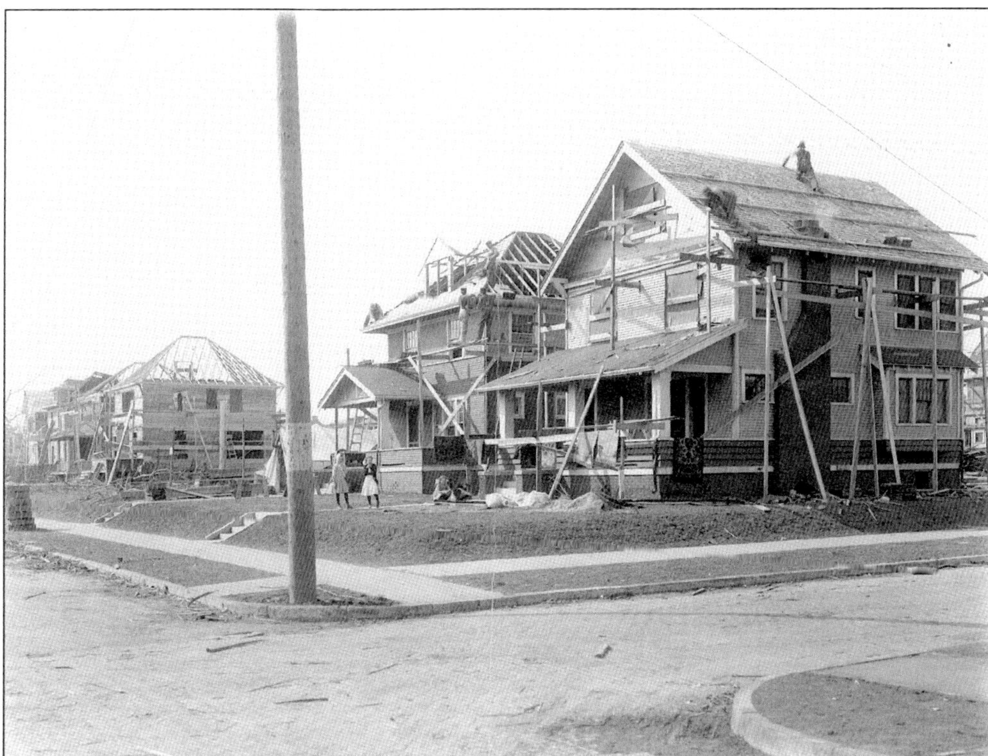

Rebuilding Kountze Place. Homes in Kountze Place are being repaired at the intersection of 18th and Locust Streets. (Bostwick-Frohardt Collection, Durham Western Heritage Museum.)

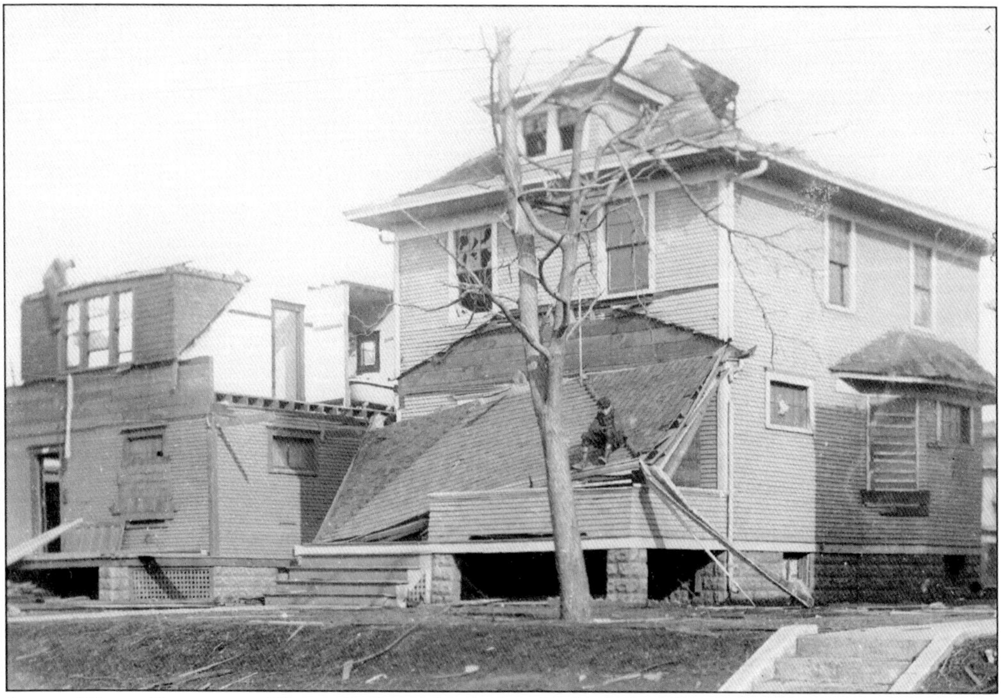

Lucas Home Damaged. This is the Lucas home as it looked after the tornado. (Bostwick-Frohardt Collection, Durham Western Heritage Museum.)

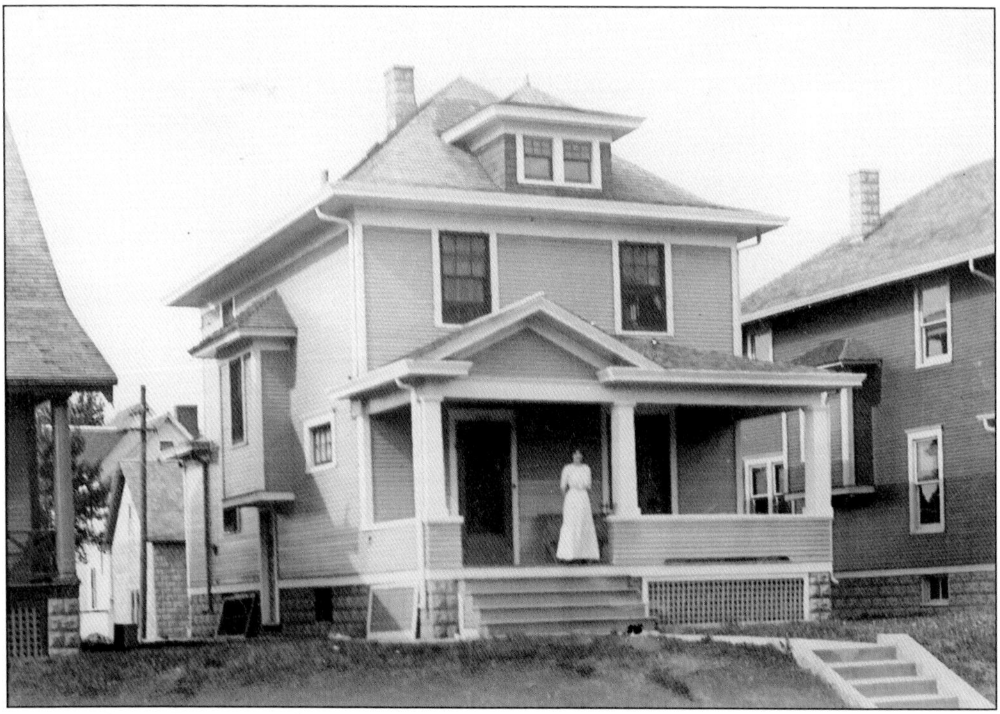

Lucas Home Rebuilt. The repaired Lucas home is pictured in the late spring of 1913. (Bostwick-Frohardt Collection, Durham Western Heritage Museum.)

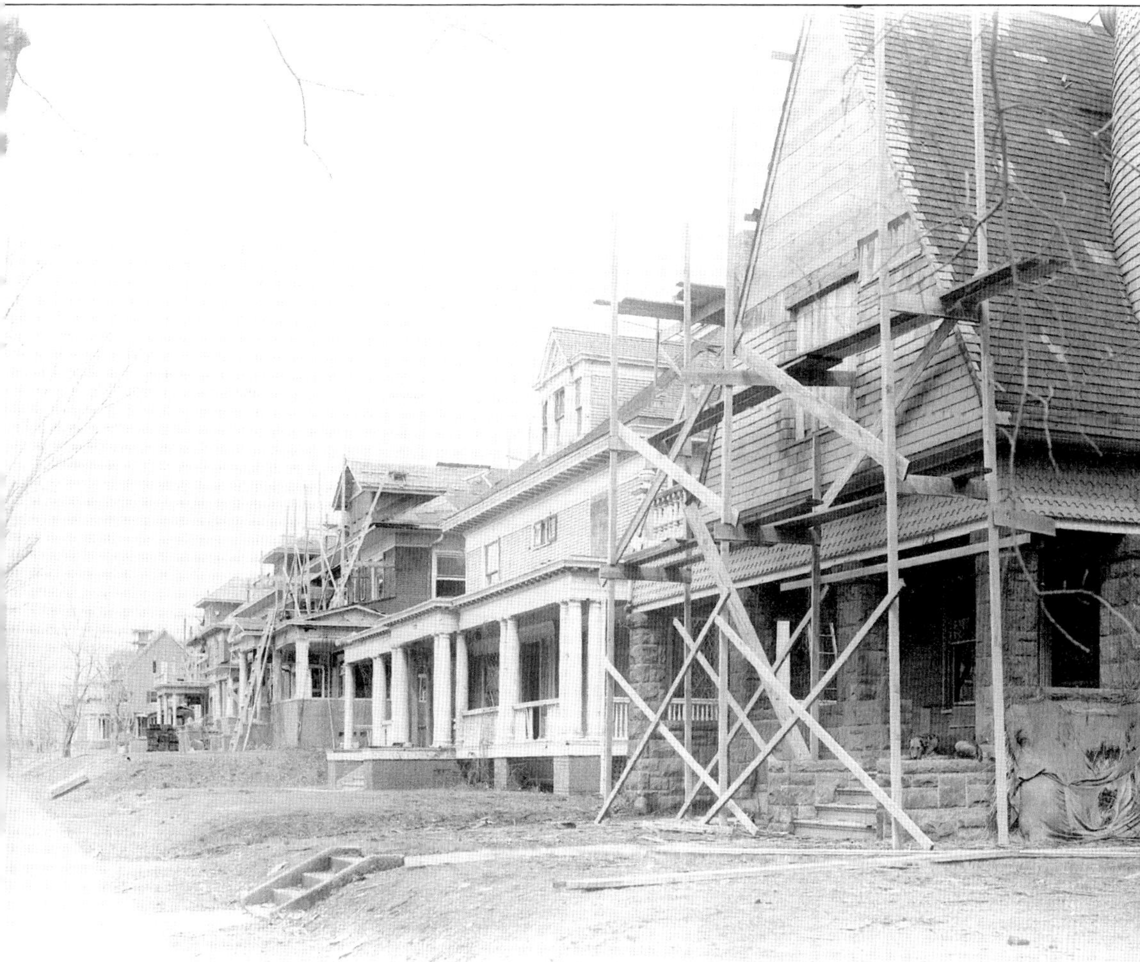

HOME REPAIRS ALONG 39TH AVENUE. Repairing and rebuilding efforts are made on a row of houses in the Cathedral district. (Bostwick-Frohardt Collection, Durham Western Heritage Museum.)

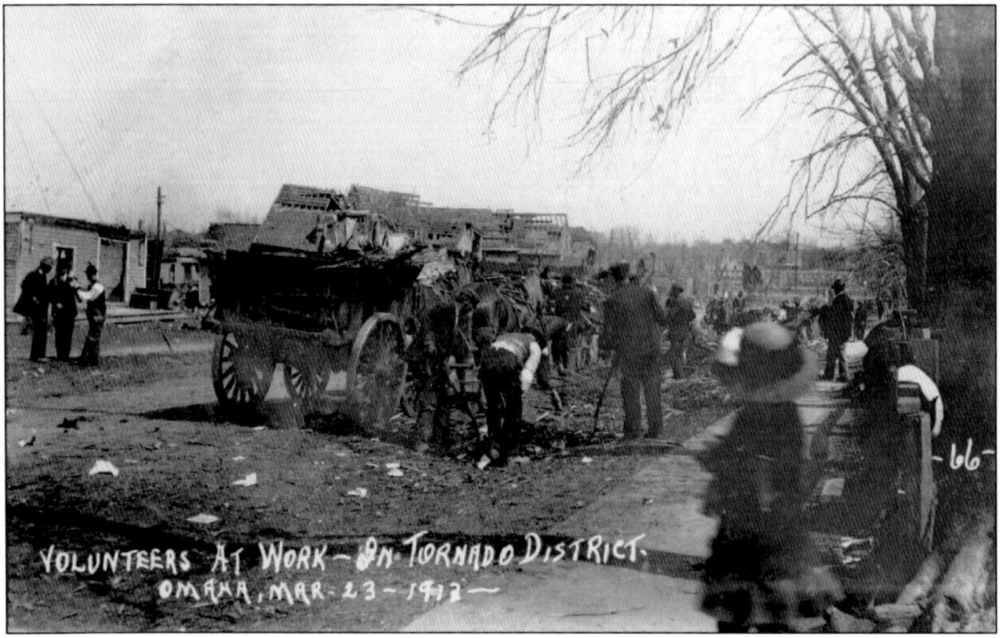

VOLUNTEERS AT WORK. Mayor Dahlman proclaimed cleanup days on April 5th and 6th. Nearly 5,000 volunteers heeded the call that weekend, over the protests of some local ministers that a Sunday was sanctioned for the event.

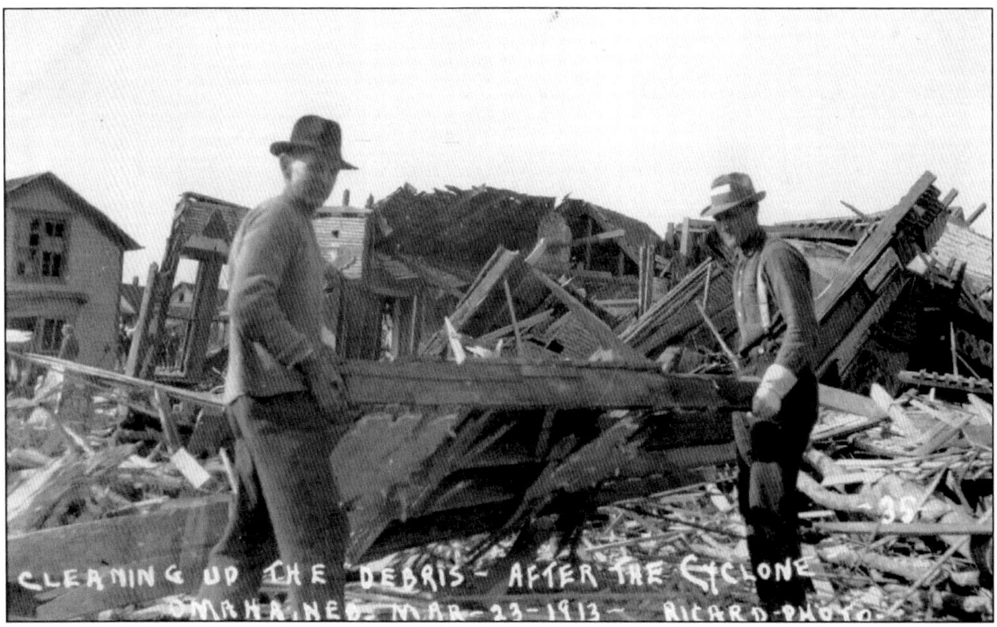

CLEANUP. These men do their part to assist the cleanup effort by moving debris.

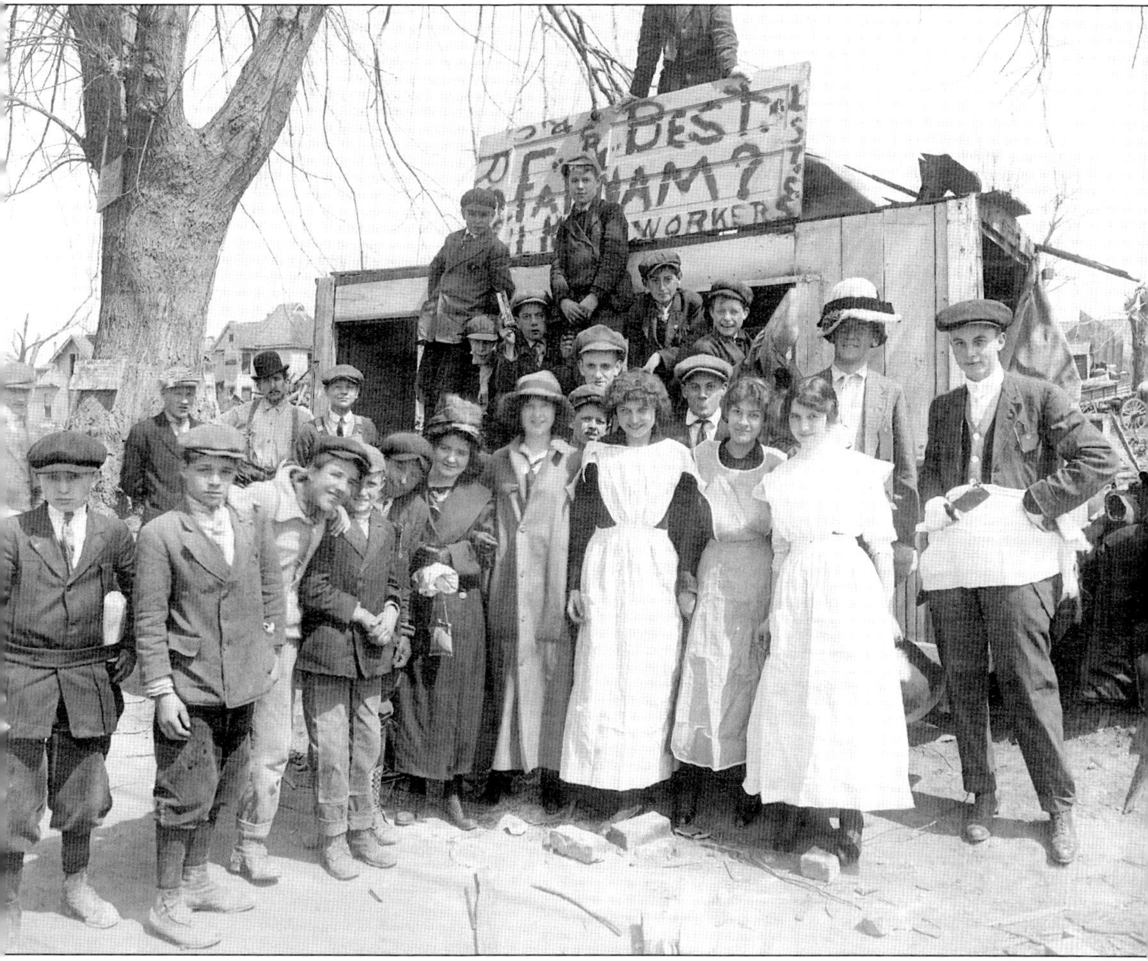

FARNAM SCHOOL. The students from Farnam School at 2915 Farnam Street do their part near 24th and Lake Streets during cleanup days on April 5th and 6th. Young ladies delivered lunch over the noon hour. Nearly 1,200 public and parochial school boys joined the effort. They were highly praised for their enthusiasm and diligent work. (Bostwick-Frohardt Collection, Durham Western Heritage Museum.)

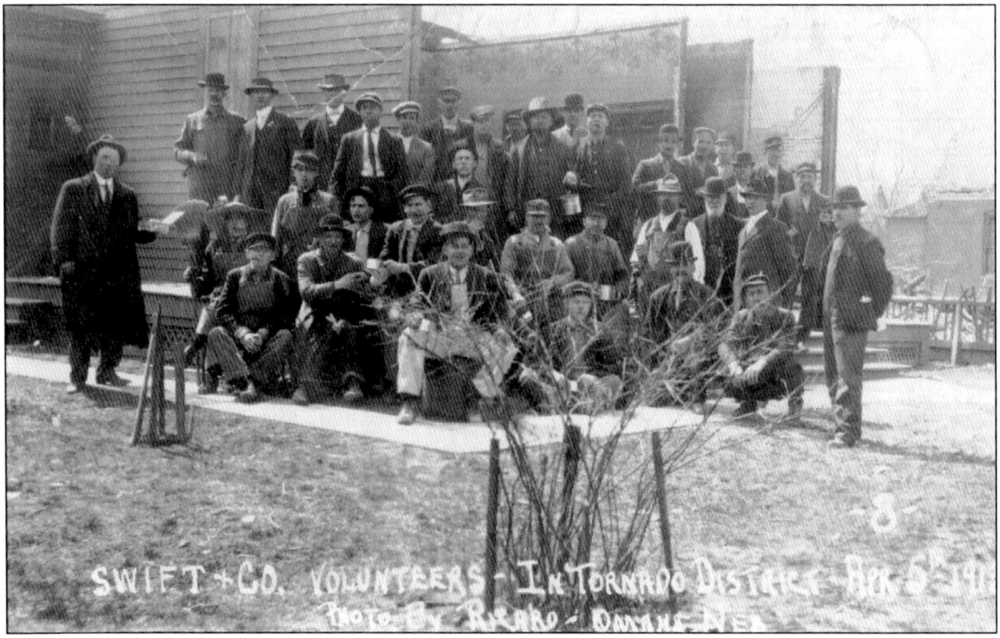

SWIFT VOLUNTEERS. These volunteers from the Swift & Company packing plant in South Omaha are aiding the relief effort.

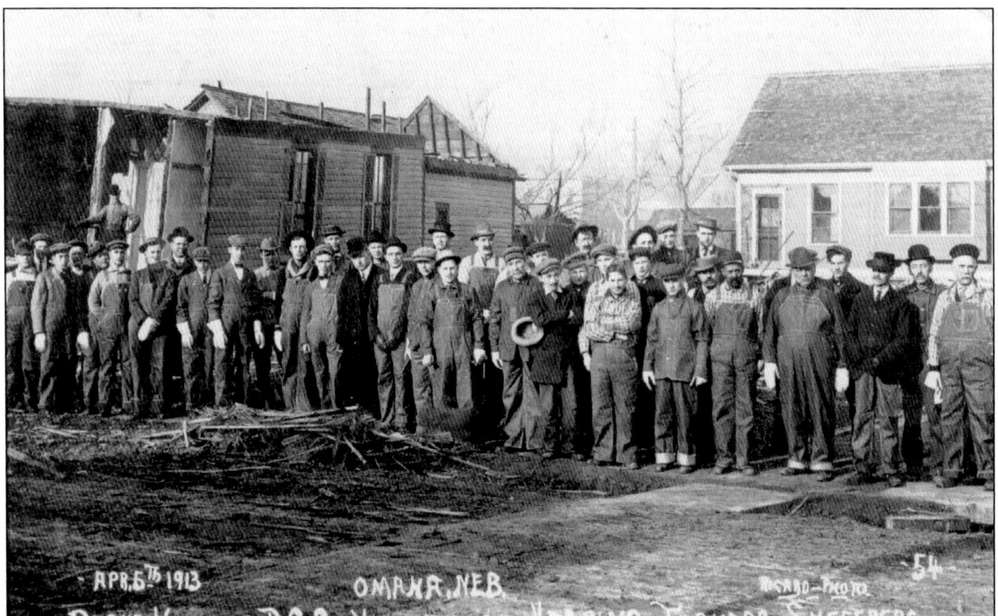

BYRNE & HAMMER VOLUNTEERS. Many local companies furnished volunteers during the city's official cleanup days. George L. Hammer, vice president of the Byrne & Hammer Dry Goods Company, was injured in the storm, and had one of his legs amputated above the knee.

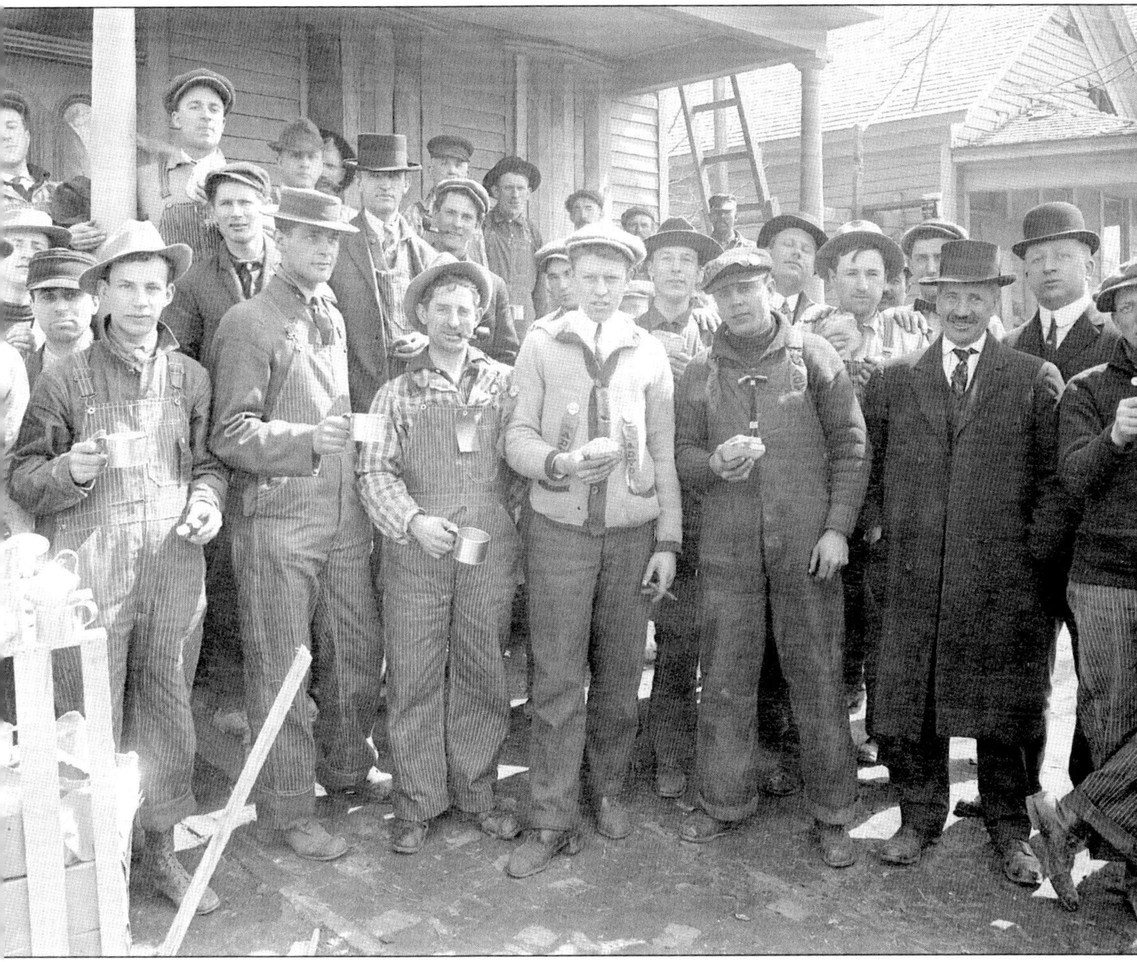

TAKING A BREAK. These men from the Byrne & Hammer Dry Goods Company are taking a break from rebuilding one of the homes damaged by the tornado at 25th and Patrick Streets. Trucks carrying food, dubbed "chuck wagons," toured the tornado district during cleanup weekend offering sandwiches and hot coffee for sustenance. (Bostwick-Frohardt Collection, Durham Western Heritage Museum.)

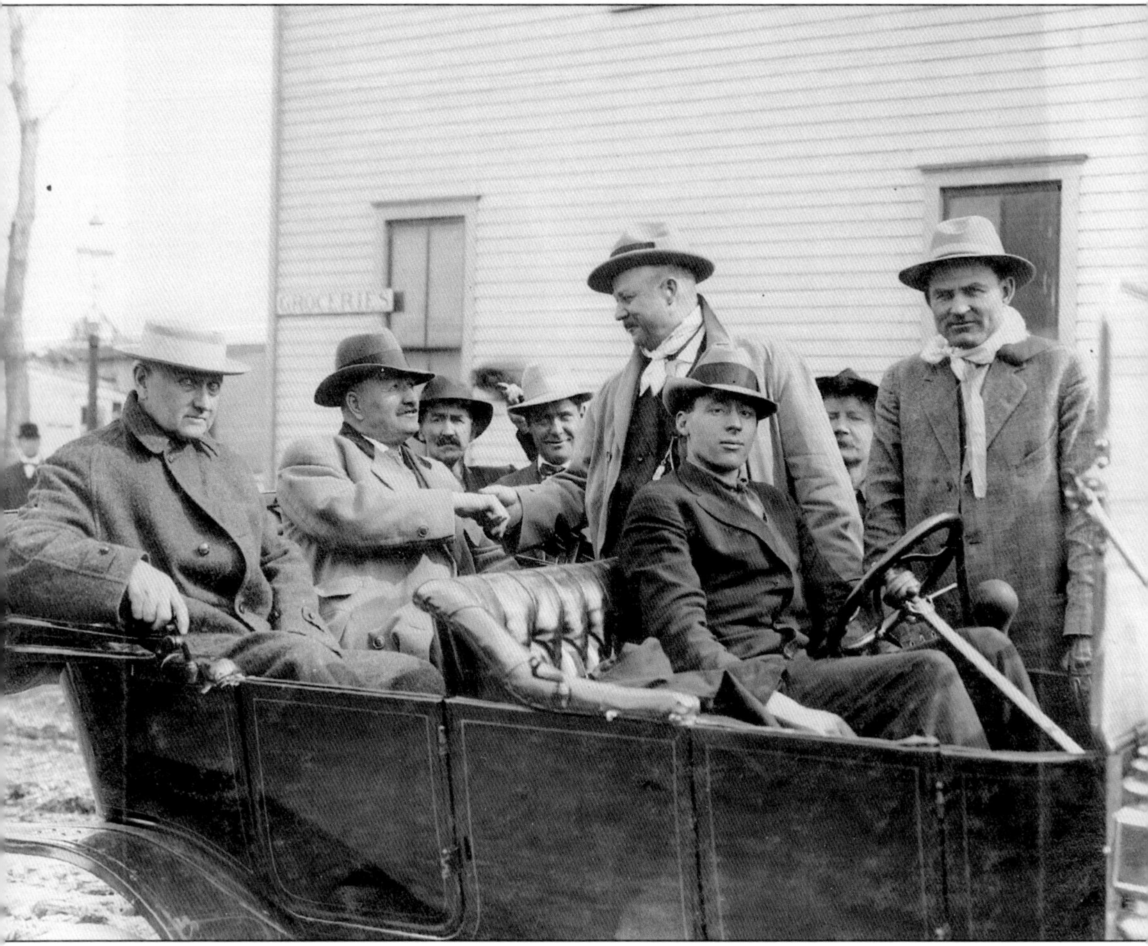

Big Bosses Tour Cleanup. Walter Jardine shakes hands with Omaha Stockyards Superintendent Jack Walters during the cleanup on April 6th. Jardine was in charge of hauling supplies to the afflicted and debris removal. Walters managed hundreds of stockyard volunteers during cleanup. Percy Ambler, at far right, was Walters' assistant. At far left is Thomas C. Byrne, the reigning AkSarBen king. Although his home in West Farnam was left a pile of splinters, Byrne aided reconstruction and relief efforts. The driver is unidentified. (Bostwick-Frohardt Collection, Durham Western Heritage Museum.)

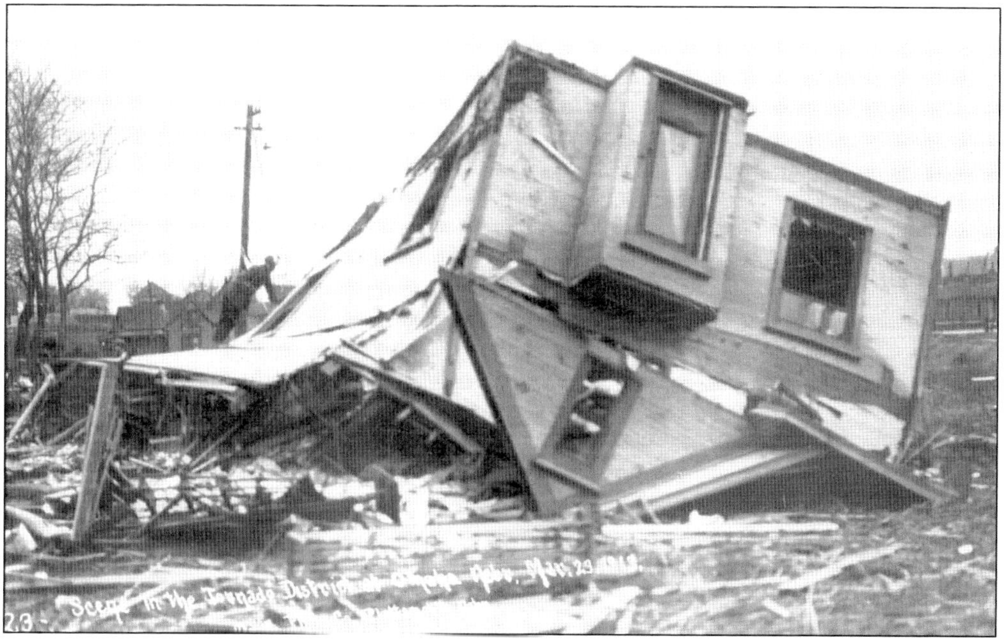

MAN ON UPSIDE-DOWN HOUSE. This man is in a precarious position upon the wreckage of his home. There were numerous reports of injuries during the cleanup and rebuilding stages, and several deaths due to collapsing ruins.

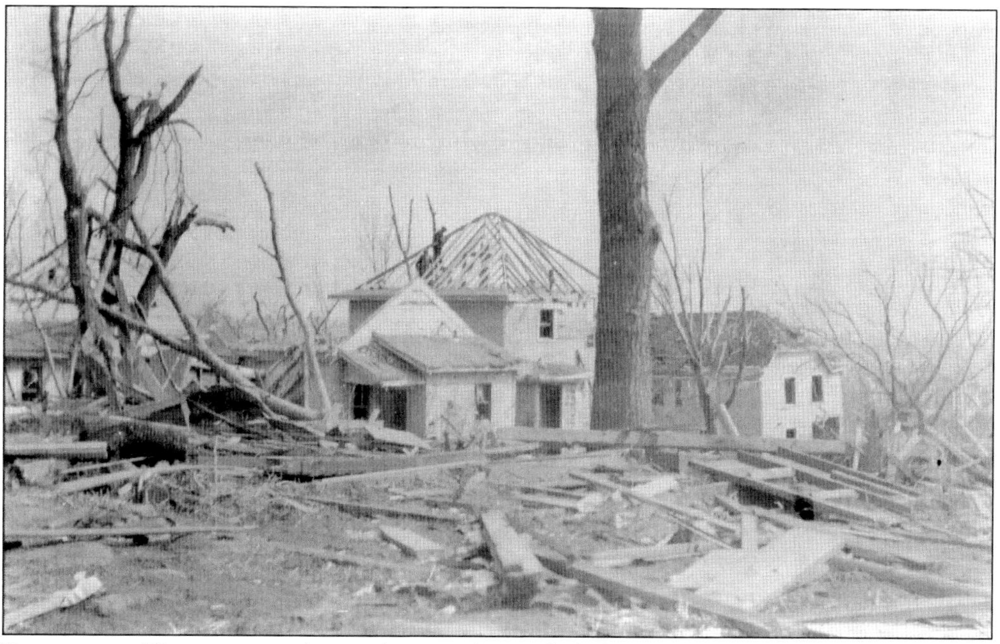

REFRAMING. These men are busy reframing the roof of a home.

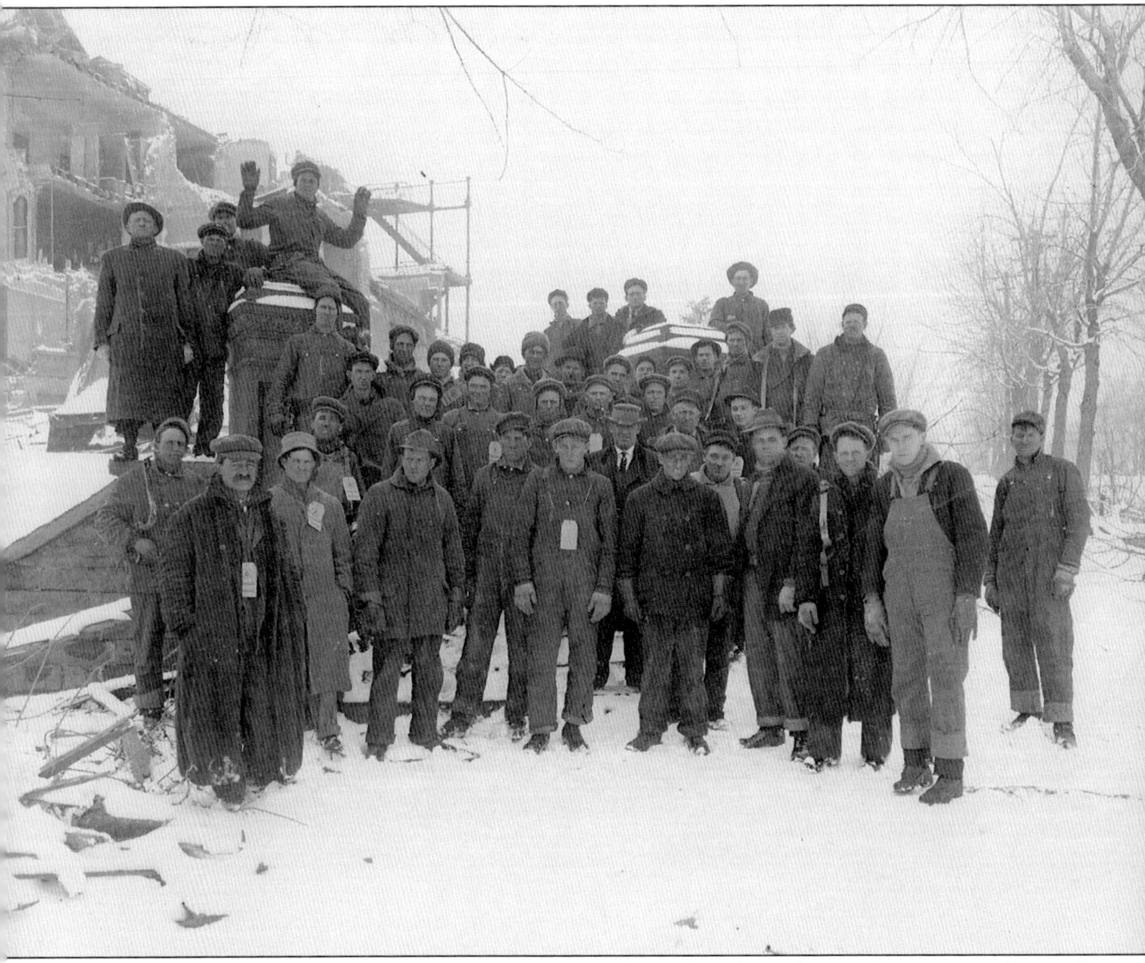

REPAIR AT SACRED HEART CONVENT. A repair crew gathered on the northeast steps of Sacred Heart Convent. Many people feared that the building would have to be demolished due to heavy damage. The Sisters raised thousands of dollars to save the building. The Sacred Heart Academy reopened in mid-September that year. (Bostwick-Frohardt Collection, Durham Western Heritage Museum.)

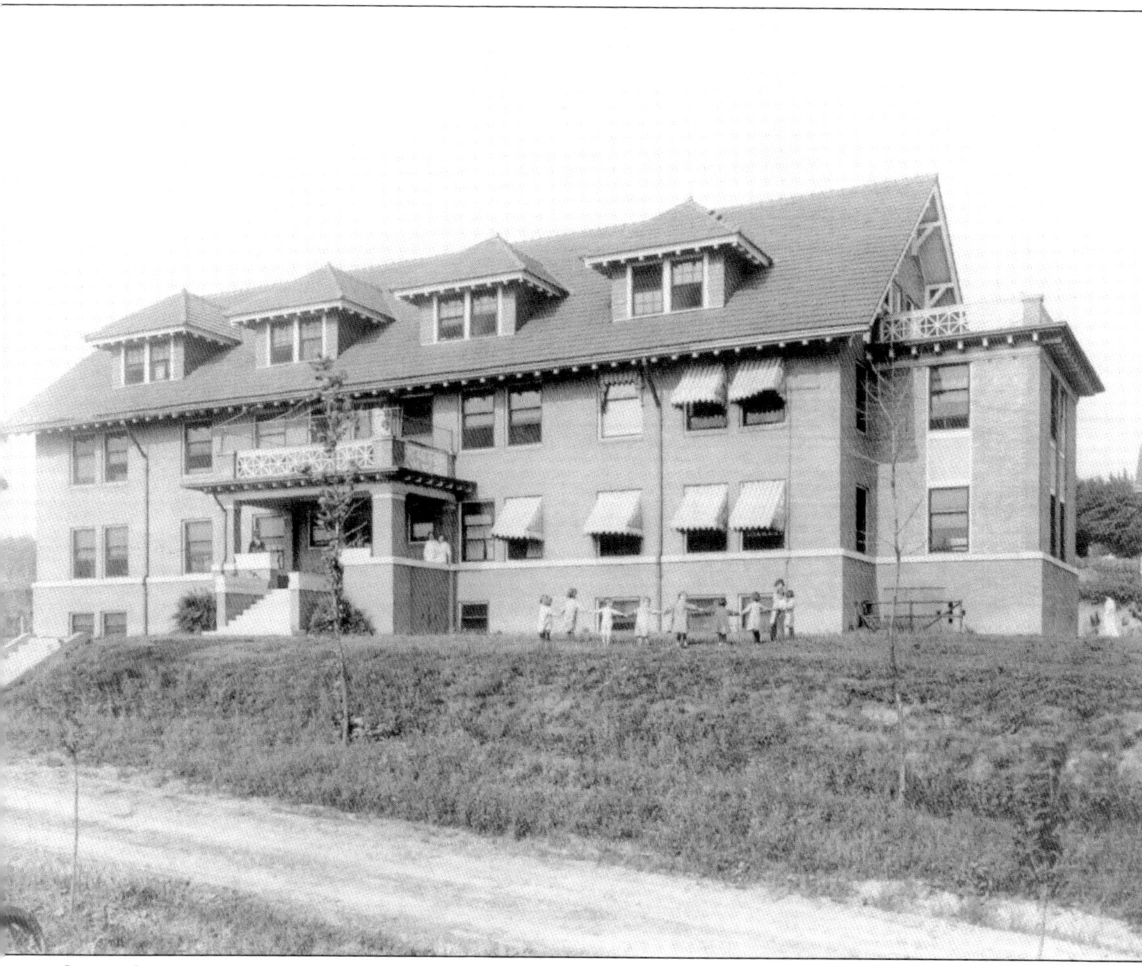

CHILD SAVING INSTITUTE REPAIRED. It cost nearly $5,000 to repair the Child Saving Institute, and the new sun room featured fewer windows. The organization watched donations shrink by $4,000 in the following year. They attributed the shortage to the tornado, as Omahans gave their money to the relief fund, or used it to rebuild their own homes and lives. (Child Saving Institute.)

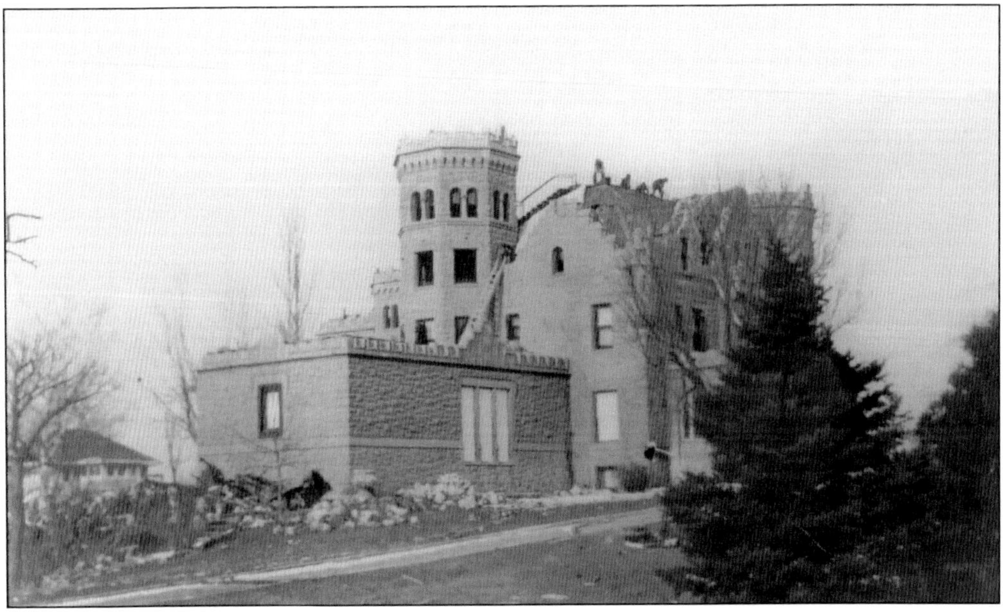

Joslyn Castle Repairs. Due to its fine construction, the Joslyn home needed only minor repairs. That fall, the Joslyns hosted a gala event for the wedding of their daughter, Violet. (Nebraska State Historical Society Photograph Collections RG 4462.)

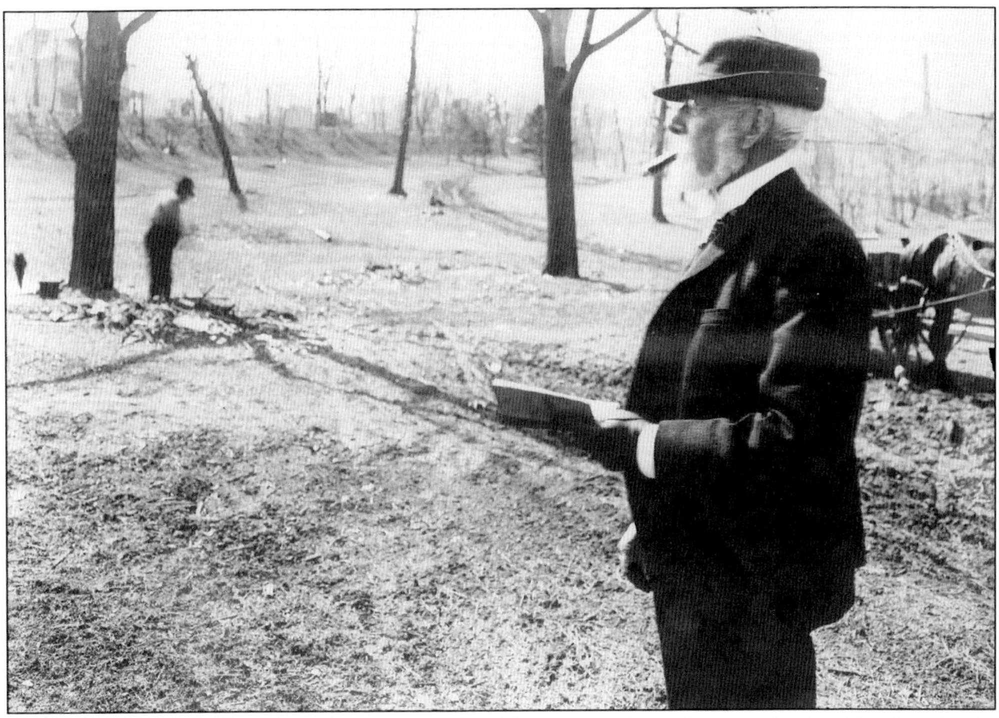

Superintendent Adams. In a considerably cleaned-up Bemis Park, Omaha Parks Superintendent W.R. Adams surveys the scene. Adams oversaw 60 men and 10 teamsters. As many trees as possible were saved, and saplings were planted to make up for lost arbors. (Bostwick-Frohardt Collection, Durham Western Heritage Museum.)

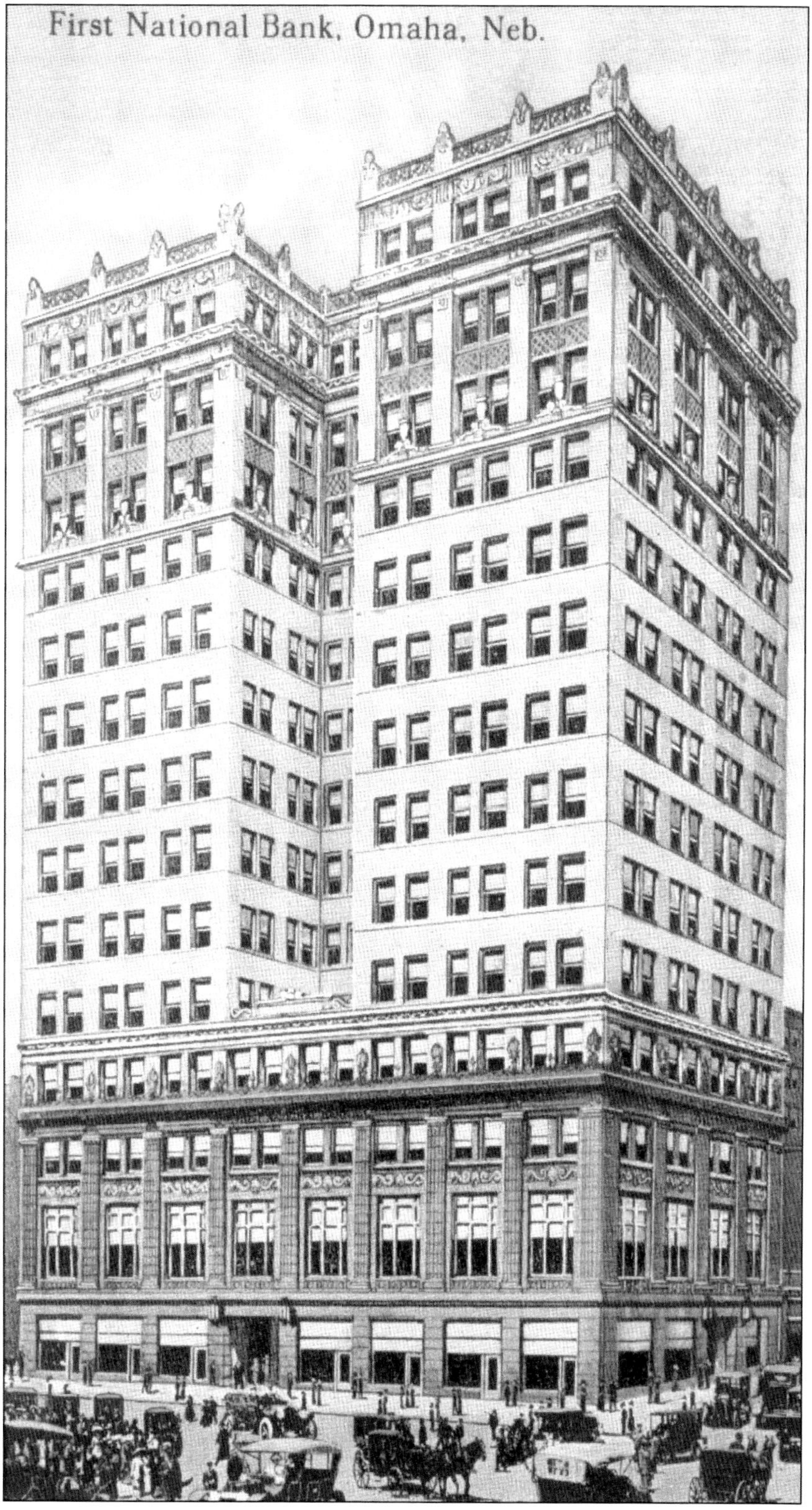

FIRST NATIONAL BANK. First National Bank at 16th and Farnam Streets was designed by the renowned firm of Graham, Burnham, & Company. Built in 1916–1917, the U-shape design was in direct response to the 1913 tornado. This skyscraper was intended to withstand the worst storm the plains could muster, and still stands in downtown Omaha.

Selected Bibliography

BOOKS

Greenleaf, Miles. *Thrilling Story of Omaha's Tornado*. Chicago: Hamming Pulishing Co., 1913.
Herbert, Thomas and J. Martin Miller, eds. *America's Greatest Flood and Tornado Calamity*. Thomas H. Morrison, 1913.
Marshall, Logan. *Our National Calamity of Flood, Fire and Tornado*. L.T. Myers, 1913.
Omaha City Directory, 1913. Omaha, Nebraska: Omaha Directory Co., 1913.
Shooter, Alice. *Early History of Ralston, Nebraska, 1865–1950*. 1987.

BOOKLETS

How Omaha Rebuilt the Tornado District in One Year. Omaha, Nebraska: *World-Herald*, 1914.
Omaha Cyclone in Pictures. Omaha, Nebraska: Mogy Publishing Co., 1913.
Picture Story of the Omaha Tornado Disaster. Omaha, Nebraska: Baker Bros., 1913.
The Omaha Tornado. Omaha, Nebraska: John L. Gideon, 1913.
The Omaha Tornado.
The Story[:] Omaha Cyclone In Pictures. Omaha, Nebraska: Arthur F. Dunn, 1913.
The Story of the Omaha Tornado In Words and Pictures. Text by Miles Greenleaf and Carl G. Eddy. Omaha, Nebraska: John L. Gideon, 1913.
Tornado. Written and prepared under the direction of Charles B. Driscoll. Omaha, Nebraska: Mogy Publishing, 1913.
The Track of the Omaha Tornado. Omaha, Nebraska: *Omaha Bee*, 1913.
Wrecked In A Night Rebuilt In A Day. Omaha, Nebraska: *Omaha Bee*, 1913.

NEWSPAPERS

Omaha Bee
Omaha Daily News
Omaha Excelsior
Omaha World-Herald